Nashville

IN THE NEW SOUTH
1880–1930

Nashville

IN THE NEW SOUTH

1880–1930

Don H. Doyle

THE UNIVERSITY OF TENNESSEE PRESS

KNOXVILLE

The paper in this book meets the guidelines for
permanence and durability of the Committee on Production Guidelines
for Book Longevity of the Council on Library Resources.
Binding materials have been chosen for durability.

Library of Congress Cataloging in Publication Data

Doyle, Don Harrison, 1946–
  Nashville in the new South, 1880–1930

  Bibliography: p.
  Includes index.
  1. Nashville (Tenn.)—History. I. Title.
F444.N257D69 1985   976.8′55   84-11976
ISBN 0-87049-446-5 (alk. paper)

FOR
Marilyn

CONTENTS

MAPS, ILLUSTRATIONS, AND TABLES

TABLES

PREFACE

This story begins with the buoyant celebration of Nashville's centennial in 1880 when the city stood at the threshold of a New South born in the aftermath of the Civil War and Reconstruction. It ends a half-century later with the devastating fall of Caldwell and Company in 1930 when the vision of prosperity and social progress the New South seemed to promise suddenly fell apart. A second volume will pick up the story of Nashville's social and political history in the 1920s and carry it forward to the city's bicentennial celebration in 1980.

Many readers of this book will be citizens of Nashville interested in the historical roots of their city, its neighborhoods, landmarks, and people. Others will come to this book with an interest in how Nashville's history illuminates urban development and social change in the South. To benefit both sets of readers I have tried to place the particulars of Nashville's history within the broader context of regional change and urbanization in America.

In recent years there has been considerable debate about the nature of the post-Civil War South. Some historians, following C. Vann Woodward's *Origins of the New South 1877–1915,* have stressed the rise of a class of "new men" led by urban industrialists and devoted to emulating the modern society that had emerged earlier in the North. Recently, other historians have argued the New South only disguised the continuation of the Old South, which was geared to plantation agriculture, marred by repression of black labor, and plagued by economic backwardness. Their reexamination of the postwar South has opened many exciting questions about the nature of the modern South and the whole meaning of the Civil War and Reconstruction in our nation's history. But until recently little had been done to test these theories within the context of the southern city. Out of consideration for my local audience I have avoided distracting historiographical forays, but those interested in the scholarly debate about the New South may profit from this book as a case study in the making of a New South city. This book is, in part, an early report on a broader comparative study of urban elites and racial policy in four southern cities (Atlanta, Nashville, Charleston, and Mobile) in the half-century following the Civil War.

Nashville is an ideal case study for an inquiry into the meaning of the New South, for it was a battleground between the forces of continuity and change in the postwar South. Nashville was the first major Confederate city to fall before the Federal invasion in 1862, and after the war and Reconstruction it became, in many ways, a spearhead for the transformation of the South in the coming decades. In the expansion of railroads, the rise of new merchants, industrialists, and financiers, and in educational endeavors, Nashville was setting trends for the region. Though Nashville's ambitious entrepreneurs were fully in accord with the new order they were fashioning in the postwar South, the city also contained powerful countervailing forces expressed in a variety of sentiments and behavior. These might be revealed in reactions to urban progress, a maudlin veneration of the Confederate's Lost Cause, or in paternalistic race relations. Like most people experiencing momentous social change, Nashvillians at once embraced and shunned the future the New South promised them.

This book began just before the city's bicentennial celebration in 1980 when I proposed to the Century III Commission, the citizens' organization in charge of all bicentennial events, to write a brief illustrated history of the city, to be prepared in the coming year. The commission members not only approved the project, they flattered me with references to the "comprehensive" and "scholarly" history they expected of me, and they granted me more time to complete my effort. To live up to their expectations, I soon put aside my other research interests to launch a long-term project devoted to as much original research as possible and aimed at producing as full a history of the city as possible.

Although this project has grown far beyond my original intentions, the craft of history necessarily involves the author's selection and interpretation of the past. No history can be truly comprehensive, and few people would want to read it if it were! I have strived, nonetheless, to relate as full and accurate a picture of the city as possible. It is a history that deals with the wealthiest business leaders and the most impoverished slum dweller, the officeholders and the voters to whom they appealed, the reformers and those they wished to reform. The picture of a city's past—even when viewed from these many angles—will always remain incomplete, however. There are dozens of unexplored paths in the city's past that await their historian, and I hope this book will serve as a stimulus to further research.

My former student at Vanderbilt, Susan Cox, first told me that the Century III Commission was contemplating sponsorship of a history of Nashville, and I appreciate all she did to help me in the early stages of this project. I wish to express my gratitude to the members of the Century III Commission, who supported this project and expressed their confidence in me. The commission launched the project with a grant from the City Council of Metropolitan Nashville and Davidson County, and it later added funds donated by many private business and individuals during the city's bicentennial celebration.

The major funding of this project came from the National Endowment for the Humanities under a grant from its Research Division. Without the support of the Endowment this book probably never would have been written. I appreciate the cooperation of the Endowment in extending the term of the grant and allowing me the opportunity to bring the project to a successful conclusion. I wish to express my gratitude to Blaine Brownell, Howard Rabinowitz, and George Rollie Adams, who supported my proposal to the National Endowment and offered their friendly advice in the beginning stages.

My thanks to Sandy Evans, who kept accounts in order for the Century III Commission during the early stages of this project. Loretta Conners, formerly with the Metro Office of Intergovernmental Affairs, did a splendid job of administering the grant after the Century III Commission disbanded. Mimi Hayes, with Metro's Director of Finance office, took over this task in the final year of the project, and I am thankful for her able assistance.

The grant from the National Endowment allowed me to utilize a number of research assistants, without whom I never would have uncovered the wealth of material that went into this effort. I wish to express my thanks to Susan Cox, Pat Miletich, Dan Smith, John Glenn, John Ellis, and Randy Horick for their good work at various times during the course of researching and writing this book. John Rumble worked for me during the early stages of the project and was always a source of reliable research and insight. Doug Flamming was a great help to me in the summer and fall of 1983 and graciously lent his expertise on religion and reform in Nashville. During her service on the project, Roz McGee compiled valuable notes from the newspapers and gathered much useful information about Nashville politics. Her knowledge of contemporary Nashville politics complemented her insights into politics of the past, and I am thankful to have had her assistance. I am especially grateful to Jim Summerville, who has served the project faithfully over the past two years. Jim brought his considerable knowledge of Nashville history and its sources to the job. He also displayed a dogged patience for tracking down the elusive fact and the appropriate illustration. He gently corrected my clumsy writing style and in numerous ways helped me maintain faith in the final product I was pursuing.

Sam Shannon, Charles Bryan, Louise Davis, May Dean Eberling, Betsie Hancock, and Marilyn Doyle all read portions of the manuscript during its evolution, and I am grateful to them for their tactful corrections of fact and style, which make the final product much better. Thanks also to David Goldfield, Howard Rabinowitz, and Carl Abbott for their expert commentary on the manuscript for the University of Tennessee Press. I valued their thoughtful criticisms highly even though I could not always satisfy them. Eleanor Graham applied her extraordinary knowledge of Nashville's history to a thorough reading of the manuscript. She saved me from numerous embarrassments and tactfully pointed out my sometimes irreverent tendencies as a historian. She was also very helpful in suggesting ways to reorganize chapters. The inevitable errors of commission and omission that remain are my responsibility.

No history would ever be written were it not for the corps of dedicated citizens, librarians, and archivists who keep the past and somehow manage to protect it from the numerous people and disasters that destroy treasures of the community's history. I discovered an encouraging number of amateur historians and archivists in the city's businesses, churches, colleges, government offices, and neighborhoods who took time to help serve history. I learned more about the business history of Nashville during a lunch with John Hardcastle of Nashville City Bank than months of reading could have revealed. Sam Shannon of Tennessee State University shared with me his deep knowledge of black Nashville and numerous aspects of the city's past. Our discussions of the temperance issue were especially helpful to my understanding of that subject. I have tried to acknowledge in the footnotes throughout the text the many other individuals who have aided my research.

The staff of the Ben West Public Library, particularly Mary Glenn Hearne and Hershel Payne in the Nashville Room, helped me and my research assistants in so many ways, it is hard to imagine how this book could have been written without them. The illustrations from this depository were reproduced by Edwin C. P'Pool. The staff of the Tennessee State Library and Archives was no less important to the success of this project. I am particularly thankful for the expert service of Fran Schell, Marilyn Bell, and Leslie Pritikin, who reproduced many of the illustrations used in this book. Finally, the Vanderbilt University Library was an important resource in the making of this book, and I am grateful to all the many members of its excellent staff who helped me and my research assistants over the course of this project. Kay Beasley of the Vanderbilt University Photographic Archive helped identify and reproduce the illustrations from that collection. Don Belcher of the

Nashville Chamber of Commerce generously gave his time to facilitate research in the Chamber's rich collection.

My interest in Nashville history began when I taught urban history at Vanderbilt. My undergraduate seminar on Nashville's past has been a continual source of inspiration for me. The roles of student and teacher often became confused in the process of directing term paper projects, and I acknowledge freely that over the years I have learned at least as much as I have taught in this seminar. I have tried, whenever appropriate, to cite the papers of my students in the book, but in a more general way I wish to express my thanks for their contributions to my understanding of Nashville's past.

Mavis Bryant of the University of Tennessee Press showed an early interest in this project, and I am most grateful to her and the entire staff at the press for helping bring this book to fruition. Thanks also are due to Barbara B. Reitt, who copyedited my manuscript with extraordinary skill.

My daughters Carrie and Kelly have grown up in Nashville over the past decade and have patiently tolerated their father's obsession with its history. They did nothing that I can think of to help me write this book, but they expect to be mentioned here, and they did help me maintain my sense of humor in this sometimes overly serious business of writing history. As for my wife, Marilyn, she too did little in the line of typing, indexing, and research one so often sees credited in scholarly books. She did read an early draft of the manuscript, raised a skeptical eyebrow in response to several embarrassing passages, and now and then gently prodded me by asking, "Just when *do* you plan to finish this book?" The dedication of the book is for all that and much more.

—Nashville
September 1983

Nashville

IN THE NEW SOUTH
1880–1930

BETWEEN TWO WORLDS:
CENTENNIAL 1880

In the spring of 1880 Nashville celebrated the one-hundreth anniversary of its founding. Nothing tells us quite so much about a community as the way it interprets its own history, for the commemoration
of major events requires formerly unspoken assumptions about the community's past to be revealed in an outpouring of pageantry, orations,
monuments, and publications.

After the Civil War many southerners revered the past as a refuge
from the present. For them history was a way of romanticizing the
South's "Lost Cause" and resisting the threatening newness of the future. Others, in tune with the rising urbanism of the New South, embraced a modern faith in history as the measure of progress. For them
the past was the story of advance from savagery to civilization, and nowhere was this story better told than in prosperous cities like Nashville. It was to these cities the railroads pulled the wealth of the countryside, and from them that an abundance of manufactured goods and
wholesale products poured forth as the South recovered from the war.
In the cities, too, were the multitude of business, charitable, and educational institutions that rose as proud symbols of the progress the New
South applauded. A vast array of new technologies—electricity, steam-
powered machinery—also made the cities showcases of modern life.
It would have been difficult for Nashvillians to resist interpreting their
history as progress, but in doing so they did not repudiate the legacy
of the Old South. Instead, the Nashville Centennial celebration became
a delicate exercise in balancing a sincere reverence for southern traditions with a buoyant vision of the city's place in a New South eager
to join the national march of progress.

THE PAST AS PROGRESS

Plans for the Nashville Centennial celebration began with the idea that it would be a purely historical commemoration of the city's founding and early history. The Tennessee Historical Society, dormant since before the Civil War, had been reorganized in 1874 by a handful of former members. Like many similar organizations that revived in the South during these years, it served as a bulwark for an older generation against the assault of a brash young crowd of New South spokesmen who were more interested in future progress than in the past. The society began working diligently not so much to repudiate the New South idea, but to make its own claim on behalf of a history for which they felt no Tennessean need feel shame. Indeed, it was the adroit skill of the Historical Society that allowed it to graft revered symbols of the past onto the progressive image of the New South. In the fall of 1874, for example, the society announced its reemergence at the fourth in a series of industrial expositions held in Nashville. Its display of an Egyptian mummy, along with other antiquities in its collection, ironically became one of the central attractions at an affair designed to celebrate the future of industrial technology.[1]

The Centennial of 1880 would amplify this juxtaposition of the past with New South symbols of progress. Two full years in advance, the society took the lead in planning the Centennial.[2] It petitioned state and city government officials for assistance in preparing for the celebration. Mayor Thomas Kercheval was authorized by the City Council to appoint a citizens' committee to work with the Historical Society in preparing for the Centennial.

At this point, the Centennial rapidly grew beyond the society's modest plans for a historical commemoration. A public meeting was called at the Library Hall on December 16, 1879, and an enthusiastic crowd turned out. Among them were many aggressive young businessmen from outside the circle of the Historical Society—men in banking, insurance, wholesale dry goods and produce, manufacturing, and the professions. These were men involved in the most vital sectors of Nashville's postwar economy, men whose economic interests linked them to regional and national markets far beyond the boundaries of the city. For them the Centennial would be "an event of great commercial as well as historical importance," an ideal opportunity to advertise to the world Nashville's promise as an industrial and commercial center just as the city was recovering from the harsh depression that began in 1873. The Citizens' Centennial Commission recommended to the audience that the anniversary be the occasion for a monumental industrial exposition that would display technological progress. It would be a testimonial to Nashville's eagerness to embrace the New South creed. Two of Nashville's older citizens addressed the crowd on the city's rich heritage and challenged the younger generation to "uphold the honor of our beautiful and magnificent patrimony that required so much courage . . . to obtain." Another put the matter in terms more familiar to the new city boosters when he announced, "We propose to take an inventory at the close of our first Centennial, and make an exhibit of loss and gain."[3]

So it was that the city's reverence for the past was joined to a cult focused on progress in the future. As it evolved, the Centennial reflected the balance that Nashville worked out after the war in making its commitment both to progress and to the past. An industrial exposition might be the focus of the celebration, but this shrine to the New South creed was also to feature events rooted in the old order. A military drill competition attracted dozens of militia companies from throughout the region and drew on powerful southern affection for military pomp that somehow survived the war. Horse races, sponsored by the Nashville Blood-horse Association, attracted competitors from all parts of the South, and crowds flocked to enjoy this traditional southern sport. Included in the industrial exposition was a large display of the Tennessee Historical Society that included personal effects of heroes of the old order. The climax of the Centennial was to be the unveiling of the equestrian statue of Andrew Jackson, whose historical image was made to bridge the gulf between the old and the new.[4]

The meetings of the Centennial Commission were conducted in strict business fashion, and no time was wasted on trivial matters. The business leaders' efficiency gave ample demonstration of the organizational skills they had acquired. Within a little over four months they planned and financed a remarkably successful series of events: an industrial exposition in a newly constructed building, a stupendous procession and fireworks display, a regional military drill competition, and other public events, all attended by thousands of visitors who streamed into Nashville.

By early January 1880 the Centennial Commission selected a site for the exposition building on the south side of Broad Street, just west of Spruce Street (now Eighth Avenue). Here the Church, Spruce & Broad Street mule-car line could bring visitors from the grand Maxwell House Hotel and other downtown hostelries and residences. The gentle hill also gave the exposition a commanding view of the river and downtown skyline. Plans were drawn by a local achitect, William C. Smith, for a large temporary building, and construction began in early February. In the meantime the finance committee, led by John P. McGuire and composed of Nashville's leading businessmen, raised $31,000 from local citizens for the exposition fund.[5] Other communities hurriedly laid the groundwork for transportation, street decorations, and a multitude of other arrangements for the grand celebration.

APRIL 24: THE PROCESSION

On April 24, 1880, the Centennial Commission's earnest efforts were revealed to all in a magnificent opening day. The date had been designated earlier by the Historical Society as the anniversary of John Donelson's arrival by flatboat at what a century before had been the site of Nashville's hazardous beginnings. There a band of settlers huddled about Fort Nashborough in dread fear of Indian attack. Now, a century later, Nashville's citizens would demonstrate how far they had come from their humble birth.

The Centennial opened with a grand nineteenth-century tradition, the public procession, the likes of which are rarely seen today. These gala parades were entertainment extravaganzas that revealed much about local society, for they were organized to show the community at its best, to display the institutions and values the community held in highest regard. The procession, as the *American* editor put it, gave "a fair picture of the social order."[6]

A one-hundred-gun salute signaled the beginning of the great day. By mid-morning different sections of the parade formed in separate locations of the downtown that had been designated well in advance by the procession committee. As the parade began a carriage with Dr. Thomas A. Atchison, president of the Centennial Commission; Governor Alfred S. Marks; Mayor Thomas A. Kercheval; and the Honorable John M. Bright, orator of the day, rolled proudly behind a squad of mounted police and the Murfreesboro Brass Band. Other distinguished guests followed in separate carriages. Behind them were representatives of the Tennessee Historical Society, whose modest plans for a small celebration had been overwhelmed by the magnitude of the affair. Next came the units of civil government: state officials, the judiciary, the City Council. Then came the Vanderbilt University faculty, honored evidence of Nashville's right to its proud claim to be the "Athens of the South" and a symbol of northern benevolence to the South at the end of Reconstruction.

Behind the officials and educators marched a handful of veterans of the Seminole wars and a larger group from the Mexican War. Local militia units—the Nashville Light Dragoons, Porter Rifles, and Rock City Guards—followed the smartly marching veterans, who were dressed in brilliant new uniforms that betrayed nothing of their former allegiance to the Confederate gray.

Next came a distinct and symbolically important unit. Led by the Reverend Nelson Merry and John H. Keeble, two leaders of Nashville's black community, the black militia companies and bands marched in their place, followed by the black fraternal societies. That these groups were segregated within the parade, and indeed within local society, was hardly more important than the fact they formed an integral part of

Figure 1. The Centennial Procession, April 24, 1880. From *Frank Leslie's Illustrated Newspaper*, May 15, 1880, courtesy James Hoobler, Tennessee Historical Society.

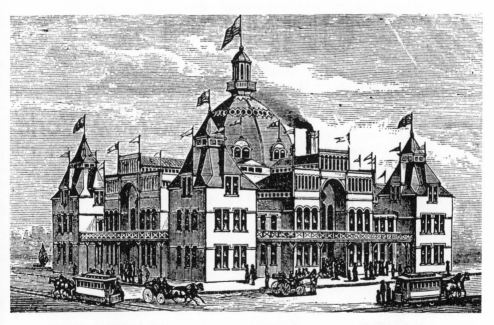

Figure 2. The Nashville Centennial Exposition Building, 1880. Tennessee State Library and Archives.

this highly articulated expression of Nashville's self-image. The idea of racial harmony was every bit as important to the New South creed as sectional reconciliation. From the outset, careful consideration was given to include black organizations in the celebration. The *American* applauded a suggestion to give the Fisk University Jubilee Singers a place in the opening ceremonies; they were "an agent for good in the elevation of a race which has just emerged from bondage." All citizens "who hope to see the race elevated and made truly citizens, interested in law and order and the prosperity of the State, and efficient co-workers" must agree, the editor argued. The Reverend Merry was given a special place at the end of the program of speakers. He played his part by testifying to the kind treatment he had been accorded by the Centennial Commission and prophesied that the ceremonies heralded a new day of racial harmony. Blacks and whites, he said, "were getting nearer to each other" in a way "his race had never seen before."[7]

Behind the black units came a long string of wagons intended to display the commercial might of Nashville. More than two hundred vehicles elaborately decorated with bunting, flags, and evergreens, filled with goods and employees, represented firms in every branch of business in Nashville. Here was the New South brandishing its commercial prosperity as the answer to past defeat.

The same prosperity and pride were exhibited to full advantage in the streets and buildings of the city itself. As the parade moved up Broad Street away from the river and through the carefully groomed downtown streets to the Public Square, it passed through a series of huge triumphal arches covered with green cedar boughs erected for the occasion at each corner of the square; others had been built on adjacent streets. Along the parade route business firms and residences showed off flags, banners, portraits, and bunting with elaborately designed floral and evergreen wreaths, horseshoes, and other displays. The "contagion of decoration," the *Daily American* editor remarked, created a "solid flare of variegated colors."[8]

The procession took an hour and a quarter to pass the thousands of spectators who thronged the sidewalks and peered out of windows from above. It could not have escaped those who watched it that what had begun as a quiet commemoration of the past now was an ostentatious celebration of the present. Nashville's history came to be interpreted during the Centennial as a benchmark from which to measure the remarkable progress the city had enjoyed.

THE EXPOSITION

Nowhere was the city's obsession with material progress more explicitly demonstrated than in the exposition building. After the parade the crowds reconvened that evening for the grand opening of the Centennial Exposition. The building was a magnificent expression of the spirit of "enthusiastic enterprise" that Nashville was so determined to show its visitors. Erected within about four months, it was an enormous two-story structure fronting 189 feet on Broad Street and extending 159 feet deep along Spruce Street. Reflecting the ambivalence of Nashville's mood toward the past and present, the architecture combined striking Victorian towers with neoclassical columns and Romanesque arches. The central feature was a large dome topped with a cupola that rose 125 feet above the ground floor. Before it was completed, the building would cost the phenomenal sum of $24,893.[9]

Because of unavoidable problems in transporting lumber, construction on the building fell behind, and only a massive last-minute effort allowed the opening ceremonies to take place nearly on time, one day behind schedule. On the two nights before the opening, April 22 and April 23, hundreds of people were at work on the exposition building. Aided by moonlight, by 1,200 gas jets, and by electric lights imported from New York for the exposition, the work continued throughout the night, and hundreds of spectators gathered around the structure to witness a spectacular sight. "This fairy hall," Centennial president Thomas A. Atchison told the crowds at the exposition's opening, was "suddenly called from out of the shapeless void of chaos by the magic, no longer mysterious, of trained minds and skilled hands."[10]

Inside the exposition hall were gathered what Atchison aptly called the "rich harvest sown by a century." It was part historical museum, part industrial trade fair, and part amusement park. For the Tennessee Historical Society the Centennial Commission allowed a large display of historical artifacts devoted chiefly to heroes of the city's and state's antebellum past, the Indians, and the generation of pioneers that pushed them aside after the city was founded. Portraits and personal effects of James Robertson, Andrew Jackson, James K. Polk, David Crockett, and others managed to obscure the few artifacts related to what was tactfully referred to as "the late war."[11] The Art Department on the second floor included paintings depicting historical events in the city's past along with other art treasures.

Also on the second floor was the school display, showing samples of work from students in the city schools. Included were exhibits of the several public "colored schools" that had emerged in Nashville since the war, as well as displays by Fisk University and Central Tennessee College. In his address at the exposition Henry M. Doak, editor of the *American*, made clear the role of education in the New South. After reviewing the slow progress of public education in Tennessee, Doak argued that the model for education could not be imported as a piece from the North but must be molded to the "changed conditions surrounding the South." "The path for ambition to tread, the rewards of the new South," he went on, were not in the "epidemic rage for the so called learned professions and other overcrowded occupations" but "in the railway field, in the factory, in the machine shop, in the mine and on the farm. . . ." He called upon the schools and colleges to take the lead in "an era of material development—a movement which will elevate those falsely called the lower pursuits."[12]

Doak's audience did not have to look far to see the enormous promise of material development. Symbolically, the displays of art and education were relegated to the second floor, whereas the products of industry dominated the main floor. "The vitality of the exposition," the *American* reported, ". . . seems to be in the machinery department. Huge engines, threshers, mills of various kinds, reapers, self-binders, twine and wire binders, all constantly at work, make the din and confusion of sounds heard during exhibition hours."[13] The Historical Society paid homage to the political heroes of the old order, but it was these noisy machines and product displays, which overshadowed the artifacts of the past, that represented the future of the New South.

Nashville's was the first of many industrial expositions that were staged in large cities throughout the New South. Modeled originally after the national Centennial in Philadelphia in 1876, these expositions took on special meaning in the South. They were designed to show northern capitalists the opportunities for industrial progress and the eager spirit of southern entrepreneurs. They also sought to demonstrate the South's commitment to education and racial harmony, which assured a skilled, industrious laboring class. Above all, these expositions sought to show northerners that the Lost Cause was forgotten; the South was reconciled to defeat in the recent war and anxious to join the national march toward industrial progress. Northern investments would never again be threatened by sectional strife.[14]

The South's industrial expositions were also aimed at the home audience. They helped disseminate the new technology of steam and electricity to urban industrialists and rural planters. Expositions served as forums for exhorting the New South creed of industrial progress, racial harmony, and national reconciliation. These expositions displayed to southerners the fruits of material progress. In the spring of 1880 people poured into Nashville from outlying farms and small towns to gaze at the array of new machines. Attendance rose steadily from over 2,000 per day to almost 13,000 by the end of the exposition. The editor of the *American* delighted in describing the crowds of "our country friends" who gawked at the electric lights and gas jets. Women milled around a large display of new sewing machines and marveled at the quality of stitching that made their hand work seem obsolete. A steam-driven fanning machine delighted adults and children as it blasted off the hats of unsuspecting passersby. Others watched transfixed by the miniature steam railroad run by young Eddie Stahlman.[15]

The new technology fascinated children and adults alike. The distinction between industrial machines and toys was blurred, as was the boundary between the serious economic purpose of the exposition and the pure fun it provided. Professor Kirtland's Orchestra and The Columbia Helicon Band accompanied the whir of machinery with popular tunes, ending each day's performance with a warm rendition of "Home Sweet Home." Punch and Judy shows kept the children entranced and made the exposition a family affair. On a wire strung across the second balcony, Professor Leon gave several tightrope-walking performances. A baby show drew dozens of competing parents. Miss Eliza Goodwin's dance class treated the crowds to a performance on another evening. The Nashville Light Dragoons gave a full cavalry drill (mercifully, on foot) to an appreciative audience, and numerous other special events assured that crowds of all ages and social classes would be entertained. Between events, those who tired of the displays could gather around the central fountain. There, amid the jets of water shooting out, two sea lions and three alligators "proved great curiosities" to the visitors. Those who wished could get a full meal in the exposition building at Venables restaurant or the Tennessee Kitchen.[16]

THE TEMPERANCE QUESTION

There was as well a steady stream of men who found refreshment of another sort behind the swinging doors of Tamble & Brothers beer saloon, tucked discreetly away in the western corner of the building. The temperance question had excited much controversy during the planning of the exposition, and it was to remain a divisive issue in the new age that the exposition heralded. A vocal group of evangelical Protestants wished to see no alcoholic beverages sold on the exposition grounds, and they warned that drunken men would spoil the exposition for families and serious businessmen.

Others disagreed with the teetotalers. An editorial in the *American* answered that "the thirsty visitor . . . will round up the century with something stronger than water, and wash down the dust of ages with the besom of alcohol in some form. . . . If he can get a glass of beer on the grounds, he will take it, perhaps; if not, he will only have to step across the street to take something and, perhaps, take two to compensate himself for the trouble." In fact, saloons in the neighborhood were advertising discount drinks at ten cents in anticipation of the thirsty crowds. A compromise was struck and the exposition committee agreed that beer only would be sold in a house adjoining the exposition building behind closed doors, "out of the way of those who may have scruples concerning the insidious liquid," quipped the *American*. The editor continued to satirize the temperance campaign and took undisguised pleasure at reporting the "constant stream of patrons who lightly spring up the saloon steps and brush open the springing doors, and then re-appear after an incredible short time."[17]

The temperance forces represented far more than simply a protest against public drinking. They became a powerful undertow of concern over the cost of progress in the New South. The Bedford County Temperance Association spoke for a large number of rural and urban south-erners when it denounced beer sales at the exposition and called for a boycott of the Nashville Centennial. The Centennial Commission members, the resolution asserted, "have shown a regard to the money-making of the occasion at the expense of decency and propriety" and have chosen to "prostitute a great and historical occasion to these baser ends. . . ." A similar tone was clear in the admonishment of Nashville's ministers, who were worried that the pressing construction deadline would tempt the Centennial Commission to allow workmen to defile the Sabbath by allowing construction on the dome of the exposition building. The Reverend John B. McFerrin's "Centennial Exhortation" warned that Nashville's progress from a wilderness of "savage men" to a "Christian city" was, alas, "too often stained with murdered blood; too many drinking saloons; too many gambling halls; too much lascivi-ousness; too many open gates leading the young to destruction." Temperance and other religious issues took on enormous importance as Nashville pursued progress in its second century, and evangelical Chris-tians continued to give voice to those who questioned the moral price of material progress. For the moment, however, that dissenting voice was all but silenced by the clatter of machinery and the hubbub of Nashville's celebration.[18]

RECONCILING WITH THE PAST

The Centennial emphasis on the present and future did not mean that Nashville's past would be ignored. On the contrary, the occasion demanded that the city's history be studied and articulated with more care than it ever received before. Those who tended to such matters fully understood the importance of local history to the city's self-image. If at times the effort given to minute details and remote artifacts sug-gested antiquarianism, the overriding purpose was to set down a ver-sion of the past that would fit the present and explain Nashville's des-tiny within the New South. The intention was to subdue mention of the Civil War and thereby avoid any revival of sectional animosity that might disturb the New South dream.[19]

Nashville's past was interpreted for the masses in a variety of forms.

The Tennessee Historical Society's exhibit at the exposition displayed the physical and literary evidence of the city's leading historical figures and their aboriginal predecessors. Centennial Orations published in the local newspaper focused on particular individuals and institutions in the city's past. The Centennial Commission also sponsored the publication of a history of Davidson County and the city, as well as a guide book with a historical sketch of Nashville. Thus for the first time an official history of the community was set down.[20] Finally, public ceremonies and unveilings of public monuments served both to commemorate and interpret the local past.

All of these various forms of history expressed a remarkably uniform point of view, emphasizing the interlocking themes of local progress and national reconciliation. Most of the historical addresses given during the celebration dwelled upon the founding of the city, the bravery and sacrifice of the pioneers. On opening day the Honorable John Morgan Bright devoted his long oration to an eloquent account of Donelson's voyage to Fort Nashborough. Another enthusiastic history of the city's founding fathers included a highly dramatic historical novel on the Robertson and Donelson parties.[21] Other laudatory speeches followed during the celebration, one on James Robertson and John Sevier, another on Andrew Jackson and John Overton. The speakers seemed conscious of their purpose in fashioning heroes in the city's past to which a new generation might look for inspiring models.

There was also the recurrent lament that the youth of Nashville did not appreciate their historical legacy. The Tennessee Historical Society saw the Centennial as a way to "stimulate a spirit of reverence for the past . . . , to impress more fully, particularly upon the youth of the State, the value of the great truths inculcated by this event, to elevate in the public mind the importance of gathering and guarding the material so illustrative of her wonderful and unexampled history. . . ."[22]

To remind these youthful minds of the dangers through which their ancestors passed, fourteen printed placards were placed throughout the city indicating where and when the pioneers of 1780 were ambushed and scalped by hostile Indians. The repeated references in speeches and publications to the "murderous tomahawk" of the Indians may have exaggerated Indian savagery, but the natives who roamed the land before 1780 served a special symbolic purpose in Nashville's local history. The red man was seen as the antithesis of the civilization Nashville had achieved by 1880. The dangers and primitive hardships the early white settlers endured had all been a prelude to progress. The distance between savagery and civilization was emphasized by repeatedly contrasting the natural wilderness ruled by the Indian and the refined urban scene Nashville presented in 1880. "The shriek of the locomotive and the hum of industry is heard instead of the howl of the wolf and the whoop of the red man," boasted Thomas A. Atchison in his opening speech. The Centennial Commission even received one suggestion to exhibit a group of Indians "in their native costumes" in order to "show to the children and rising generation the great contrast between then and now."[23]

By keeping the focus of local history on the contrast between the beginning and end of the century, the progress of civilization was allowed to dominate the stage and become the paramount theme. The central crisis of Nashville's, and the South's, past—the Civil War—was pushed backstage, but not ignored. The subject was a delicate one, not only for the potential it had in reviving sectional hostility and scaring northern capital away, but because Nashville itself had been internally divided during the war. Indeed, before the firing of guns at Fort Sumter, Nashville was a strong pro-Union city. With the opening of the Louisville and Nashville Railroad (L&N) in 1859, the city began to serve as a major avenue of commerce between the North and South. Its distance from the Black Belt and the relative sparseness of large slave plantations in the city's environs made Nashville a poor breeding ground for the fanatical defense of slavery that flourished in the Deep South. In the presidential election of 1860 Nashville's voters expressed overwhelming support for John Bell and the Constitutional Union Party, who promised to keep the South within the Union. To be sure, when the secession issue was forced to its violent climax at Fort Sumter, much of the pro-Union support rapidly shifted, and the local vote to join the Confederacy was overwhelming.[24]

Nashville's destiny was never firmly tied to the Confederacy, however. Within less than a year Federal troops under General Don Carlos Buell marched to the door of the city. As the Confederate forces hastily evacuated they sought to impair Nashville's value as a supply center. Steamboats were destroyed or taken away, military provisions were given away, and some called for the wholesale destruction of machinery and buildings to leave the Federals nothing but ashes to claim. But when the Confederate soldiers put the torch to the suspension bridge and the L&N railroad bridge that spanned the Cumberland, angry citizens protested.[25] Here were Nashville's vital links to northern commerce— the lifeblood of the city.

When Union troops marched into Nashville, they were not welcomed with open arms, but their presence did mean that the war would make the city grow and prosper as a supply center for the Union troops that invaded the South. The railroad bridge was easily repaired, and the L&N Railroad resumed its important role as a link between North and South by transporting supplies for the advancing Union troops. Nashville, which also manufactured some of those supplies, thus held considerable strategic importance. The Confederates fully understood this and twice attempted to recapture the city. After the war Nashville's boosters occasionally expressed perverse pride in all the blood that was spilled over control of their city, for it proved the extraordinary natural advantages of the city as a center of commerce in peace as well as war.[26]

The large numbers of Federal troops that swelled Nashville's population during the war had a permanent effect not only on the city's growth but on its image as a border state metropolis whose leadership would help reunite the North and South. Many Federal soldiers stayed on in Nashville, a good number of them to settle down with local brides.[27] The gifts of Commodore Vanderbilt and George Peabody to Nashville's educational institutions underscored the city's role in the educational reconstruction of the South after the war. Above all, the expansion of the railroad network, particularly the vast L&N system, made Nashville a key point in the interchange of northern manufactured goods and southern agricultural staples. The city, and most of the South, would also depend on northern capital to help underwrite the New South dream of industrial growth and agricultural diversification. For all these reasons the South's Lost Cause had to be recognized —even enshrined—but in such a way as to repress all traces of the ideological furor that led to massive violence two decades earlier. One way to deal with the "late war" was simply to ignore it as much as possible. Charles Edwin Robert's official *City Guide,* sponsored by the Centennial Commission in 1880, led off with a lengthy historical sketch of the city but allowed only one short paragraph about the war. This was only to mention Nashville's key position as the "gateway" to the South, a fact reflected "in its present vast importance as a railroad, commercial and educational center."[28]

The most important historical publication to come out of the Centennial in 1880 was Professor W. Woodford Clayton's *History of Davidson County,* sponsored by the Tennessee Historical Society. As though to be sure that the history would be free of sectional feeling, the author was brought in from Philadelphia. The nation's Centennial had spawned a minor industry in local history publications. All across the nation in the late 1870s and 1880s small towns and large cities commissioned professional histories to be done. These reasonably accurate publications provided buoyant chronicles of community progress. Criticism of unsavory aspects of the local past was carefully avoided, and laudatory sketches of the lives of leading citizens were included for those who were willing to pay the price. Clayton's treatment of the "great Civil War" was brief and tactful. After a succinct discussion of the issues preceding secession, Clayton turned to a long discussion of the military operations in and around Nashville. This fascination with military strategy and battles helped, paradoxically, to distract from the ideological divisions that brought the North and South into violent conflict.[29]

The same effect was achieved by the military drill competition during the Centennial celebration. Militia companies "of chivalrous soldiers from all sections of the country" came to Nashville to join the "magnificent military displays, consisting of reviews, tournaments, competitive drills, and sham battles. . . ." Prizes were announced for the "friendly competition" to be held out at the fairgrounds on Harding Pike (now Centennial Park). The editor of the *American* described the hundreds of brilliantly dressed soldiers who poured into Nashville for the drills: "Today those . . . who thundered at the portals of Nashville, or sternly resisted the advancing columns, are gathered here in friendly spirit, under one flag, devoted citizens of one Government." "The results of your meeting," John F. Wheless told the soldiers, "will be a mutual respect, confidence and friendship, the influence of which will be the restoration of harmony and the promotion of national greatness. Your meeting will be that of soldiers; your parting, we hope, will be that of comrades."[30]

The Old South's love of military valor was joined skillfully to the New South's dream of "the restoration of harmony and the promotion of national greatness." The marriage was solemnized with a beautifully orchestrated pageant toward the end of the Centennial celebration. May 20 was selected for "the crowning event of the Centennial jubilee." A grand military procession and review would be followed by the unveiling of the equestrian statue of Andrew Jackson at the Capitol. For the occasion, General Joseph E. Johnston, a warmly loved Confederate hero, was invited as a distinguished guest. A reception committee of Confederate veterans met the general's train in Tullahoma, stopping en route for Johnston to deliver speeches to the crowds at each station. At Nashville a large contingent of brass bands and veterans followed Johnston from the railroad station through the downtown streets. Loud cheers and throaty rebel yells from the thousands of veterans testified that the Lost Cause was not forgotten. "No cause is a failure," the *American* observed after Johnston's reception, "which can hold thousands to heroic and self-sacrificing endeavor." Johnston played his role perfectly. His speech at the Capitol the next day alluded to the war and "seemed to revive memories that spoke with no need of interpretation in the glowing faces and beaming eyes of the ex-Confederates in the audience." A loud applause greeted his claim that "the old Confederate soldiers made now the best and most loyal citizens of the Union, however much it might be that they cherished deep and sweet recollections of their own Cross of St. Andrews."[31]

On the morning of May 20 General Johnston rode in the same carriage with Union General Don Carlos Buell, conqueror of Nashville in 1862. A long parade of Centennial officers, government officials, and distinguished guests was followed by the militia companies and veterans' organizations that had come for the military drill competition. Behind them thronged "a jostling, pushing, shoving mass of people" through

Figure 3. Dedication of the Andrew Jackson Statue, May 20, 1880. Tennessee State Library and Archives.

Figure 4. Edmund W. "King" Cole (1827–1900). W. Woodford Clayton, *History of Davidson County, Tennessee* (Philadelphia, 1880).

the streets of the city to the east side of the Capitol building. Perched on fences and balconies, leaning from ledges, a "mass of humanity, a great sea of upturned faces," some 25,000 people, crowded in to witness the unveiling of the Jackson statue, which was now surrounded by a military guard.

The band played "Dixie" and the crowd cheered for General Johnston. The old warrior came forward and bowed to the enthusiastic response. Then the crowd shouted for General Buell, who also came forward to loud applause. After welcoming addresses and prayer by Vanderbilt's Bishop McTyeire, Congressman John F. House was given the stage for a long speech on Andrew Jackson, the Hero of New Orleans and this day the Hero of Nashville.[32]

The center of attraction, the Jackson equestrian statue, was the third of its kind cast by sculptor Clark Mills. One was placed in Lafayette Park in Washington, the other in Jackson Square in New Orleans. Before the war, efforts to acquire the third statue for Tennessee had failed. Now, with the city's Centennial, the Tennessee Historical Society took up the cause once more and raised money to bring the statue to Old Hickory's home town.[33] Jackson was the ideal symbol for Nashville's historical spirit. His political career was launched in the "howling wilderness" of Tennessee, and his fortunes rose with those of his state. As a military hero Jackson was associated with national expansion in the Old Southwest and was untainted by sectionalism. "Since he closed his eyes on a peaceful and happy country our land has been drenched in fraternal blood," House told the crowd around the statue. "But these unhappy days are past, and it is to the interest of all that the passions and animosities that marked them should also pass away." House closed with the famous words that now made Jackson a hero for the New South: "The Federal Union—it must be preserved." The band blared out the "Star Spangled Banner" as the crowd exploded in applause. An ode to Jackson, sung by the Harmonic Society, followed as the statue was unveiled to the admiring crowds.

That evening Nashville's citizens and visitors reconvened to watch a magnificent fireworks display. Toward the end the flares produced a portrait of the Hero of New Orleans, surrounded by sun rays. The "most notable day of the Centennial celebration" closed with a "grand allegory": Fiery letters spelled out "1780 NASHVILLE, MAY 20, 1880." Above the letters waved "the starry banner" and to each side were revolving globes "representing the Old and New World."[34] At that moment in its history Nashville surely stood between two worlds, one old, the other new. In its celebration of the past century the city had demonstrated its determination to join the new world of cities, railroads, industry, and commerce. But at the same time Nashville revealed an equal determination that this new world would be a southern world, a world that would build upon its past.

THE STRUGGLE
FOR COMMERCIAL EMPIRE

Nashville's growth in the years following the Centennial seemed to fulfill many of the ambitious boasts of the day. From a population in 1880 of 43,350 clustered within a mile of the waterfront, the city swelled outward, filling a radius of almost four miles. The census of 1910 showed 110,364 people within the city borders and another 39,114 in the surrounding county. (For city and county population figures, 1860–1980, see appendix A.) The historical pattern of growth was erratic. During the 1880s the population increased almost 76 percent (accelerating from a 68-percent gain in the 1870s), but a severe depression in the 1890s hit Nashville particularly hard and the growth rate plummeted to a little over 6 percent in that decade. The next ten years saw Nashville recover from this slump to acquire 36 percent more people within its borders. Citizens were reassured by city boosters that Nashville—the "Rock City"—was experiencing steady growth on a solid foundation, unlike the kind of "mushroom" growth experienced by rivals like Atlanta, Birmingham, and Memphis. But this was little solace in the face of news that all these cities, aided by superior transportation facilities along with vigorous commercial and industrial expansion, had passed Nashville by 1900 or 1910. Beginning at a rank of fortieth among United States cities in 1880 and rising to thirty-eighth by 1890, Nashville fell to forty-seventh by 1900 and regained only slightly by 1910, when it stood forty-fifth in size.[1]

Whatever Nashville's relative position among southern rivals, the city shared in a vital burst of economic growth among the interior cities of the South, which all benefited from a radical shift in patterns of trade. Seaports like Charleston, Savannah, Mobile, and New Orleans, dependent upon vast river systems to drain the South of cotton, tobacco, and other export commodities, once dominated the commerce of the region without challenge. Now the expansion of the railway system pulled trade away from the rivers toward interior cities, which enjoyed central location and direct access to the North.

Nashville's strategic location was appreciated fully by the management of the L&N Railroad. The empire this giant constructed in the late nineteenth century made it one of the most powerful systems in the South. Nashville's commercial strength was supplemented by the Tennessee Central Railroad, a home-owned rival, and the Cumberland River steamboat trade. But the L&N dominated Nashville's commercial growth, and the L&N — controlled by outside interests — also set the limits of growth.

The stream of wealth drawn from commercial activities flowed into diverse economic channels: manufacturing, banking, insurance, and education. Each branch of Nashville's new economy met in some way the particular needs of the New South as it struggled to move away from its dependence upon the North.

The creation of this new economic structure in Nashville owed much to the accidental blessings of central geographic location and other forces external to the city. But it was also the product of an ambitious crowd of "new men" whose vision and entrepreneurial skills propelled Nashville into a leading position in the emerging economic structure of the South. These were men who linked their insatiable drive for individual success with the collective effort of city building. They set the tone of the times, creating a vigorous climate of enterprise that opened the city to new ideas — and new money.

KING COLE AND THE L&N OCTOPUS

Precisely as Nashville prepared to celebrate its Centennial in the winter of 1879–80, the city rejoiced over a stunning coup by hometown railroad entrepreneur Edmund W. Cole. Against all odds "King" Cole had put together a through line from St. Louis, the rising emporium for western grain and meat, all the way to Atlanta, and from there to the Atlantic Ocean at Savannah. The heart of this new system was the Nashville, Chattanooga and St. Louis Railroad (NC & stL), a line nurtured and owned primarily by Nashville's own capitalists. Cole, a farm boy from Giles County, came to Nashville in 1845 at the age of eighteen, began as a store clerk, and educated himself at night. Eventually he worked his way up from bookkeeper for the old Nashville and Chattanooga Railroad in the 1850s to become its president in 1868. He rapidly turned a dilapidated small line into a formidable railroad enterprise by 1880.[2]

In December 1879 King Cole unveiled his grand scheme to the world. Grain and meat that previously flowed from the Midwest to New York before coming South now would funnel into St. Louis and through Nashville to all parts of the South. Cole, the "Deliverer of the South," would create for Nashville a role of central commercial importance.[3] Cole's new kingdom, however, intruded into the realm of the L&N, which until now had dominated the central South without serious challenge. Many Nashville merchants resented the powerful influence of the L&N on their city's trade. Louisville interests controlled the company from the outset, and the road was run to the advantage of the northern terminal city. One by one, several small rail lines serving Nashville had been taken over by the L&N. Now, with a second major railroad system entering Nashville, and one controlled by local interests, Nashville could expect competitive rates from the L&N as well as a huge increase in the combined volume of trade.

King Cole's dream and Nashville's heady vision of sharing this commercial empire vanished almost as rapidly as they appeared. Just as Cole was putting the finishing touches on his grand plan, the NC&StL attorney, Godfrey M. Fogg, who had been privy to all Cole's negotiations, left Nashville suddenly for a secret meeting. Fogg told Cole he was rushing to Washington to defend the company in a lawsuit, but he went instead to New York. There he met with his uncle, Vernon K. Stevenson, former president of the NC&StL, Thomas Evans (both former citizens of Nashville and friends of Cole), and financier Christopher Baldwin. The four men went into secret negotiations with Victor Newcomb and L&N President E.D. Standiford to arrange a sale of NC&StL stock to the L&N. Acting on rumors of the meeting, Cole telegraphed Stevenson and pleaded with him to hold his stock while Cole tried desperately to buy up other shares to keep from the L&N. His efforts were in vain, and on Saturday, January 18, 1880, Cole received a conciliatory telegram from Newcomb informing him that his company had been bought out by the L&N.[4]

Cole's "magnificent idea" for Nashville and the South was dead. The news swept through Nashville, and "on the streets . . . the subject [was] being discussed in all its bearings by all classes." Merchants called an "indignation meeting" to publicize their outrage at the L&N. Effigies of Stevenson and his cronies were publicly burned, and threats were made to burn the L&N depot. Fogg was compared to Judas Iscariot. The whole affair was interpreted locally as a betrayal of friendship and treachery against an honorable city, but it is better understood as a product of the L&N's aggressive strategy to expand and monopolize its southern territory.

Newcomb's territorial strategy led to a series of takeovers; the NC&StL would be only the first of several small fish the octopus would capture. By the summer of 1880 Newcomb had expanded the L&N's network to 2,348 miles. It was now a regional giant far ahead of all competing southern roads.[5] The very strategy that led Newcomb to expand his system required the company to raise more capital on Wall Street. Control over the L&N consequently shifted from Louisville to New York by 1880. The company fell into the hands of northern financiers residing in the North rather than southern railroad managers, and the new breed of young entrepreneur that emerged in the 1880s saw the company as a vehicle for financial speculation rather than an instrument for southern economic development.[6]

In 1884 New York-born Milton Hannibal Smith took over as president of the L&N, a position he held until 1921. Smith first gained his railroad experience working for Union-controlled roads during the Civil War. He brought to the L&N an aggressive design to expand the company's southern empire. Under his leadership the L&N's track mileage increased two and one-half times, to over 5,000 miles by 1921. In 1886 the L&N, in a Herculean effort, reworked every mile of track and every axle on its freight cars and locomotives to bring the system into conformity with the northern standard gauge of 4 feet and 9 inches.[7]

Smith also came to personify the imperious attitude of the railroads toward the local interests of cities like Nashville. In his 1896 correspondence with Samuel Spencer, president of the Southern Railway, which dominated the Southeast, he likened them both to Spanish conquistadors:

> PIZARRO (Smith): How shall we divide the New World?
> CORTEZ (Spencer): I will take North America and you can have all of South America, . . . and neither of us will do anything to the Isthmus without notice to and cooperation of the other.
> PIZARRO: While Patagonia is not a very large or important part of the world, yet, perhaps, it is as much as I can tote.[8]

As control over the southern rail system shifted into the hands of the northern conquistadors, Nashville merchants grew increasingly resentful of the monopolistic stranglehold the L&N had on their commercial fortunes. Without northern capital the full expansion of the L&N would have been impossible, and without this vast system Nashville never would have grown as it had into the commercial center of the central South. Indeed, the L&N's strategy favored Nashville's dominance as distribution center for a large territory in southern Kentucky, much of Tennessee, and northern Alabama.[9] Nevertheless, Nashville's business leaders persistently pursued a strategy of developing alternative transportation systems for their city. One course was to nurture a home-grown railroad independent of "foreign interests." The other was to exploit in new ways a traditional avenue of commerce, the Cumberland River.

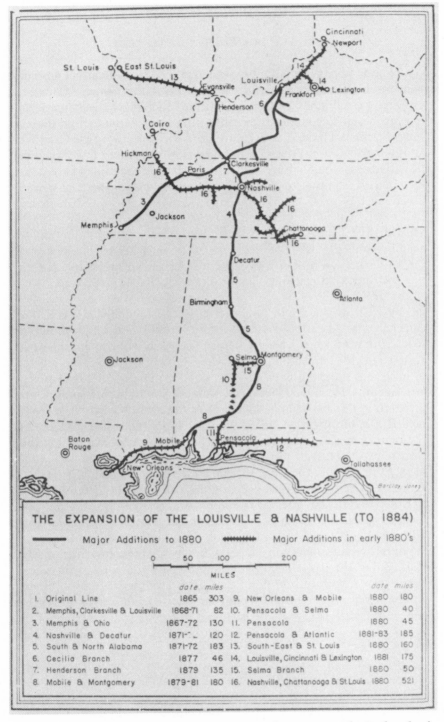

Figure 5. Map: The L&N System, 1880s. From John F. Stover, *The Railroads of the South, 1865–1900: A Study in Finance and Control* (Chapel Hill, 1955), 216.

JERE BAXTER AND THE "LIBERTY LINE"

No one was better suited to redeem King Cole's dream of an independent, locally controlled railroad than Jere Baxter. When Baxter first organized the Tennessee Central Railroad in 1893, he was just forty-one years old. The son of Nashville's prominent jurist and politician, Judge Nathaniel Baxter, he came of age in the city during the Civil War and Reconstruction. After a schooling at Montgomery Bell Academy, he defied his father's advice, and with $500 from the sale of two mules he sailed off to Europe to put together an ambitious commercial scheme involving European exports to Central America. He was stranded in Berlin, where he taught English for two years before returning to Nashville in 1874. He immediately began a promising career in law and legal publishing (*Baxter's Reports* remains an indispensable reference tool for Tennessee lawyers). On the side he engaged in innovative real estate ventures that spawned Baxter Block on Union Street and Baxter Court on Church.

By 1879, at the age of twenty-five, Baxter launched a whole new career as railroad entrepreneur with the Memphis and Charleston Railroad, which he served briefly as the youngest railroad president in America in 1881 and 1882. At the same time he organized a company of local and northern capitalists to develop the coal fields of northern Alabama. He helped found and promote Sheffield, Alabama; South Pittsburgh, Tennessee; and Arkansas City. In every way Jere Baxter embodied that omnivorous entrepreneurial spirit that took hold among the rising generation in the cities of the New South. Everything this "steam engine on legs" put his hand to seemed to succeed. But when he went up against the octopus, Jere Baxter met his match.[10] Baxter's Tennessee Central Railroad was originally designed to link Nashville to Knoxville on the east and Memphis on the west; above all, it was to give Nashville its own railroad free of L&N control. By the 1890s six railroad lines reached Nashville, every one under L&N control.[11] Baxter began raising funds and constructing the eastern branch of the new line in 1893, but the Panic of 1893 dashed the new company to ruins and left it over a half-million dollars in debt. Finding little enthusiasm among Nashville capitalists, Baxter turned to St. Louis, where over the course of nearly two years he managed to persuade a syndicate of investors to buy the bankrupt Tennessee Central and reinstall Baxter as its president.[12]

By September 1898, against all odds, the eastern branch was nearly complete. Baxter invited two hundred of Nashville's leading businessmen to join him and the St. Louis capitalists on an excursion along the new "Liberty Line" to survey the commercial domain they now commanded. As all the pompous prophecies of wealth the railroad would bring to Nashville circulated, however, the giants were already

Figure 6. Jere Baxter (1852–1904), president of the Tennessee Central Railroad. Tennessee State Library and Archives.

Figure 7. Exterior of the L&N's Union Station, completed 1900. Tennessee State Library and Archives.

aroused by the challenge Baxter posed and were well along in a plan to destroy the Tennessee Central. Baxter's line was an east-west route that cut across the territory of two major north-south lines, the L&N and the Southern. Baxter, in other words, had crossed the "isthmus" these two rivals had agreed not to invade, and in doing so he threatened to wreck the territorial balance worked out earlier. Samuel Spencer of the Southern wrote to Milton Smith in February 1896, playing on the conquistador metaphor Smith had introduced earlier.

> PIZARRO (Smith): Since our last conversation the division of the New World between us had made some progress.
> CORTEZ (Spencer): Yes, you seem to have acquired Patagonia, and I have secured a considerable part of North America . . . ,but it seems to me you have acquired a considerable neck of the Isthmus which is the connecting link between us. Was it understood that connecting links which touched both of us should be a matter of consultation before acting or not?[13]

Spencer was alluding to some "defensive mergers" the L&N had engineered already on the western arm of Baxter's new line. Would not the L&N, pursuing this defensive strategy, be forced to buy up the entire Baxter line, penetrate the isthmus, and thus bring the conquistadors into a massive territorial battle? Smith and Spencer were keenly aware of the cost such a battle would mean to their companies, and they agreed neither would try to acquire the Tennessee Central or any other lines that cut between them. Instead, they would let such challengers "stew in their own fat," that is "if any fat be found in them."[14]

The most serious blow the L&N struck against Jere Baxter's railroad came later when the Tennessee Central was excluded from terminal facilities at the new Union Station. Nashville's passenger facilities had long been a symbol in the eyes of critics of the shabby treatment the city suffered from the L&N. The move for a new depot began as early as 1886, when the old L&N station north of the Public Square burned, and the parent company was forced to share cramped quarters with its subsidiary, the NC&StL, in its depot on Walnut (now Tenth Avenue) between Church and Union. The L&N Terminal Company incorporated in 1893 (the same year Baxter organized the Tennessee Central) and announced plans for a grand depot in the gulch south of the existing station. During debate in the state legislature certain amendments to the Terminal Company's charter, which would have kept the station open to all railroads, were defeated with the help of concerted pressure and the influence (some would say bribery) of free passenger passes from L&N lobbyists.[15]

The City Council was less easily manipulated at first. The city controlled rights of way on streets crossing the proposed site, and the council's consent was delayed for five years during which several bills and

amendments were fought over intensely. In June 1898 Mayor Richard
Houston Dudley approved the "Depot Bill," which in the end included
no provision for access by the Tennessee Central.[16] The L&N had scored
another hard-won victory. Construction began immediately on Union
Station, and by the fall of 1900 this magnificent structure opened its
doors to Nashville's citizens.

Union Station was one part of a conscious effort by the L&N to win
good will among the people of Nashville. The extravagant use of interior space and elaborate ornamentation seemed to refute the sinister
image of an octopus squeezing the economic life out of the community. The station was designed in the fashionable Richardsonian Romanesque style. Its main tower soared over 200 feet into the sky, adorned
with a modern digital clock and a statue of Mercury, the mythical messenger of the gods. The main waiting room walls were covered in oak
and marble; the ceiling had an ornate skylight that flooded the room
with sunshine. On one end two young female figures in bas-relief represented the cities of Louisville and Nashville with arms outstretched
to one another. Opposite them, two other figures represented Time and
Progress. No modern-day public relations firm could have found a more
pleasing combination of environment and symbol to assuage popular
distrust of the railroad.[17]

Opening day was a grand occasion for the company to cultivate the
good will of the people who gazed approvingly at this lavish gift of corporate wealth to the citizenry of Nashville. The ceremonies began with
a gala procession which wound through the streets of downtown and
finished at the new depot. Inside, listeners were treated to many speakers, all of whom applauded the munificence of the railroads to Nashville. It would have been easy in the midst of this splendid new palace
and all the pompous speeches to forget that Union Station would exclude Nashville's own railroad, the Tennessee Central, and was in truth
a symbol of the L&N's control of the city. But when it came time for
Mayor James M. Head to perform the rites of his office in welcoming
the company's guests to Nashville, he gave the crowd a jolt. Head, a
zealous opponent of corporate monopolies, made a bold speech that
blasted the L&N for shutting out Jere Baxter's railroad and denying Nashville its right to economic freedom. Nashville, Head warned the city's
eminent guests, is not a "lemon to be squeezed" by outside capitalists.
He left his stunned audience with a subtle but pointed allusion to the
myth of Mercury, whose likeness stood atop the station tower: "May
the winger messenger of the immortals, whose figure adorns the top
of this building, in his eagerness to promote the blessings of commerce
and the harmony of social intercourse, forget the discord which the theft
of the fifty oxen produced in the mythical history of the god it represents." The opening of Union Station coincided with the beginning of

Figure 8. Interior of Union Station. Tennessee State Library and Archives.

Figure 9. Jere Baxter's proposed depot for the Tennessee Central Railroad. It was to be near the foot of Broad, but Baxter's difficulties with the L&N prevented it from being completed in this grand style. From Elmer G. Sulzer, *Ghost Railroads of Tennessee* (Indianapolis, 1975).

a pre-Lenten carnival and street fair that thousands attended. Amid the revelry and the imposing beauty of the new station, Mayor Head's bitter words were momentarily forgotten.[18]

Jere Baxter escalated his fight against the L&N by trying to meet the company on its own terms, with political manipulation and newspaper propaganda. Prior to the ceremonies at Union Station, Baxter and Mayor Head staged a mass meeting in the Union Gospel Tabernacle (later named Ryman Auditorium) to stir public support for what would be the western branch of the Tennessee Central. The meeting took on the tone of a religious revival, with converts in the audience pledging to support Baxter's plan, which would involve $5 million, including $1 million in city funds. The City Council promptly put the question to the public in December 1900, and the vote showed overwhelming support for Baxter.[19]

Four men brought suit against the city's plan to purchase the $1 million in railroad stock, and they won an injunction. Baxter quickly reorganized the railroad as the Nashville and Clarksville to conform with the court ruling against city support of interstate roads. In August 1901 the City Council put the $1 million question to the people again, and again the voters gave strong support to Baxter. Another suit was filed by J. Craig McLanahan of Pennsylvania and other nonresident Nashville taxpayers, this time alleging election fraud. Later it was revealed the NC&StL was behind the suit.[20] When construction finally began on the western branch of the Tennessee Central, which was to go along the river on Front Street (now First Avenue), Baxter was blocked by another court injunction, which forced the Tennessee Central to take a long detour around the south edge of the city.[21]

In his battle to win popular support for his railroad, Baxter found no help from the city's leading newspapers, for both were heavily influenced by the L&N. The *Banner* was published by Edward B. Stahlman, former general freight agent and vice president for the L&N. The *American* had been taken over in 1895 by Eugene C. Lewis, president of the L&N Terminal Company and chairman of the board for the NC&StL. The "old roads" (as Baxter always referred to the L&N and the NC&StL) "bottled up" the press as thoroughly as they had the commerce of Nashville. Baxter started his own *Daily News* just before the second city election on the stock subscription in the summer of 1901. He used it effectively as a forum from which to blast his enemies and arouse public sentiment in favor of his plans, often with his own florid rhetoric. Baxter's indignant polemic, "In the Grip of Monopoly," compared Nashville's situation to the classical statue of the Laocoön, which depicted an old man and his sons ensnared by serpents: "The old man is Tennessee; the two children are Statesmanship and Commerce, choked and throttled into submission by the twin serpents, the two great common carriers . . . acting together with a single understanding, prosperous, powerful, pompous, but pitiless."[22]

Jere Baxter's finest day came in the spring of 1902 when the Tennessee Central entered Nashville for the first time. An estimated 10,000 people greeted the train at the new Tennessee Central depot near the river south of Broad; another 5,000 lined the tracks coming into the city. Baxter, Mayor James M. Head, and other company officers mounted a special platform attached to the front of the locomotive as the train steamed into town. A portrait of Baxter, surrounded by garlands of evergreens, adorned the front of the engine, and the hero of the day blew the "liberty whistle" loud enough to be heard all the way to Union Station.

A large procession formed at the depot, led by mounted police, the Gray and Dudley Band, several fire and militia companies, and Baxter atop a spirited black horse, behind him a string of fancy carriages carrying Governor Benton McMillin, the City Council, and various other dignitaries. In their own carriages came a large contingent of lavishly gowned ladies, and behind them, led by their own brass band, came the "colored" lodges, militia company, and assorted citizens in carriages. The parade moved up to the public square and then out Broad, tauntingly close to Union Station before it returned down Broad to the Union Gospel Tabernacle. Mayor Head congratulated the people of Nashville on this great day for their support of the Tennessee Central: "They [the L&N] bought out the press, entered the halls of the Legislature and finally tried to corrupt the ballot box, but thanks to the manhood and integrity of Nashville's citizens, they didn't succeed." Baxter then held the audience for over an hour, promising them "the forty years of gloom that have hung over the city of Nashville like a dark cloud have now passed away."

An elegant victory banquet sponsored by the Retail Merchants Association and Chamber of Commerce followed that evening, when more congratulations streamed forth. "Free at last, thank God!" one joyous citizens summarized the day. Baxter has "bearded the octopus in his den, and like Bosco, eaten him alive. They have snatched us from the tentacles of the monster—and only charged us a million dollars for the job."[23]

In the same year Baxter strengthened his political attack on the L&N by running successfully for the Davidson County seat in the state Senate. He began by pushing through a bill ratifying the contested city election, thus securing the million-dollar stock subscription. He also sponsored the terminal bill, which would have forced Union Station open to any railroad entering Nashville and, in the process, would have strengthened state regulation of railroads. The "Baxter bill," as it soon came to be known, was debated intensely in the winter of 1903, and both sides worked hard to win public favor and legislative votes.

In the end the bill was defeated, and so, finally, was Jere Baxter. During hearings on the Baxter bill the attorney for the NC&STL, Claude Waller, mentioned one reason for the unwillingness of the "old roads" to accommodate the Tennessee Central: Baxter's slanderous attacks on Smith and Lewis. Baxter had become persona non grata. Jere Baxter adroitly seized this opportunity to make a dramatic public resignation as president of the Tennessee Central in order to "give place to someone who was not obnoxious to the two old roads. . . ."[24] Baxter's strategy was to reduce the whole conflict to a personal dispute, deftly remove that issue by resigning, then publicly embarrass the L&N into negotiating with the Tennessee Central for access to Union Station. The L&N did not rise to the bait, and it became clear it was not Jere Baxter but the threat of an independent railroad that was, in fact, obnoxious to the L&N.

Within a few months of his resignation Baxter fell ill with kidney failure. He died February 29, 1904, at fifty-four years of age. A massive public funeral took place in the Tabernacle on March 1. All business in the city was suspended for the day, and a crowd of 4,000 to 5,000 gathered in the building where Jere Baxter once aroused their enthusiasm for the railroad.[25]

The next year the Tennessee Central leased its western branch to the Illinois Central and the eastern branch to the Southern Railway. Even these giants were repelled by the L&N. When they laid plans to jointly purchase the Tennessee Central and build modern terminal facilities on the river in North Nashville, the L&N quickly erected next to Union Station a modern warehouse complex known as Cummins Station, which drew businesses away from the riverfront and made the North Nashville plans far more risky.[26] The Illinois Central and Southern withdrew interest in the Tennessee Central in 1908, and by 1912 the company went into receivership. It was revived in 1922 and managed to survive the growing competition from trucks and highways until 1968, when it folded. The old roadbed surrounding the city again became embroiled in controversy as the proposed route for Interstate Highway 440, an ironic end for Jere Baxter's dream.[27]

Baxter's admirers had in mind a more fitting tribute to their hero when they raised money for a statue that was unveiled in 1907. It stood at the intersection of Broadway and Sixteenth, where West End Avenue begins. For years, before it was removed to Jere Baxter School, his statue stood amid the passing trolleys and autos, his eyes gazing to the east where his railroad rose into the Cumberlands, the view partly obstructed, appropriately enough, by the rising tower of Union Station. Even in victory the L&N could not resist a final blow to its former adversary. After the statue was unveiled, Eugene C. Lewis, a member of the City Park Commission, arranged for a marker to be erected in Centennial Park honoring one John Murrell, a legendary horse and slave thief in early Tennessee, who compared favorably, Lewis thought, with the man who sold the city one million dollars of near-worthless railroad stock.[28]

TOM RYMAN AND THE STEAMBOAT ERA

The mixed blessing of the L&N's monopoly on Nashville's railroad service turned many leaders toward the original source of the city's commercial life—the Cumberland River. Before the 1890s the river provided Nashville with a natural market that tapped over 500 miles from the mouth at the Ohio River to Burnside, Kentucky, near the navigable headwaters. The hilly terrain of the territory upriver from Nashville was forbidding to railroads, and there the steamboats for a time could run free of competition from their iron adversaries. Downriver, where the Cumberland flowed through a less hilly and richer agricultural hinterland, the railroads lured away much of the trade the steamboats once commanded.

Cotton, the mainstay of the antebellum steamboat trade, quickly receded from middle Tennessee with the collapse of the slave plantation system. A more diversified pattern of agriculture took its place. The new leading crops, corn, oats, wheat, and hay, were all semiperishable, and the growing volume of cattle, hogs, poultry, and dairy products also required the more rapid and dependable service of the railroads. Even the expansion of the tobacco crop, which might have offset the decline of cotton, was slowly taken over by the railroads after the L&N built a main line through Clarksville and a series of branch lines across the dark-fired tobacco fields of Tennessee and Kentucky.[29]

The single most important cargo on the river was the grain that flowed in huge volume out of the Midwest on the Mississippi and Ohio rivers and then upstream to Nashville. The railroads quickly extended their tentacles to cut off this flow of grain and redirect it along the rail lines. The NC&StL and the L&N provided free use of grain elevators to shippers and offered privileged rates on grain coming into Nashville. Not only did the privileged rates give the railroads a distinct advantage over the steamboats, it gave grain merchants in Nashville a decisive advantage over those in rival southern cities. Around these railroad rate privileges Nashville would build a major center for grain processing and distribution of flour and meal throughout the region. The "Minneapolis of the South," as the boosters touted their city, owed its advantages to the competition between river and rail shippers.[30]

The railroads and steamboats established an unspoken agreement to avoid cutthroat price competition and maintain the status quo, in which the railroads allowed steamboats a portion of the grain trade to

Figure 10. The Lower Wharf and Front Street (First Avenue North) in the late nineteenth century. Tennessee State Library and Archives.

Figure 11. Captain Thomas G. Ryman (1841–1904). Byrd Douglas Papers, Tennessee State Library and Archives.

Nashville. The "Cumberland Compromise" was not the product of any soft-hearted generosity toward the steamboats; it was an effort by the L&N to protect the railroad privileges for Nashville and maintain their control over the southern grain, flour, and meal markets. The grain privileges were just one aspect of the L&N's strategy to establish Nashville as the major distribution center for a vast territory below Louisville and Cincinnati on the Ohio River extending from Jackson, Tennessee, on the west, to Decatur, Alabama, on the south and over to Chattanooga and the Applachian Mountains on the east. Within this large territory freight rates were designed by the L&N and its subsidiaries to discourage direct shipments to all points except Nashville. While Nashville businessmen were complaining about the octopus and the lack of competition within their city, rival cities complained just as loudly about the favoritism Nashville enjoyed under L&N rate policies.[31]

With the passage of federal regulatory acts, particularly the Interstate Commerce Act in 1887 and the Sherman Anti-trust Act of 1890, the national government began to act as a referee of the marketplace. Now rival cities could complain about Nashville's privileges—not just to the L&N, but to the Interstate Commerce Commission—and complain they did. In the face of government challenges the L&N was able to justify its favorable rates to Nashville by pointing to the fact that it was a river city, and that steamboat competition required lower rates than to cities that had no navigable river. But steamboat competition had to be be genuine. In 1892, in response to a Chattanooga complaint, one Interstate Commerce Commission member argued there "was no more water competition in Nashville than there was on top of the Rocky Mountains." The railroad rate privileges, designed to annihilate steamboat competition, now required the continued presence of the steamboat in order to be protected.[32]

But the steamboats could continue in the lucrative grain trade only by token competition for a fraction of the market. If the steamboats were to survive and prosper, they would have to turn upriver beyond reach of the octopus. Competition both from railroads and other steamboat operators on the lower river forced many of the small operators out of business during the 1870s. In the 1880s Captain Tom Ryman built his line of packet steamboats into the dominant force on this part of the river.

Captain Tom Ryman was the waterborne counterpart of railroad entrepreneurs Edmund Cole and Jere Baxter. Born in South Nashville in 1841, Ryman was raised on the rivers of Tennessee. He worked with his father as a commercial fisherman in Chattanooga for ten years before he returned to Nashville during the Civil War to take advantage of the booming demand for fish among the military population. His father died penniless in 1864, and Ryman "set manfully to work" to support his mother and her four other children. By 1865 he bought his first steamboat and began hauling cargoes along the Cumberland. Beginning in 1875 he organized three packet lines, consolidating them in 1885 as the Ryman Line. He built a magnificent mansion on Rutledge Hill overlooking his steamboat empire. Then in 1885 Tom Ryman suddenly got religion when Methodist evangelist Sam Jones converted him. Ryman eliminated the lucrative saloons on his boats and led a drive to build the Union Gospel Tabernacle, which became the nerve center of Nashville's religious and political life in this period.[33]

During the 1880s Ryman was able to drive out many of his competitors, but by this time the competition of the railroad overshadowed all else. With its improved grain elevators and privileged rates, the railroad forced Ryman, who was still in the prime of his business career, to consider several cruel choices about his future on the river. He could, of course, take on the L&N in a price-cutting war, but time would be on the side of the giant corporation in this game. Others thought Ryman should refit his steamboats to work as tugboats and haul barges of grain on contract. But converting the packets into tugboats would be enormously costly, and there was considerable risk in the venture. Besides, Captain Ryman had no taste for dismantling his floating palaces and less for making himself into an operator of an unglamorous fleet of tugboats.[34]

The strategy Ryman pursued instead was to maintain whatever share of the trade on the lower river the railroads allowed and turn upriver to expand his empire. The upriver trade was filled with several small, independent operators, many of them owners of single boats, who often picked up trade as they went with no scheduled packet service. These independent operators resented Ryman's entry into their territory, and they promised a vicious battle for control of the upper river. The independent boatmen met Ryman in a bitter, highly personal battle to defeat him and the monstrous railroad they saw allied with him. Every boat Ryman sent out was followed by an independent boat. When Ryman cut rates, they followed. Freight rates fell drastically in the 1890s from fifteen cents per hundred pounds to ten cents and finally to five cents. Profits necessarily fell too, for now increases in volume could not make up for the decline in rates. This was a war that would leave both sides mortally wounded. So, precisely as the steamboat operators confronted their formidable adversary on the lower river, they faced one another in a more vicious and ruinous struggle in the only region the railroads could not yet penetrate.[35]

The Upper Cumberland Valley contained some 400,000 people in this period, and they depended solely on the river to bring them a wide variety of goods they were unable to manufacture locally: hardware, farm implements, stoves, patent medicines, clothing, boots, and shoes. In return, the people of the valley sent downriver a growing volume of produce, meat, livestock, eggs, dairy products, tobacco, furs, and molasses.[36]

One of the most important products of the upper Cumberland—lumber—came downriver without the steamboat. The Cumberland Mountains were covered with virgin forests of oak, hickory, ash, poplar, and other hardwoods. About 13 million acres of forest lay waiting to be harvested, milled, and manufactured. Some of this timber was rough cut in the small saw mills upriver and taken by boat down to Nashville. But as the lumber business boomed in the 1880s it was found the best way to handle this product was to haul the felled timber by mule or short rail spur to the river, lash the logs into a huge raft, and float the raft down to the large saw mills that lined the eastern banks of the river opposite the main wharf. The raft was usually 200 (sometimes 250) feet long and required extraordinary agility to control around curves and obstructions in the river. A crew of six gritty hill men guided the raft with huge rudders or "sweeps" at front and back. The men slept in turns in a crude lean-to lined with straw, cooked their food on board, and arrived in Nashville after two weeks of floating, a grisly, fearsome-looking breed who enjoyed "taking the town" by celebrating their arrival in the saloons and vice dens along the waterfront.[37]

During high season, after the river rose in the spring, one could see tied up along the banks of the river, for miles above and below the city, up to 50 million board feet of timber. By 1882 the *Southern Lumberman*, a newly established journal for the industry published in Nashville, reported that 56 million feet of lumber worth nearly $3.4 million had been milled in Nashville that year. By 1903 annual footage stood at 400 million feet, worth $4.8 million.[38]

Along with the rafts of timber came coal mined in the area above Burnside, Kentucky, and floated downriver by barge to Nashville. Smith's shoals, which dropped 65 feet, presented a treacherous obstacle to the small barges and many were lost, but the coal trade to Nashville was profitable enough to justify the risks. The coal barge crews were a notoriously rough-looking bunch. The coal dust blackened their faces and apparently created a powerful thirst for whiskey, which they quenched lustily at the end of a long trip to Nashville. The coal barge and timber raft crews would return to their homes in the hills on the steamboat packets going upriver from Nashville. With nothing else to do, they whiled away the time playing cards, shooting craps, drinking raw whiskey, and matching one another in outrageous cursing. The saloons on the steamboats no doubt recaptured for the boat owners a good deal of the income they lost in lumber and coal cargoes. After Captain Ryman got religion in 1885, he ended this lucrative source of profit by banishing the saloons on his boats; he also must have given up a good number of passenger fares from the upriver raft and barge men.[39]

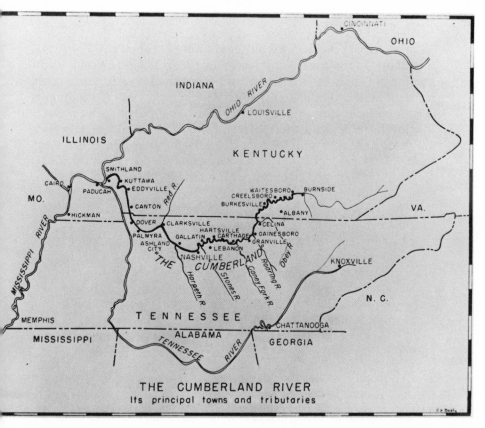

Figure 12. Map: The Cumberland River Valley. Byrd Douglas Papers, Tennessee State Library and Archives.

Figure 13. The launching of a new oil barge at Nashville's wharf, August 1919. One of the last of the upriver steamboat packets is on the left. Byrd Douglas Papers, Tennessee State Library and Archives.

The critical problem for all these lines of trade was the seasonal fluctuation of the river. Below Nashville the river was navigable about six to eight months of the year, and some shallow-draft boats could ply these waters throughout the year. Upriver, only four to six months permitted navigation to Burnside, usually beginning in December.[40] Moreover, the opening and closing of the river varied radically from one year to the next, making it particularly risky for producers of vegetables, dairy products, and eggs, who relied on the river. Nature, it seemed, had provided a bountiful hinterland for Nashville and at the same time denied reliable access to it.

The answer was to build locks and dams and to canalize the river to allow year-round navigation, but no combination of steamboat, merchant, and farmer interests was sufficient to underwrite such a costly project. Beginning in 1889 Nashville merchants forged a coalition to bring pressure to bear upon the federal government to take on this task. They sponsored a convention that fall with about two hundred delegates from Nashville and other points along the river. The Cumberland River Improvement Association was organized to serve as an ongoing lobby for merchants interested in river commerce. Throughout this period the association worked diligently to pressure the federal government to increase funds and speed work on a series of locks and dams. But the locks and dams came too late to save the steamboats. Annual tonnage skidded from a high of 1 million in the 1880s to 375,000 after the turn of the century. The romantic era of the steamboat, its captains, roustabouts, and colorful passengers, gave way to the utilitarian barge that hauled sand and gravel, dredged from the river bottom, to Nashville's building materials merchants—this being one of the few cargoes the railroads could not steal from the river.[41]

Captain Tom Ryman died in the twilight of the steamboat era, December 23, 1904. He died from injuries incurred in a collision on the viaduct near Union Station, when horses, frightened by the locomotives, rammed a wagon into Ryman's buggy. Like Jere Baxter, who died earlier the same year, Ryman was honored with a magnificent public funeral in the Tabernacle. Sam Jones returned to eulogize his convert in the building they both worked to raise. The Tabernacle would be named after its founder following the funeral, and it remains one of the few lasting monuments to Ryman and the empire he once commanded.[42]

What Ryman and Baxter failed to do in their struggle with the L&N the federal government now pursued with new fervor. Ryman's successors decided to withdraw from the marginally profitable downriver trade, leaving the railroads without the token river competition to justify the privileged rates on grain. By 1910 a group of Atlanta merchants successfully petitioned the Interstate Commerce Commission to investigate what they considered the unfair advantage Nashville enjoyed because of rate discrimination. The case dragged on for three years and was decided against the L&N and against Nashville's rate privileges. The L&N and the city's grain dealers were dealt a terrible blow, for the privileges, in effect, were ruled illegal. Merchants who had complained about the L&N's unfair treatment of Nashville now had reason to wonder what this defeat would mean for the prosperity of their city. Following the grain case of 1913 the southern grain industry began to disperse to other railroad centers, and the former "Minneapolis of the South" had a hard time living up to its boast.[43]

The grain case was one of several rulings made by the Interstate Commerce Commission between 1912 and 1921 against Nashville's privileged rates. In 1912 business interests in Bowling Green, Kentucky, pointed to the new improvements on their Green and Barrier river systems and successfully attacked Nashville's railroad freight rate advantage, based as it was on the claim of river competition that was in fact far inferior. In 1919 the Murfreesboro Board of Trade, on behalf of several small cities surrounding Nashville, overturned the system of rates that had discriminated in favor of Nashville. By 1921 the Interstate Commerce Commission mandated a thorough revision of rates in Nashville's territory, not only eliminating the city's once-favored position but raising freight costs across the board for Nashville shippers.[44]

Coinciding with the grain case defeat, the L&N came under investigation by the Interstate Commerce Commission, which was probing charges involving the railroad's monopoly of trade in Nashville and its influence in politics, particularly through the company's use of free passes. Behind this investigation was a scrappy young senator, Luke Lea of Nashville, who began a personal crusade in behalf of all the enemies of the L&N. Born to an old Nashville family, Lea made a startling political debut in 1906, and by 1911, at age thirty-two, he was the youngest man in the U.S. Senate. He bought the *Tennessean* in 1907 and later engaged in a bitter personal feud with rival *Banner* publisher Edward B. Stahlman. The L&N and Stahlman helped to end Lea's Senate career in the election of 1916, but not before Lea pushed the Interstate Commerce Commission to expose the corruption of the railroad in public hearings that year.[45]

The investigation produced a voluminous record of the L&N's shameless manipulation of politicians and the press through heavy use of free passes and financial loans to publishers. The railroads, the commission summarized, "have dipped into practically every domain of public and private life. . . ." President Milton Smith responded callously for the railroad: "Society, as created, was for the purpose of one man's getting what the other fellow has, if he can, and keep out of the penitentiary."[46] Senator Lea certainly brought public condemnation against the L&N, but in the end, the Supreme Court of the United States upheld the right of the L&N to exclude the Tennessee Central from Union Station.[47]

The railroads' abuses could easily obscure an understanding of their remarkable achievements in this era. They had laid out a vast system of commercial arteries that extended enormously the range of markets Nashville and other southern cities could serve. The railroads also tapped coal, iron, and other raw materials and made the mass production of industrial goods possible for the first time. Nashville's merchants and manufacturers had every right to complain about mistreatment at the hands of the L&N. Rivals of this giant, whether on rail or river, also deserve sympathy for their hopeless struggle to overcome the L&N monopoly. But all must have understood that Nashville's growth and economic transformation in this dynamic stretch of history depended on the very company these less powerful actors vilified.[48]

COMMERCE AND INDUSTRY
IN THE ROCK CITY

The expansion of Nashville's transportation system not only extended its range of commercial markets, it required radical innovations in the organization and strategy of the city's business firms. Like the railroads, Nashville wholesalers sought to ensure increased profits by enlarging the territory they served and removing competition through price cutting. The changes in the size of the marketplace also called forth a new scale of enterprise. The nineteenth-century business firm was typically based on the family unit; a father and his son, two or three brothers, perhaps uncles and nephews formed the core of most small business houses. Partnerships with non-kin were often consolidated by the marriage of sons and daughters. These small family-based firms were suited well enough to most of the demands of an economy organized around local markets and handicraft manufacturing, and this type of family capitalism was to prove remarkably durable in Nashville. But the new economic order created by the railroad and the factory required large firms, typically organized through incorporation. Only these large enterprises could amass sufficient capital to serve extensive markets, pay for the new technology, and compete successfully in a marketplace that demanded of its participants cutthroat competition with low prices and huge volume.

This new marketplace also rewarded constant innovation in marketing strategy. Behind all the changes in organization, scale, and strategy was an ambitious class of entrepreneurs who worked as individuals to build personal fortunes and collectively to build their city.

MERCHANTS OF CHANGE

Nowhere were these changes better illustrated than among the city's wholesale merchants. Nashville grew in this period primarily by its strength as a central distribution point for groceries, dry goods, boots and shoes, liquor, agricultural implements, hardware, drugs, and a wide range of other goods. Table 1 shows the relative importance of the leading wholesale activities ranked by their value in 1882 and 1907.[1]

Table 1. LEADING COMMERCIAL ACTIVITIES, BY VALUE OF RECEIPTS, 1882, 1907 *($ millions).*

1882		1907	
1. Groceries	$12.8	1. Grain	$26.6
2. Flour and grain	7.7	2. Groceries	12.1
3. Cotton	6.0	3. Dry goods	11.0
4. Dry goods	6.0	4. Lumber	9.7
5. Cigars, tobacco	3.0	5. Boots, shoes	9.5
6. Drugs	2.0	6. Livestock	6.7
7. Lumber	2.0	7. Hardware	6.5
8. Clothing	1.8	8. Publishing	5.5
9. Provisions	1.5	9. Fertilizers	5.5
10. Boots, shoes	1.5	10. Furniture	4.0
		11. Tobacco	4.0

SOURCES: *Manufacturing and Mercantile Resources of Nashville, Tennessee . . .* ([Nashville], 1882). *Year Book of the Nashville Board of Trade, Nashville, Tennessee* (Nashville, 1908), 15–16.

Central to most of this wholesale activity was Nashville's key role as a processor and distributor of agricultural goods, especially grain, groceries, produce, and meat. Throughout this period the wholesale grocery trade was one of the leading sectors of the local economy, and it spawned several of the new fortunes that emerged in the city during this time. Earlier, the grocery trade was restricted largely to staples: sugar, flour, corn meal, salt, lard, and the like. Even city dwellers depended heavily on the kitchen garden and hog pen to supply most of the family's diet. But with the advent of rapid railroad transportation, breakthroughs in refrigeration and canning, and the growing density of the urban population, a whole new market appeared for a diverse line of commercial food products, and the kitchen garden and larder were no longer essential. One recently arrived Nashville family was visited by their grandmother from the country who, on seeing the sparse pantry, promptly burst into tears for fear the family would starve when winter came.[2] Nashville's grocers, meat packers, grain millers, and others sprang to the opportunity during the 1880s and came to dominate a vast market extending north into southern Kentucky, east into the Cumberlands, south into northern Alabama, and west to the Tennessee River.

Rival cities on every flank competed for this domain: Louisville and Memphis on the north and west, Birmingham from the south, and Atlanta, Chattanooga, and Knoxville on the east. But early on, Nashville's wholesalers established a position in the marketing of food to a large area within the central South that was not easily undone.

The success of this trade depended heavily on the drummers or sales agents Nashville's merchants sent out in legions to the rural hinterland. They traveled by horse, boat, and rail from one small country store to the next, offering samples, taking orders, collecting debts, and maintaining a personal link between merchants in the metropolis and retailers in the hinterland. Arch Trawick, an "old-time drummer" in the late nineteenth century, began his career with Morris White wholesale grocers. With his new suit, derby hat, white vest, ascot tie, patent leather shoes, umbrella, and a "very imposing" set of whiskers, he represented to thousands of country folk the flashy, aggressive Nashville drummer.[3] Trawick's colorful memoirs recount his experience with two men in Nashville's grocery trade who represented the bold entrepreneurs who typified this era. One was Joel O. Cheek, who came downriver from Burnside, Kentucky, and began work as a drummer for one of Nashville's grocers at the age of twenty. By 1890 Joel Cheek was ready to begin his own wholesale grocery firm with his cousin, Christopher Tomkins Cheek.

During the late nineteenth century the grocery trade became fragmented as dealers in liquor, tobacco, and coffee, for example, began to specialize. Coffee, long the favorite of wealthy urbanites, became a staple consumer item during this period. Earlier, coffee had been sold as green beans to be roasted and blended at home. Now the Cheeks' new company, Nashville Coffee and Manufacturing, introduced a prepared coffee, already roasted, blended, and—later—even ground and canned, ready for home use. In 1892 Cheek began experimenting with various combinations of high-quality coffee beans. With the help of coffee connoisseur Roger N. Smith (who had lived in Brazil with Confederate exiles), Cheek found a perfect blend, but it would cost far more than rival brands. Instead of competing at a disadvantage in the same market, Cheek sought a prestige market. He persuaded Nashville's elegant Maxwell House Hotel to serve his coffee, and then he borrowed the hotel's name for his brand label. When President Theodore Roosevelt visited the hotel in 1907, he immortalized Cheek's coffee with his endorsement that it was "good to the last drop," which quickly became the brand's slogan. By 1904 the Cheeks had gone into partnership with James W. Neal, another former drummer. With more capital they expanded operations, building roasting plants in Houston, Jacksonville, Richmond, Brooklyn, Los Angeles, and Chicago, as well as a new plant in Nashville's Cummins Station. Maxwell House Coffee eventually captured one-third of the American coffee market.[4]

Figure 14 (left).   Joel O. Cheek (1852–1935), founder of the Maxwell House Coffee empire. Nashville Chamber of Commerce, *Nashville in the Twentieth Century* (Nashville, [1900]), Tennessee State Library and Archives.

Figure 15.   Horace Greeley Hill (1873–1942), wholesale and retail grocery entrepreneur. John Trotwood Moore and Austin P. Foster, *Tennessee, The Volunteer State, 1769–1923,* vol. 3 (Chicago, 1923).

Horace Greeley Hill, another of Trawick's contemporaries, was born to the grocery trade. His father ran a large retail store at Market (now Second Avenue) and Lafayette. As a youth, Hill toured the Pacific Coast to study an innovative development in retailing, the "chain store." In 1893, at the age of twenty, he began a bold strategy of buying auctioned lots of wholesale groceries on credit and covering his bills with profits from Saturday "closeout sales" offered direct to the public at a 20-percent discount. Next, he began buying up small retail groceries. With twenty stores in his chain, Hill was able to buy at wholesale prices. He also introduced strict cash sales and avoided the extra costs of carrying customer accounts for a full year, the usual practice among retailers in every line. Hill was among the first to introduce the "groceteria," where customers picked out their own packaged food from shelves instead of waiting for the clerk to serve them from behind a counter. Hill's discount prices annoyed competing retailers no less than the wholesalers who were bypassed by his direct buying strategy. Wholesale grocers made efforts to boycott Hill, but his innovative system was bound to succeed with the public, and Hill quickly rose as one of the wealthiest products of Nashville's new entrepreneurial spirit.[5]

Nashville's most important role in the processing and distribution of food for the South came in the 1880s with the railroads' privileged rates on grain. In 1880 the city's flour and grist mills produced about $1.5 million in flour and meal; by 1910 the flour industry alone brought in close to $6 million. It was the leading product in Nashville's wholesale trade.[6] Coinciding with the introduction of favorable transportation rates on grain came a new technology of milling, the "Hungarian process," involving a series of procelain rollers rather than stone wheels. These roller mills required huge initial capital outlays and therefore to be profitable had to be designed for large-volume production. As grain and flour elevators were built to accommodate this fast-growing industry, Nashville soon acquired transportation, milling, and storage facilities unmatched by any other southern city. The proximity of Nashville's grain market also accelerated the transformation of Middle Tennessee agriculture as it shifted from cotton to grain and livestock. After the railroad privileges were taken away in 1913, Nashville lost its claim as the "Minneapolis of the South," but it remained a center for local grain farmers.[7]

Oscar F. Noel was the first to build a modern roller mill and elevator when in 1883 he established his plant in South Nashville, near the NC&STL depot. The Noel Mill and Elevator Company, together with brother Edwin T. Noel's American Mill Company, could produce over 2,500 barrels a day. The Noels drove many of the old low-capacity stone mill companies out of business. Soon a number of large modern roller mills, the most important being William Litterer's Model Mills, joined in competition with the Noels for a share of Nashville's booming grain industry.[8]

The radical change in the scale of enterprise brought by railroads and new industrial technology was reflected in changing marketing strategies as well. In 1895 the new Owsley Milling Company became the first in the South to market a premixed "self-rising flour." This product was a daring innovation at the time but eventually won favor throughout most of the South. Nashville mills using the process made much of their "secret recipes," which gave the city an ongoing advantage in this new line. In 1898 W.L. Smith's Ford Flour Company made an equally venturesome departure by producing five- and ten-cent packages of flour designed for direct sale to consumers. Within a decade this practice became widely imitated in the South.[9]

The meat-processing industry experienced a similar pattern of growth, corporate concentration, and innovation. Earlier, most livestock was shipped out of Nashville by boat or rail and slaughtered as close to consumer markets as possible. The development of refrigerated railroad cars by Gustavus Swift of Chicago allowed the centralization of slaughtering and packing in major cities. Nashville became the meat supply center for a large market extending at least 150 miles in all directions.[10]

Most of Nashville's early slaughtering and meat packing took place in North Nashville's "Butchertown," where German butchers organized the industry in small backyard enterprises and used the river to dump their waste. The new competition from the large midwestern meat packers forced reorganization of the local industry. Butchers formed a cooperative stockyards, slaughterhouse, and hide-processing plant. Small family firms either expanded operations or folded.[11] Henry Neuhoff came to Nashville from St. Louis in 1896 when he was just twenty-six years old. By 1906 he was operating three meat markets in partnership with his brother Lawrence. The Neuhoffs introduced to Nashville the boneless ham, which quickly caught on with local restaurateurs and housewives. At first they would buy up hams at wholesale, then bone, smoke, tie, and market them as "Neuhoff boneless hams." Neuhoff moved into preparation of his own hams in 1902 when he opened a slaughterhouse. In 1906 the Neuhoff Abattoir and Packing Company was incorporated with $40,000 in capital. It began on a modest scale, employing only four workers, but rapidly expanded to 150 employees. By the time the Neuhoffs sold out to Chicago's Swift & Company in 1931, they had built a major component of Nashville's meat-packing industry.[12]

Other industries grew on the rich natural resources on Nashville's hinterland. The timber that came primarily by river spawned several large mechanized saw mills on the east bank of the Cumberland. Prewitt, Spurr & Company began in 1866, and by 1890 it had a steam-driven

Figure 16. The Cumberland Flour Mills on "Roller Mill Hill" in South Nashville, the center of the "Minneapolis of the South." *American Journal of Commerce* [n.p., 1898?].

Figure 17. James C. Warner (1830–1895), iron manufacturer, industrialist, and New South entrepreneur. Joseph B. Killebrew, *Life and Character of James Cartwright Warner* (Nashville, 1897).

plant with three hundred hands busy manufacturing lumber and wooden buckets. The Edgefield and Nashville Manufacturing Company began in 1874, specializing in cheap office furniture. The Cherry, O'Conner Company, established in 1871 and reorganized in 1878, also produced inexpensive furniture and the Tennessee wagon, which was sold widely throughout the South. Located near the old state penitentiary on Stonewall, this company made use of convict labor and became a target of political controversy. Nashville Sash & Door, one of the city's oldest firms today, also emerged in this period as a leader in the wood manufacturing industry. A number of other manufacturers made boxes, caskets, plow handles, ice boxes, wooden pumps, and building supplies from the hardwood that flowed downriver into the city.[13]

The foundries that emerged in this period also took advantage of local natural resources in coal and iron. Iron production had a long history in the Nashville area, but most of it was limited to small firms using crude methods located in outlying areas, such as Cumberland Furnace, near raw materials. The railroads allowed coal and pig iron to be brought to foundries near large urban populations of laborers and consumers. In Nashville the foundries lined up along the NC&StL tracks west of Capitol Hill. The leading firm was Phillips & Buttorff Manufacturing Company, established in 1866 and incorporated in 1881. By 1890 it employed 425 hands in a large plant covering 6 acres, one of the largest plants in the industrial strip that formed in this location. Phillips & Buttorff made tinware, hollowware, mantels, grates, house furnishings, and lamp goods, but its best-known product was a line of heating and cooking stoves, which could be found in homes throughout the South.[14]

One of the most important ventures in iron manufacturing was the Tennessee Coal, Iron, and Railroad Company (TCI&R), which was organized by Nashville capitalists and maintained headquarters in the city but had an impact that went far beyond the borders of the city. The company had its roots in the Sewanee Mining Company, organized before the Civil War. Arthur S. Colyar, a leading industrialist of Nashville, reorganized the company after the war, and with the help of three young Nashville entrepreneurs, James C. Warner, Alfred M. Shook, and Nathaniel Baxter, Jr. (brother of Jere Baxter), the company became a leading producer of coke and iron by the 1880s. It was TCI&R that entered the northern Alabama coal and iron fields, bought up several small companies, built modern blast furnaces, launched the southern steel industry, and made Birmingham into a leading industrial center of the New South. By 1907, when Birmingham threatened to rival Pittsburgh as a steel producer, TCI&R was swallowed up in a controversial merger with U.S. Steel, which thereafter restricted Birmingham to a secondary role in the nation's steel industry. Birmingham nonetheless grew far more rapidly than Nashville, whose capitalists had done so much to build the industrial launch pad for the "Magic City."

James C. Warner's role in the iron industry went beyond his activities in TCI&R, which he served as president in the 1880s. Warner, a tailor's son from Gallatin, began in Nashville in 1847, at the age of seventeen, as a clerk in a wholesale grocery store. In 1873 he toured the North with Alfred M. Shook to study new methods of producing coke and brought back plans for the first modern blast furnace in the South, built by TCI&R at Tracy City. The Warner Iron Company, established in 1880 in Hickman County, west of Nashville, became a model of new industrial technology. Warner introduced new chemical tests of ore and steam shovels for mining; he also built schools, churches, and commissaries for workers, and organized the whole plant around modern principles of efficiency and industrial paternalism. Later, he built a much larger plant, the Aetna Furnace, in the same area. By the late 1880s Warner was one of Nashville's leading capitalists; he became involved in a variety of industrial ventures, including a textile mill in Nashville and street railways in Nashville, Chattanooga, and Birmingham. Before he died in 1895, after a long history of feeble health, Warner and his business associates, Shook, Baxter, and Colyar, had done much to mold the industrial spirit of Nashville and the New South.[15]

The emergence of the cotton textile factories in Nashville was perhaps the most significant symbol of the New South's struggle to end its former role of supplying raw materials to northern manufacturers. In the New South era an almost evangelical fervor to "bring the cotton mills to the cotton fields" set off a trend that radically shifted textile manufacturing southward, away from New England. The cotton mills came, in fact, not to the Deep South cotton fields, but to the rising railroad centers and Piedmont mill towns of the upper South, where fuel, water power, railroads, along with an abundant supply of cheap white labor, made cotton manufacturing profitable.[16]

These natural and human resources would have counted little without the bold "industrial spirit" that the new entrepreneurs stirred up in cities like Nashville. Modern textile manufacturing required huge capital investments that could be formed only by pooling money in corporations. As early as 1869 Samuel D. Morgan, a leading dry goods merchant in Nashville, along with a number of other local capitalists, founded the Tennessee Manufacturing Company. In 1871 they completed an enormous four-story brick mill in North Nashville. By 1890 the mill had expanded to house over 1,000 looms with 35,000 spindles, tended by eight hundred operatives, mostly young white women.[17]

The stunning success of the Tennessee Manufacturing Company lured more adventurous capitalists into the field. In 1881 two more cotton mills were incorporated. The National Manufacturing Company built its works on the industrial strip along the NC&StL tracks west of Capitol Hill. Edward B. Stahlman, the L&N executive, was the founding president of the mill. The company attracted $300,000 from local capitalists, employed nearly three hundred hands by 1890, and produced a variety of finished cotton goods along with coarse sheeting, which was a southern specialty.[18]

The Nashville Cotton Mills were also established in 1881 by Godfrey M. Fogg, lawyer with the NC&StL, and Trevanion B. Dallas, a wealthy cotton manufacturer with interests in Huntsville as well. By 1890 the original mill at Clay and Clinton, along the same western industrial strip, was supplemented by a second mill down the line at Robertson Street. Together these mills operated with about six hundred and fifty hands by 1890, and the company pioneered in the southern production of fine brown cotton sheeting. A series of other factories cropped up around these large mills to make men's overalls and shirts, women's dresses, cotton bags for the flour millers, mattresses, and a wide assortment of other cotton goods.[19]

Publishing became another important component of Nashville's increasingly diversified economy before 1915. The growth of the local publishing industry was intimately connected to the competitive expansion of evangelical Protestant denominations in the late nineteenth century. Methodists, Baptists, Presbyterians, and Christian churches all sought to enlarge their spiritual empires. To do so required massive production of religious tracts, Bibles, hymn books, Sunday school texts, and periodicals to maintain communication with far-flung preachers, missionaries, and laymen.

The Methodist Episcopal Church, South, established its Publishing House in Nashville as early as 1854 following the dispute with northern abolitionists. It occupied a large building on the Public Square, rebuilt in 1874 with no less than seven stories on the rear portion, served by a steam elevator. A huge stream of periodicals reaching almost 1.2 million subscribers by 1890 poured forth from the Methodist press, which became the core of a thriving industry in religious publishing.

The Cumberland Presbyterian Board of Publishers also made Nashville its permanent home in 1889 and soon erected its press on Cherry Street (now Fourth Avenue) near Church. The Gospel Advocate Publishing Company, organized by David Lipscomb of the Church of Christ in 1866, expanded during the 1880s under the direction of the Reverend J. Clayton McQuiddy and printed four periodicals in addition to its popular interdenominational hymn book. In 1896 Dr. Richard H. Boyd established the National Baptist Publishing Board for the black churches. Other religious presses joined the growing cluster: the Southern Baptists, African Methodists, Pentecostal Mission, and Seventh Day Adventists all brought presses to Nashville. By 1908 some $5 million had been invested in Nashville's publishing industry, making it the fifth largest publishing center in the country.[20] The advantages of good quality presses, skilled laborers, cheap supplies of paper and ink, and central geographic location (particularly important when postage was geared to distance) all worked to attract a growing cluster of religious and secular presses to Nashville.

Education soon became another small but vital industry in Nashville. Along with the publishing houses, the city's colleges and schools gave Nashville a special role within the New South as a transmitter of new ideas and new values. The major educational institutions—Fisk, Meharry, Vanderbilt, Peabody—were all funded by northern philanthropy and were part of a program to reconstruct the mind of the South. These schools would help to create a new generation of leaders in politics and the professions and to train a legion of teachers who, in turn, would transmit the new skills and values to the coming generation. Nashville's prosperity, its central location, and the cumulative advantages of its having a cluster of colleges, all combined to make the city a regional educational center. The accumulation of large and small educational institutions, with their growing endowments, student bodies, and staffs, gave the economy a unique kind of diversity. More important, Nashville's colleges lent a certain tone of refinement and cultural amenities that boosters of the "Athens of the South" never failed to note.

NEW MONEY

The enlarged scale of commerce and industry meant that southern banking and insurance had to pursue innovative methods to mobilize the large pools of capital required. The South remained desperately short of capital because of the dominance of agriculture, conservative attitudes toward banks, and continuing dependence on northern financial institutions, which siphoned off investment capital from the South. Nashville, like other rising cities in the New South, tried vigorously to break with these traditions and develop financial institutions that would be independent of the North.[21]

Before the Panic of 1893 Nashville's booming economy had spawned a good number of seemingly healthy banks. Most were organized and directed by the city's wealthy wholesale merchants and industrialists, who themselves were increasingly dependent on local capital to finance their economic ventures. During the 1880s the same process of consolidation and expansion evident in business firms was seen in Nashville's financial sector. By 1890 the city boasted four nationally chartered banks. The Fourth National, with Samuel J. Keith (a former wholesale grocer) as president, was the most powerful in the city and one of the leading banks in the South, with deposits totaling over $2 million by 1892.

The lists of officers and directors in all the large banks reveal a definite pattern: the leading wholesalers, particularly in groceries, along with industrialists were moving into banking in the late nineteenth century.[22] Their involvement in banking was natural, perhaps, since these men constituted the new wealth of Nashville. But more important, these were men who understood that their fortunes were being made in a new economic order that required new mechanisms for capital formation, mechanisms that exceeded the capacity of traditional modes of family capitalism, partnerships, and private loans.

The same logic led to a growth in the scale of banking through mergers. The First National Bank, established in 1863 and reorganized in 1884, swallowed up the Mechanics National and Merchants National Banks and rose to become the second largest bank in the city. The American National, established in 1883 by Edmund W. Cole and others, absorbed the old Third National in 1884. John Kirkman, a former hardware merchant, took over as president of the American National until his untimely death in 1888, when Edgar Jones succeeded him. Commerce National, organized in 1884, was led by Marcus A. Spurr of Prewitt, Spurr & Company, lumber manufacturers.

Together these large, nationally chartered banks controlled about $5.5 million in deposits, and Nashville's other state-chartered banks, trust companies, and small savings companies, designed primarily for home loans that the national banks could not finance, claimed another $1 million in deposits. This $6.5 million constituted about one-third of the state's total bank deposits, demonstrating that Nashville was a banking center for a good part of the state, and parts of Kentucky and Alabama as well.[23]

The Panic of 1893 had harsh, lasting effects on the local economy. Commerce National, the smallest of the national banks, folded when a major loan went into default. Other small banks also failed, and a growing uneasiness among the public was evident in the streets of Nashville by the summer of 1893. Memories of the devastating Panic of 1873, and the milder one in 1884, still lingered in the minds of a public long suspicious of banks. On the morning of August 10, 1893, large crowds of depositors milled outside the bank doors, anxious to redeem their savings. Earlier, the American National staved off a run by piling money in the window to assure the public of its solvency. This time the crowds were more skeptical; within the first thirty minutes after the doors opened more than $1 million had been withdrawn from the city's banks. Even the largest banks had to suspend—or at least limit —payments before the bank run subsided. The Panic of 1893 was the prelude to a deep depression (the second most severe in America's history), which dragged on into 1897. Bank deposits recovered slowly, from $6.5 million in 1890 to $8.1 million by 1899.[24] Bank clearings, the total amount of money passing through all local banks, followed a similar trend, rising from $43.4 million in 1894 to $69.2 million by 1899 (see Appendix B).

In the wake of this depression Nashville's financial institutions rebuilt, stronger than ever. Deposits jumped to $23 million by 1906, then rose slowly to $25.3 million by 1915.[25] Bank clearings more than quadrupled between 1900 and 1915. Luxurious new buildings were erected to house many of the large banks along Union Street, which later came to be touted as the "Wall Street of the South." Samuel Keith's Fourth National Bank remained the largest. In 1907 it moved into elegantly furnished quarters in the Stahlman Building, Nashville's striking new skyscraper. In 1912 the Fourth's largest stockholder, James E. Caldwell, engineered a merger with the First National and became the new president.[26] By 1915 the Fourth and First together with its affiliate, First Savings Bank and Trust, controlled nearly $10 million in deposits, about 40 percent of the city's total.

James E. Caldwell, with his dark striped suit, white vest, gold-headed ebony cane, and neatly trimmed beard, walked Union Street in gentlemanly splendor. For all his aristocratic bearing, Caldwell was in many ways the banking world's counterpart of the upwardly mobile "new men" who shaped the city's commercial and industrial sectors. Caldwell's *Recollections of a Life Time* is one of the few autobiographies this generation left behind. Caldwell, the son of a former Memphis-area plantation owner, left his parents in Franklin, Tennessee, in 1870 at age sixteen and came to Nashville. He clerked for a wholesale grocery firm, roomed on Cherry Street (now Fourth Avenue), and steeled himself to resist the temptations that beckoned in the saloons and theaters along that notorious street. He attended Bryant and Stratton Business College in his spare time and, with his new skills, moved into bookkeeping jobs. Caldwell's adventure in the world of finance began at age twenty when he captured the local market in millet seed and made a handsome profit. He continued to "shave notes" on the side and also took over a wholesale hardware business. By 1876 Caldwell went into the fire insurance business with William C. Nelson, and from this vantage point he became involved in a number of financial ventures. In 1883 he joined other capitalists in the Cumberland Telephone and Telegraph Company, which soon branched out to Louisville, Memphis, and New Orleans as the new technological wonder took hold in the South. Caldwell served the company as president for several years before he sold out to Southern Bell in 1913.[27]

Caldwell's move into banking in 1912 symbolized the national shift from entrepreneurial capitalism to finance capitalism, which accelerated in the wake of the 1890s depression. Before the 1890s wholesale merchants and industrialists organized banks on the side to serve their goals as businessmen. Now, increasingly, financiers took a leading role in underwriting large corporate enterprises, arranging mergers, and con-

Figure 18 (above left). James E. Caldwell (1854–1944), telephone entrepreneur, banker, president of Fourth and First National Bank. James E. Caldwell, *Recollections of a Life Time* (Nashville, 1923).

Figure 19 (above right). Cornelius A. Craig (1868–1957), founder of National Life and Accident Insurance Company. National Life and Accident Insurance Company.

Figure 20. Andrew Mizell Burton (1879–1966), founder of Life & Casualty Insurance Company. D.D. Moore et al. eds., *Men of the South* (New Orleans, 1922).

trolling the marketplace by controlling the finances of the major companies in nearly every sector of the economy.[28]

The Nashville Trust Company, founded in 1889, survived the depression well because it dealt exclusively in trusts and had no savings or checking accounts for depositors to withdraw. The trust company represented an important innovation in specialized financial service that responded to the needs of Nashville's new men of wealth and their heirs. The inspiration came from Herman Justi, a bright, young wholesale hardware dealer. Much of the financial backing came from Charles Nelson, owner of the Greenbrier Distillery. Like Justi, Nelson was German-born and was uneasy with the rising temperance movement, which was frequently linked with antiforeign sentiment. As a bank president Nelson adopted a more respectable image and acquired a safer haven for his whiskey fortune. After Nelson's death Joseph H. Thompson took over as president. Thompson represented one of the several links forged between the older elite (the Thompson family owned Glen Leven on Franklin Pike) and the New South entrepreneurs. His presence lent a tone of conservative stability to Nashville Trust, which helped it weather the Panic of 1893 and, afterward, grow into one of the city's most durable financial institutions.[29]

Beneath the large, nationally chartered banks several smaller banks, trust companies, savings and building loan associations cropped up in the wake of the 1890s depression. Among these were two small institutions, the One Cent Savings Bank and Trust, founded in 1904, and the Peoples Savings Bank and Trust, set up in 1909, both founded by black business leaders and designed to serve the growing numbers of mostly small depositors from Nashville's black community.[30]

Whether they were collecting the pennies and nickels of the working class or the growing profits of merchants and industrialists, these banks all successfully established methods of capital formation that the new economic order demanded. The deposits were invested or loaned to railroads, trolleys, factories, businesses of all kinds, as well as to home builders and owners. Without these large pools of capital, Nashville's growth in this period could never have taken place with such speed.[31]

Nashville's most important innovation in the struggle to gain some financial independence from the North appeared in the inauspicious founding of two small insurance companies after the turn of the century. The changes that swept through most of the postwar South created a new market for insurance sales. As the plantation system eroded and as migrants moved into the cities and towns, a new class of wage earners swelled. Traditional sources of personal security rooted in the rural community—kinship, church, and older forms of racial paternalism—were left behind by these urban migrants. Black sharecroppers and tenant farmers who remained on the plantations also turned to low-premium insurance for security.[32] A multitude of fraternal associations and mutual-benefit associations tried to fill the void with casualty and death benefits, but they were small, financially weak, and tainted by many fraudulent operators who took advantage of the insecurity and ignorance of the poor.[33]

Beginning about the turn of the century, these fraternal associations were crowded out by large-scale insurance companies that sold policies especially designed for the working class. Industrial insurance had been invented in England in 1854 and was imported to America in 1875, when the Prudential Insurance Company of New York introduced a weekly premium policy costing as little as a nickel with benefits to cover a few weeks' wages or the cost of a modest funeral.[34] The insurance industry—indeed the whole world of finance in America—was dominated by New York City, with other northern cities competing for a share of the market the giant New York companies did not control. Many firms selling ordinary life insurance, along with commercial and fire insurance, to the wealthier classes had moved into the South and were accused of draining capital out of the region. But the large northern companies specializing in industrial insurance—Prudential, Metropolitan, and John Hancock—had not tapped the growing population of southern black workers. Nor did the "old line" life insurance companies selling ordinary policies seem willing to step into this peculiar southern market. Furthermore, after 1900 southern reformers were beginning to restrict the "foreign" insurance companies in their midst.[35]

The National Sick and Accident Company began in Huntsville, Alabama, in 1897, selling industrial insurance solely to blacks. The company was reorganized in Nashville in 1898 under the guise of a fraternal association to escape taxes, and it rapidly expanded by selling policies to white as well as colored "lodges."[36] When controlling interest in National Sick and Accident stock was put up at auction sale in December 1901, it took a group of ambitious young men to see the company's potential. The business of selling "Negro insurance" did not attract the interest of Nashville's established wealth, in any case.

Cornelius A. Craig was just thirty-two, a farm boy from Giles County, who ran a drug store in Pulaski before he came to Nashville in 1897 to work in the office of state treasurer and insurance commissioner. Craig noticed the dominance of northern insurance companies in Tennessee and was eager to develop a home-based enterprise. Craig and his older brother Edward pooled their small resources with a group of others, mostly young men from rural villages: William Ridley Wills, C. Runcie Clements, Thomas J. Tyne, and Rufus E. Fort. With the financial backing of Newton H. White, a wealthy landowner in Giles County, they launched what was to be one of Nashville's Cinderella stories in the coming years. They changed the name to National Life and Accident in 1902 but immediately decided not to market ordinary life insurance, concentrating instead on industrial health and accident policies.[37]

A similar story of audacious youthful ambition lay behind the founding of Life and Casualty Insurance Company in 1903. Andrew M. Burton was born in rural Sumner County, Tennessee, in 1879. He came to Nashville in 1896 and took his first job as a day laborer at the Tennessee Centennial Exposition grounds. He went into insurance sales and at age twenty-three was promoted to state agent for the Traders Mutual of Illinois, just before Tennessee revoked the company's license, part of the attack on "foreign" insurance companies in the state. With a sales force of fifty men, Burton had a good business going. He went to Cincinnati to ask another insurance company to take over the Traders Mutual policies in Tennessee. "Young man," the company president blithely suggested, "why don't you go home and start a company of your own?"

Burton needed capital if he was to follow this advice. He had $1,000 in savings, and Helena Haralson (later Johnson), a former cashier for Traders Mutual (and former stockholder in National Sick and Accident), put in another $1,000. Burton approached businessmen in Nashville and quickly raised $24,000 from Guilford Dudley, Sr., an insurance broker and banker; Dr. J.C. Franklin; and Pat M. Estes, a young lawyer (who had been partners with Thomas Tyne before the latter joined National Life).

Initially, Life and Casualty also concentrated on industrial insurance. A field of twenty salesmen moved into Nashville, Memphis, and other Tennessee cities and towns. The first sick claim was filed by an old Negro woman in North Nashville whose hand had become infected when she snagged it on a washboard. President Burton and the whole Nashville sales force went out to the woman's home, paid her claim of $2.25 with great public ceremony, then canvassed the neighborhood, picking up $7.50 in new policies.[38]

Industrial insurance required a unique style of personal marketing. Agents walked door to door through their "debit" or territory each week writing new policies, renewing old ones, and paying claims. It also involved cutthroat competition as more companies entered the field. About 1905 one anonymous agent hired a palm reader who set up a tent in a black slum behind Capitol Hill and warned superstitious clients that a black bird on their wall was a bad omen, and a one-eyed man who wrote with his left hand would bring them luck. The National Life emblem was then an eagle, and industrial policies were often tacked on the walls of holders. The one-eyed southpaw, of course, was the agent who hired the palm reader.[39]

National Life rapidly built up a sales force supervised by branch offices in the major cities of Tennessee, northern Alabama, and Kentucky, and then moved into Louisiana, Mississippi, Georgia, Virginia, and the lower Midwest. By 1912 the company entered into a booming market in Texas from which many large eastern companies had retreated following the enactment of restrictive laws against outside firms. By early 1913 National Life had at least fifty-seven branch offices in large and small cities across its vast territory; about a third were in Tennessee. The company's assets had grown from $23,000 in 1901 to $2.3 million by 1916.[40]

Life and Casualty also expanded beyond Tennessee beginning in 1909 when salesmen entered Mississippi, selling primarily to the huge dispossessed black population of sharecroppers on the large plantations. Life and Casualty entered Louisiana in 1911, then Arkansas and South Carolina in 1913. The company's assets had grown to about $112,000 by 1909.[41] Andrew Burton took a personal hand in building the aggressive sales force required to market industrial insurance. His 1911 pamphlet *John Smith and His Success* was part practical guide to sales technique, part Horatio Alger story of personal ambition.[42] Burton experimented with a special agency of black salesmen to cater to the company's large black market. He saw the insurance industry as a means of educating the southern people in modern ideals of health, thrift, and personal moral improvement.[43]

The nickels and dimes collected by National Life and by Life and Casualty trickled back to Nashville to form a deep pool of capital by the 1910s. Some profits went into stock dividends and new buildings to house the growing home office workers, but the capital amassed by these companies was also invested locally and was instrumental in building the city. The insurance companies invested heavily in Nashville real estate loans, city bonds, street railway stock, and other large enterprises that might never have been launched had it not been for the availability of this capital.[44]

THE CITY BUILDERS

Nashville's growth in this period was due to more than the mere sum of individual enterprises in transportation, commerce, industry, and finance. Neither was it due simply to the natural advantages of geography and resources or to external forces of national development. The city's business leaders and newspaper editors constantly reminded one another that their city's economic welfare must be pursued aggressively. Whatever their disagreements might have been on the L&N or politics, businessmen in every field shared a faith in the central goal of urban growth. Population growth measured economic vitality, and to make the city bigger was, without question, to make it better. The business of city building required cooperative effort through some collective agency. Before the late 1890s there was general agreement that planning and promoting the city's growth were far too important matters to be left in the hands of municipal government. Instead, private voluntary organizations were designed to form a broad, solid platform upon which businessmen from all sectors of the economy could work together to pursue goals that transcended their daily drive for individual gain.

Paralleling the pattern of corporate mergers in the business world, Nashville's commercial associations experienced a series of organizational changes between 1880 and 1915. In 1877 the new Merchant's Exchange was formed to ally with the Cotton Exchange, Tobacco Board, and others, and to create a "union of interests." Open to businessmen, bankers, and manufacturers, the organization was led largely by wholesale grocers, meat packers, and others involved in the thriving wholesale food industry. The exchange was more a mechanism for regulating wholesale markets than for promoting the city. Members occupied desks on the main floor of a large building on South Market Street, where they showed product samples and offered bids that were posted on a call board.[45]

By 1888 the Commercial Club was formed to "promote more intimate social relations among the businessmen of Nashville, to encourage and promote the commercial and manufacturing interests of the city, to advertise its diverse advantages . . . to foster and encourage a public spirit which will benefit the city. . . ." This more ambitious organization set up a number of standing committees to concentrate on such issues as immigration and city development, as well as to plan their own entertainment. The club was led by a more diverse group of younger businessmen who represented the retail merchants, salesmen, attorneys, and wholesalers in dry goods. They envisioned a broader public role for an energetic commercial association and took up their mission with zeal. They met one evening each week and built up a strong membership of over 500 by 1900.[46]

The earnest efforts of these businessmen were rudely shaken by the Panic of 1893, which left the Merchant's Exchange in ruins. In October of that year a few "brave spirits" picked up the pieces, canvassed the business community, and reorganized as the Board of Trade. The board merged with the Commercial Club in April 1894 and became the Chamber of Commerce. Throughout the depression of the 1890s the chamber tried to put the best face possible on local economic distress. It sponsored a steady stream of booster pamphlets filled with statistics and hyperbolic rhetoric describing Nashville's unique advantages and the wonderful opportunities that awaited men of enterprise. It was during these hard times that the slogan "Rock City" came into common use in the booster press. It alluded to the city's limestone base, but more propitiously to the solid economic foundation Nashville's boosters claimed. "There are no mushroom concerns here . . . [we do not] attempt to play brass band music on a tin whistle. And it might here be added that if Nashville has a serious fault it is her conservatism and yet it is this that makes her the solidest city in the resplendent South." The Panic of 1893 was a temporary inconvenience, the chamber insisted: "there is not a city in the United States that weathered the storm more nobly than Nashville." Now, it was claimed in 1895, "the channels of trade are throbbing with activity, and the smile of prosperity rests upon the city."[47]

The chamber provided more than puffy rhetoric and trade statistics. During the 1890s and 1900s it worked diligently to offset the devastating effects of the depression. It was instrumental in the early planning for the Tennessee Centennial Exposition of 1897, which was being promoted by the chamber as early as 1894. This exposition displayed in a dramatic way the growing willingness of business leaders to transcend their private pursuits and cooperate in collective efforts to build their city. The exposition, the chamber predicted in 1895, would reinvigorate the local economy: "Thousands of people from all parts of the world will visit Nashville. . . ." "Millions of dollars . . . will be shot through her channels of trade like a golden stream. . . ." "Nashville's rapidly and steadily increasing population will receive an influx that will place her, by the end of the century, among the greater cities of the United States."[48]

These prophecies, of course, failed despite the success of the exposition. The census of 1900 showed rivals Atlanta and Memphis well ahead in the population race, and Nashville's ascendancy before the depression appeared to be lost. By 1910 upstart Birmingham passed Nashville in population. The growth of all three rivals was fueled by a rapid expansion of railroads and industry and by a quality of energy and cooperation that somehow had failed to take firm hold among Nashville's business leaders.[49] The chamber continued to churn out ebullient pamphlets and books boosting the "Rock City," but an unspoken mood of demoralization descended on the business community. Membership in the chamber sagged to a little over three hundred by 1903, and the president carped about poor attendance at meetings.[50]

A separate Retail Merchant's Association had been formed in November 1898, which, no doubt, affected the chamber's strength. By February 1906 these two organizations merged as the Nashville Board of Trade, touted as "the strongest and most aggressive organization Nashville ever had." In truth, the new Board of Trade never became more than a loosely bound federation of almost a dozen specialized trade associations. The Builders Exchange, Grain Exchange, Real Estate Exchange, Manufacturers Association, Retail Merchants Association, Jobbers Association, Lumbermen's Club, Credit Men's Association, the Industrial Bureau, Booster Club, and several other pursued their particular interests with no coherent authority vested in the board to speak effectively for Nashville as a whole.[51]

Divisions among the officers of the board hindered its efforts to deal with the pressing matters before Nashville in this period. The board was dominated by older men, and a large number of young businessmen withdrew into their own social club, calling themselves the "Young Turks."[52] One of their complaints was the lack of social conviviality offered in the board's pleasant but sterile offices in the Stahlman Building. "You can not develop an *esprit de corps* among any body of men who never come in contact with one another," one businessman explained.[53]

In 1912 these young men split off from the board and formed the Commercial Club, a more ambitious revival of the one organized in 1888. The club's building on Third Avenue North included handsomely fitted reading and billiards rooms and a first-class dining room that served sumptuous meals for members and their visiting clients. The elaborate menus, prepared by a French chef, became a point of considerable pride among the membership. The club published a chatty monthly newsletter, the *Tattler*, which advertised the amenities of the club and kept members informed of one another's activities and the issues affecting Nashville's economy. Despite criticism from the Board of Trade, the Commercial Club thrived and attracted over 1,500 members immediately. With its facilities for dining and entertainment, the club quickly became the nerve center of Nashville's business community as a meeting place for the various trade associations.[54] But the Commercial Club did not overcome the problem of fragmentation. The grain case of 1913, the losing battle to remain ahead of rival cities like Birmingham, and the growing concern with municipal reform, all seemed to demand a coherent voice for the city's business leaders.

Beginning late in 1913 the leaders of the Commercial Club, Board of Trade, and ten other commercial associations met to work out plans for consolidation that were consummated in 1914. These men were impatient with the wasteful inefficiency of competing organizations, and they compared their plan to a corporate merger. "Jealousy and distrust will give away to harmony and cooperation, waste and reduplication of expenses will be displaced by economy . . . ." It was, in effect, a merger ruled by the progressive young men of the Commercial Club, whose name was adopted by the new organization. More than 1,800 members joined the new Commercial Club in 1914 after a concerted membership drive. Within two years plans were laid to refurbish new headquarters in the former Vanderbilt Law School building.[55]

The consolidation of 1914 was an essential step in the long and frustrating effort to weld Nashville's business leaders into a coherent body capable of directing the city's erratic economic course. The history of fragmentation among Nashville's business leaders was not over, as the events in coming years would demonstrate, but the Commercial Club, renamed the Chamber of Commerce in 1921, became a permanent force with which to pursue the goals of the city's business community.

THE TRANSFORMATION
OF THE CITY CORE

Nashville's economic growth between 1880 and 1915 generated a massive physical expansion of the city. In 1880 Nashville was still a compact city clustered near the river's wharves and the railroad depots, with workplace and residence, rich and poor, necessarily overlapping. The limitations of intracity transportation required people to live close to where they worked, and that, in turn, created a jumble of social enclaves within the city. By 1915 it had become a modern city, with clearly defined residential and commercial zones and with neighborhoods segregated by ethnicity, race, and social class far more than had been possible before. The process of segmentation was partly the result of the new scale of enterprise and the new technologies of transportation, which were transforming cities across America in similar fashion. It was also the product of growing social tensions across ethnic and class lines. Though Nashville followed patterns familiar to most medium-sized cities in this period, it was shaped most by the peculiar features of its topography and by the multitude of human decisions made by real estate and transportation entrepreneurs and the residents they served.

At the heart of the modern city was the central business district, filled with new retail stores, financial offices, government buildings, and, nearby, wholesale warehouses. An industrial ring along the river and railroad tracks also took shape around the central business district in this period. Adjacent to these zones of bustling economic energy emerged squalid slums filled with white and—more often—black workers who lived with their families in abject poverty and faced the constant threat of disease. Small ethnic enclaves of Irish, Germans, and Jews, as well as larger black concentrations, used their neighborhoods and institutions as the bases for separate subcommunities and as staging grounds for the entry of some into suburban middle-class life.

The economic growth of the city also produced rich, ambitious families eager to establish themselves as members of a social elite. These parvenues, together with members of old Nashville families, forged a new upper class in the late nineteenth century, a class defined not simply by wealth but by a thick network of new clubs and intermarriage, and by their opulent new suburbs. The segmented city that emerged in this period was divided as never before by social class, race, and ethnicity. At the same time, it was integrated by the new technology of electric trolleys that made suburban life possible. In the modern city each neighborhood, each social group, became more interdependent than ever, and more segregated than ever.

THE FORGING OF AN UPPER CLASS

The growth of Nashville's economy between 1880 and 1915 generated a good number of new fortunes. The entrepreneurs whose exploits have been described in earlier chapters were only a sample of the crowd of new men who, along with their wives, rose to positions of wealth and social standing in the city. By the turn of the century these new men had coalesced into an identifiable new upper class, an integrated network of families linked by intermarriage, clubs, commercial associations, and neighborhoods.

There was some continuity with the old families of wealth and prominence of antebellum times, as the persistence of names like Lea, Overton, McGavock, and others suggests. More characteristic of the men who rose to wealth and power after the Civil War was their newness, their lack of connection to the old landed gentry or the mercantile elite of antebellum Nashville. Many of the old elite families, whose mansions had symbolized the prestige of the old order, failed to produce a generation of leaders in the New South. Their fortunes eroded; their mansions fell empty or were taken over by the newly rich. Jackson's Hermitage was rescued by the Ladies Hermitage Association, the Hardings' Belle Meade estate was subdivided into surban lots, while Polk Place gave way to downtown development.

A profile of the ascending upper class at two different times can be sketched from collective biographical data. From the 1880 city directories the names of 126 directors and major officers of leading banks, insurance companies, railroads, streetcar companies, and manufacturing corporations were included among the economic elite. Of those, about half were selected as the most active and prominent business leaders, and these were scrutinized more carefully in newspaper obituaries and other biographical sources. Another collective biography of 71 economic leaders was drawn from entries in the 1911 publication

Who's Who in Tennessee. Together, these sources give us a clear picture of the post-Civil War elite at its early and more mature stages. The aggregate statistical portrait of these men presented in Table 2 may blur the colorful details of individual personalities, but it helps us better understand the pattern into which these men fitted.

Reflecting changes in the local and national economy, the occupa-

Table 2. SOCIAL CHARACTERISTICS OF NASHVILLE'S ECONOMIC LEADERS, 1880 AND 1911.

	1880	1911
Age		
Median	52	48
percentage over 59	32	25
percentage under 40	16	25
(N=)	(52)	(68)
Birthplace (%)		
Nashville-Davidson Co.	21	25
Other Tenn.	28	36
Other South	32	18
North	11	14
Foreign	8	4
(N=)	(53)	(71)
Occupation (%)		
Wholesale	39	9
Retail	10	9
Finance	20	37
Manufacturing	16	18
Professions	8	18
Transportation	8	10
(N=)	(51)	(71)
Education (%)		
No schooling	56	0
Grade school	19	36
High school	9	26
College	12	22
Post-baccalaureate	4	15
(N=)	(57)	(69)
Religion (%)		
Presbyterian	28	30
Methodist	50	23
Baptist	11	15
Episcopal	0	19
Other Protestant	0	6
Catholic	11	4
Jewish	0	4
(N=)	(36)	(53)

NOTE: All percentages are only for those with known data, as the variations in N indicate.

SOURCES: *Nashville City Directory, 1880*, lists of officers and directors of leading economic institutions, as explained in text; newspaper obituaries on 1880 leaders; *Who's Who in Tennessee* (Nashville, 1911).

tional base of Nashville's elite shifted from wholesale merchants, who led in 1880, toward banking, insurance, and other occupations in the financial sector. Notable too was the rapid demise of the transportation sector, caused by Nashville's loss of local autonomy in the railroad network. Otherwise, the occupational base of economic leaders remained stable.

Over half (57 percent of 126) of the 1880 elite could be located in Nashville's city directories before the Civil War, but the biographical sketches reveal that most came from outside the city. About a fifth in 1880 and a quarter in 1911 were born in Davidson County. Most of the remainder came from small rural towns or farms in Middle Tennessee or southern Kentucky. The 1911 data tell us that they were typically sons of small-town merchants, lawyers, or farmers—a mere 7 percent claimed fathers who were planters. There was also room for Yankees and other foreigners in Nashville's rising elite, and they contributed about one-fifth to each sample of business leadership.

On the whole, these were men who had left home as youths and come to the city to work their way up a social ladder that was remarkably unobstructed by entrenched old families. The emergent elite gave room to the ambitions of youth, as the data on age suggest. Even as this nascent upper class matured, in the early twentieth century, the median age actually dropped from fifty-two years in 1880 to forty-eight in 1911. Most of these men owed little of their status and wealth to formal education. Only a handful of the 1880 elite claimed college or professional school education, and many had not finished high school or private academy. Most had only a rudimentary education in the country common schools or were "self taught," as they frequently noted in their biographies. The increasing importance of formal training is evident by 1911, when close to 40 percent claimed college or professional school degrees. Vanderbilt University's role in training and certifying status among the new elite is also evident, for about one-eighth of the 1911 elite held degrees from that institution.

One of the more intriguing features of the new elite was the strong religious leaning toward the evangelical Protestant denominations. The Episcopal church, which was often the denomination of the South's antebellum elite, contributed none to the 1880 sample and less than a fifth to the 1911 group. This, of course, reflects the group's social origins, from middling levels of rural society. Also, the spirit of the Methodists and other Protestant evangelical churches was more in tune with the aspirations of these rising new men. The emphasis in these churches on personal moral discipline, salvation through sudden conversion, charity, good works, and revivalism all provided a set of spiritual ideals that reinforced the more earthly goals of these men as ambitious self-made men and civic boosters. In other ways, as we will see, the Methodists were particularly responsive to the challenges of urban life and social change in the New South.[1]

The stories of how these new men rose from humble origins to positions of wealth, power, and social prestige were celebrated proudly in the local press. Beginning with the centennial historical volumes by Clayton and Woolridge, there was a constant effort to bring the lives of these men to public notice, to announce the arrival of—and at the same time to define—a new upper class. *Chat*, a short-lived society magazine, printed a "Leading Citizens Series" in 1895, providing biographies of more than three dozen outstanding men of enterprise in Nashville. *Chat* also provided the social set of Nashville in the 1890s a steady stream of news on parties, visiting, engagements, and weddings among the city's elite. The *Evening Herald* also ran a series of biographical tributes to "well-known Nashvillians" in 1889. The other daily newspapers, the *American* and *Banner*, frequently paid homage to business leaders with lavish praise for the virtues of industry and perseverance they embodied. These biographical sketches served not only to define the new elite, they helped transmit an ethos of enterprise to a large audience in the city.[2]

In 1896 the first local social register was issued, preliminary to the Tennessee Centennial Exposition. Crozier's *Nashville Blue Book* identified a large number of eminent families and listed the city's most prominent clubs. In 1900 Dau's *Nashville Society Blue Book* presented a more selective guide to the city's social elite, complete with references to club associations, children's names, and the days of the week visitors were received. In 1911 Mrs. William W. Geraldton improved on Dau's with her *Social Directory*, which included the names of debutantes and eligible sons among the rich and prominent of Nashville society. These social directories thrived on a combination of snob appeal and a certain degree of anxiousness among rising families, whose listing in the blue books gave assurance that they had arrived. After World War I these directories disappeared as quickly as they had come on the scene. By this time the core of Nashville's upper class was securely established.[3]

Whatever the details of the lives revealed in the newspapers and society magazines, they all tended to fit predictable formulae wherein wealth and prestige were the well-deserved rewards of personal virtues: industry, innovation, moral self-discipline. Edmund W. Cole was described in Woolridge's 1890 *History of Nashville* as a poor farm boy from Giles County whose father died when he was but three, leaving a family of ten to take care of itself. After years of hard work on his mother's farm, Cole came up to Nashville at the age of eighteen and learned to "rely on his own resources." Beginning as a clerk, he worked his way up slowly at first, "studied to improve himself" during "every spare hour," and resisted the temptations that beckoned to youth in a dangerous city. Thanks to the strictures of his good Methodist mother, young Cole "never danced a step, never was intoxicated, and never gambled."[4]

This kind of laudatory biography announced the arrival of new men and new money in Nashville, but more was involved. These new men were welding together the associational foundations of a new upper class. The efforts to unite businessmen through commercial associations pursuing concrete economic goals has been traced in the previous chapter. These associations had explicit economic functions, but the Commercial Club was successful because it also provided social conviviality and good dining. Other, more exclusive, downtown lunch clubs began to appear for the first time in the late nineteenth century. Previously, merchants walked home for a leisurely midday meal with the family. The exodus of wealthy families to the suburbs and the more hurried pace of postwar business life help explain the demise of this tradition. By 1904 the *American,* announcing the opening of a new downtown restaurant, lamented the trend: "More and more are the businessmen of the city falling into the habit, which prevails so extensively in the North, of eating their midday meal in the city."[5] More than northern habits were responsible, for prominent businessmen were now utilizing lunchtime and evenings at clubs that brought them together, away from their private spheres of family and business and into a common orbit within which they identified the common values and goals they shared.

The most prominent of the downtown men's clubs was the Hermitage Club, established in 1882 and housed in a gracious antebellum mansion on North High Street (later Sixth Avenue) above Church. It was famous for its plush decor, sumptuous meals, and elaborate balls that drew the city's eminent families.[6] The University Club, established in 1895, occupied the old John Hill Eakin mansion on Church Street. It was composed of a small but fast-growing coterie of men who had attended college. The Standard Club, founded in 1884 by Nashville's Jewish merchants, served a similar function as a social gathering place for a small but important minority.[7]

The making of Nashville's new upper class also owed much to the wives of these business leaders, for by the 1880s and 1890s they were constantly busy in the social activities of a number of new ladies' clubs that formed a thick web uniting the families of the new upper class. The Ladies Hermitage Association, established in 1889 to preserve the Old Hero's mansion, became the most prestigious of the women's clubs. Its list of officers provide a feminine mirror of the city's business leaders. In 1892 the ladies honored Jackson's famous victory at New Orleans with a lavish ball at the Ponce de Leon Hotel in Saint Augustine, Florida, which one thousand invited guests attended, many brought in from Nashville by privately chartered railroad. The Jackson Day Ball on January 8 became an annual affair sponsored by the Ladies Hermitage Association at the downtown hotels in Nashville. They were occasions which every family with social aspirations could not afford to miss.[8] The Centennial Club, established in 1905, was an outgrowth of the Women's Department at the 1897 Tennessee Centennial Exposition. Its early identity as a civic club devoted to social uplift signaled the advent of the civic-minded clubwoman, who would eclipse the society matron during the early twentieth century.[9]

Nashville in this period spawned dozens of small literary societies and recreational clubs that served to connect the new elite and many less wealthy middle-class families. Two of the oldest literary societies, the Round Table (established 1884) and the Old Oak (established 1887–88), linked leaders in law, business, and the clergy to Vanderbilt's academic community. These clubs symbolized the growing identity of Vanderbilt with the local elite and reinforced an affinity for cultural refinement amid all the commercial boosterism of the day. The subjects discussed at their fortnightly meetings indicate these clubs were fully engaged in the public issues of the day as well as more remote topics in art and history. The Old Oak Club's agenda in 1889, for example, included papers by John T. McGill and William L. Dudley on "The Race Question in America," George W. Chambers on "The Commercial Value of Art to a City," and D. Rankin Stubblefield on "What are the Real Grievances of the Workingman?"[10] These and dozens of less formal discussions over lunch at the Hermitage Club or Commercial Club informed specific policies and, more generally, tended to imbue Nashville's new leaders with a common view of the world.

THE TRANSFORMATION OF THE DOWNTOWN

The rise of a new elite was paralleled by the physical transformation of the city center. Once the home of the local upper class, the city's core became a more concentrated commercial district that pushed most residential land use away as it expanded. On the periphery of the central business district emerged mean slums that were plagued by poverty, disease, crime, and vice; these problems repelled the wealthy families at the same time they drew the intense concern of social reformers in the progressive era. The lure of the suburbs, and their new accessibility by streetcar, accelerated the transformation of the old city into a central business district surrounded by slums.

The advent of animal-powered streetcars immediately after the Civil War had already drawn many young merchant and professional families away from the central city. The process began slowly, and in 1880 the major features of the old city were still highly visible. At that time it was a densely packed city with people who sought living space within

Figure 21.   View from the Capitol looking east, early 1880s. The County Court-house and City Hall to the right, Edgefield in background. Tennessee State Li-brary and Archives.

Figure 22.   View from the Capitol looking south, in the early 1880s. Cedar (now Charlotte Avenue) and High (now Sixth Avenue) streets in the foreground, the towers of the First Presbyterian Church on Spring (now Church) Street in the background. Tennessee State Library and Archives.

an easy walk to their place of work. The centripetal force of this "walking city" meant that most of the city's people would be packed within one-half to three-quarters of a mile of the Public Square.

The older city center was also mixed in a way unknown to the modern segmented city that was to dominate the twentieth century. Commercial and residential land use intermingled casually, and many merchants, professionals, and artisans lived with their families in loft apartments above their shops and offices. In the single block bounded by Market, Broad, Front and Church—the heart of the waterfront wholesale district—the census taker in the summer of 1880 found 158 people residing there. Among them were three dozen children belonging to the families on the block. About half the population consisted of lodgers and servants, who generally roomed with the families. Wealthy lumber merchants shared the block with transient riverboatmen. Three dozen blacks lived cheek by jowl with their white neighbors. Nine foreign countries were represented on the block. Outside on the streets and in the shops wholesale merchants, saloon keepers, prostitutes, and laborers all sought their livelihood in this heterogeneous environment.[11]

A few blocks away from the teeming life of the waterfront, on high ground west of the river, Nashville's streets of fashion—North Vine (now Seventh Avenue) and Spruce (Eighth Avenue), and Park Street, near the Capitol—harbored the wealth and prestige of the old city. Vine Street was capped by Polk Place, a magnificent antebellum mansion where in 1880 the widow of former president James K. Polk still reigned as grande dame of local society. The other brick mansions on these streets were three and four stories and designed in neoclassical, Italianate, and various Victorian fashions, usually with iron fences guarding small front gardens. The refinement and wealth of these streets of fashion stood in sharp contrast to the raffish slums south of Broad, but both were characteristic of an older, compact, mixed urban life that was to almost disappear in the next two decades.

From within the city core the expansion of a central business district pushed residential land use aside. In 1880 Nashville's main business center was the Public Square, as it had been since antebellum times. Wholesale warehouses and publishing companies occupied space on the east and north side of the square, but most of the shops surrounding the square were retail stores selling clothing, dry goods, boots and shoes, and other consumer goods to the population that concentrated close to the old city center. The retail shopping district had spread north along College (Third Avenue) and west along Union in the decades following the Civil War. On Lower Broad and along Market Street (Second Avenue) a smaller cluster of retail shops vied for customers amid the wholesale firms. Had it not been for the special circumstances of Nashville's topography, the expansion of the business district might

Figure 23. View from Rutledge Hill looking north, c. 1880. Market Street (now Second Avenue) and the Nashville Medical College in foreground, the Capitol in background, Black Bottom between. Tennessee State Library and Archives.

Figure 24. Market Street (now Second Avenue), looking north, in the early 1880s. A mixed neighborhood of warehouses, shops, and residences filled with rich and poor, black and white, native and foreign, families and vice. Tennessee State Library and Archives.

Figure 25. Vine Street (now Seventh Avenue), looking north, c. 1900. One of the streets of fashion in the old downtown. *Art Work of Nashville, Tennessee* (Chicago, 1901).

Figure 26. Summer Street (now Fifth Avenue) looking north from Church Street, c. 1900. *Art Work of Nashville, Tennessee* (Chicago, 1901).

easily have moved south from the square and north from Broad, leaving the mansions to the west untouched for decades. But the rather steep incline separating the square from Broad encouraged retailers to expand westward along Union, then down what became Fourth and Fifth avenues, and finally along Church Street, all reasonably level streets that pedestrian customers could easily traverse from one shop to the next. Lower Broad would become isolated from this main thrust of retail activity. There, lower property values afforded the extensive space required by furniture retailers, who set up a near-solid row of shops along Lower Broad, expanding away from the river and paralleling the westward pattern of the main business district.[12]

About the turn of the century the shift of retail activity west and south of the Public Square was accelerated by two important innovations in retailing. One was the modern department store, pioneered in Nashville by Castner-Knott Dry Goods Company. Founded in 1898 by William Knott and Charles Castner, the first store, located on Summer Street (later Fifth Avenue) near Church, helped make this street the heart of the new retail district.[13] "Everything from the Kitchen to the Parlor can be found for home or person," a 1903 advertisement for the store boasted. In 1906 Castner-Knott pushed the retail frontier westward along Church Street by opening a large new store at Seventh Avenue and Church, the former site of the Demoville family mansion.[14] In 1903 Paul L. Sloan, John E. Cain, and Patrick H. Cain formed a partnership and took over Kalmbach's Beehive, a popular dry goods store on Summer Street. After Castner-Knott moved to its new location, the Cain-Sloan Company took over the store at Fifth and Church.[15]

The development in 1902–1903 of a pedestrian shopping arcade between Cherry (Fourth Avenue) and Summer (Fifth Avenue) streets south of Union strengthened the trend of retail activity away from the square. The Arcade was the idea of Daniel C. Buntin, a "progressive young real estate dealer" who was to leave a definite mark on the face of the city in the years to come. Buntin had been impressed with similar glass-covered arcades in Italy and in northern cities, where they had become quite fashionable. The concept was similar to the department store. In one large, attractive mall forty stores of every variety were available to shoppers who could stroll unmolested by horses, wagons, and trolleys, and be protected by a glass roof from the elements. After a series of legal squabbles, the Arcade opened in spring 1903, a major event in downtown development. "The Nashville Arcade is one of the show features of the City," the *Daily News* trumpeted. It is to Nashville "what the Rialto was to Old Venice." Built at a cost of $300,000, the Arcade was heralded as clear "evidence of the progressiveness of the city," and a sign of "a new spirit—one of industrial enterprise, of financial activity, of prosperity."[16]

The expansion of retail shopping away from the square and to the

Figure 27. Church Street between what is now Fifth and Sixth avenues, c. 1900. *Art Work of Nashville, Tennessee* (Chicago, 1901).

Figure 28. The Arcade on opening day, 1903. Ridley Wills private collection.

5TH AVE. NORTH TOWARD UNION S.

Figure 29 (opposite).   Fifth Avenue at night, c. 1915. A lively center of the new retail district. Tennessee State Library and Archives.

Figure 30 (opposite below).   The Nashville skyline, c. 1915. Some of the old mansions survive along Eighth Avenue in foreground. Tennessee State Library Archives.

Figure 31 (below).   The Nashville skyline, c. 1915. This continues the panoramic view from the roof of the Methodist Publishing House. Tennessee State Library and Archives.

west accelerated after the depression of the 1890s and soon encroached upon the streets of fashion once guarded by Nashville's wealthy families. Already in 1893 a project to widen Deaderick Street brought destruction to a long row of old mansions, once the homes of "eminent jurists . . . noted politicians . . . and the leaders of the press." The demolition was noted in the city's annual report with mixed emotions: "We gaze in wonder upon the splendor and magnificence of the city, which in its enlargement, and progress, and increase in population, has wiped out the scenes so prominent in the eyes of those who were with us more than half a century ago."[17]

With the death of Mrs. Polk her home, another downtown landmark, would give way to progress. It was Daniel C. Buntin who arranged in 1898 the sale of Polk Place by its owner, Jacob McGavock Dickinson, to J. Craig McLanahan, a Philadelphia capitalist connected to the L&N. McLanahan quickly tore down the magnificent old mansion that had been a crucial anchor for the downtown upper-class neighborhood and built Polk and Watauga Flats, which provided fashionable downtown apartments popular among young newlyweds and retired couples. These apartments later deteriorated into seedy tenements as the downtown decayed in the twentieth century.[18]

A RING OF SLUMS

As retail and other commercial ventures expanded into downtown residences from the center, new industrial, railroad, and commercial facilities impinged on these downtown neighborhoods from outside. To the north and west, in low-lying ground along the NC&STL tracks, a corridor of heavy industry, mainly iron foundries, manufacturing plants, slaughterhouses and the like, created a sooty, odorous barrier to residential expansion. To the west the construction of Union Station and Cummins Station, a large warehouse facility, brought noise, soot, and a huge stream of wagons catering to the passengers and warehouses that cropped up around the depot. To the south the concentration of flour mills, breweries, and other agricultural processing plants centering on the NC&STL South Yards and "Roller Mill Hill" created another expanding industrial buffer on the downtown residents. On the east, of course, the river with its wharves, steamboats, lumber mills, and the new Tennessee Central Depot near the base of Broad Street completed the ring of industrial and commercial land use surrounding the old central city. The very sources of wealth that spawned Nashville's newly rich families would force them out of the central city.

Between the expanding central business district and the industrial-transportation belt surrounding it, there emerged a band of squalid

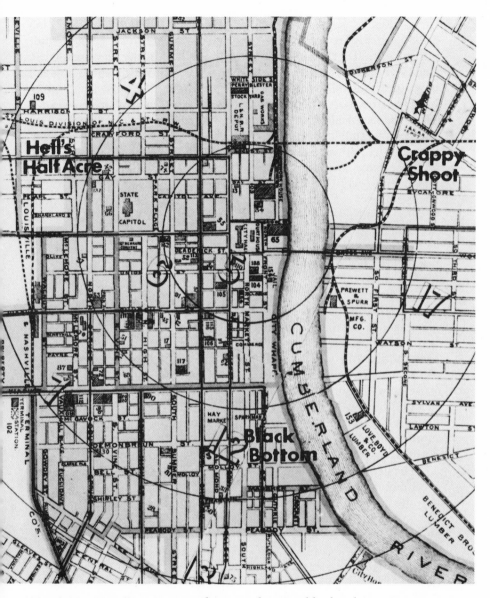

Figure 32. Map: Downtown and surrounding neighborhoods, c. 1900. Marshall and Bruce Co., 1900. Tennessee State Library and Archives.

slums filled with ramshackle housing, saloons, brothels, and gambling dens. Nashville's riverboat crews had always demanded a certain amount of commercial vice, and the soldiers quartered in the city during the Civil War produced a booming business in prostitution, which lingered long after 1865. Nor was poverty new to the city, but these social problems became more visible, more concentrated, as the city grew after 1880. The new scale of transportation, industry, and commerce required large pools of labor living nearby. The expansion of the central business district and industrial belt left a wide swath of old housing ripe for real estate speculators who rented to the poor while waiting for opportunities to develop the land. Nashville's social geography also conformed closely to topography. A ring of low drainage land stretched from north of Capitol Hill west along the railroad gulch, and south of Lower Broad, and was frequently flooded by the river and heavy rainfall. These low-lying areas became the preserve of the poor, concentrated as never before near the city center and close to the sites of their industrial and unskilled jobs.

The worst of these slums was an area known as Black Bottom, located in the low land south of Broad from the riverfront up to about Fifth Avenue, where the land ascended along with rental prices. Filled largely with blacks, as its name implied, the area was home also to a fair number of poor whites and Irish and Jewish immigrants. As early as 1888 conditions in the area had become bad enough to provoke a suggestion to remove the residents and turn it into a "delightful park."[19] In 1893 the city condemned portions of Black Bottom near the river for a city haymarket, a project designed to remove the "country trade" from the Public Square as well as to displace the tenements of Black Bottom.[20]

The depression that began that year only expanded and intensified the squalor and poverty of Black Bottom. By 1905 Black Bottom had become a permanent sore on the edge of the downtown, described by one indignant citizen as "a conglomeration of dives, brothels, pawnshops, second-hand clothing stores, filthy habitations . . . accompanied by the daily display of lewdness and drunkenness on the sidewalks and redolent with the stench of every vile odor . . . no city in America or Europe can present a more disgraceful or sickening aspect of modern civilization. . . ."[21] The ongoing struggle to "reclaim" or eradicate Black Bottom continued through the 1900s and 1910s. In 1907 the South Nashville Women's Federation, a group initiated by the Centennial Club, lobbied for a city bond issue to underwrite a large park and a new bridge across the Cumberland, both intended to "eliminate Black Bottom."[22] The Sparkman Street Bridge was built, terminating near the Haymarket and displacing many of Black Bottom's tenements as new warehouses and industrial activities cropped up around the bridge.[23] A bond issue to develop a park in Black Bottom was defeated in 1910, however, in

Figure 33. A rare glimpse of life in Black Bottom, 1909. *American,* August 8, 1909.

part because of fears that slum dwellers would only migrate to middle-class neighborhoods.[24]

Poverty and vice were not restricted to Black Bottom. Another largely black slum grew up under the trestle of the NC&STL tracks west of the downtown. By the 1880s a sprawling area filled with shacks and lean-tos spread up the western and northern slopes of Capitol Hill. Known as "Hell's Half Acre," it rivaled Black Bottom for its vice, epidemics, and desperate poverty. Along Line Street (later Jo Johnston Avenue) a series of "fancy houses" catered to a mixed clientele of white and black men, while along Criddle Street in North Nashville, near the slaughterhouses and cotton factories, another red-light district thrived. Cutting through the heart of the downtown along Cherry Street (Fourth Avenue) and College Street (Third Avenue) was the "men's quarter." The famous Southern Turf, a well-known gambling spot, and the Climax and Utopia saloons, along Cherry Street, catered to middle-class men, while a strip of more seamy dives clustered along Cherry down the hill toward Broad. Respectable women wishing to dine at the Maxwell House Hotel, which faced Cherry Street, avoided this masculine turf by using the lady's entrance on Church Street.[25]

SUBURBAN FLIGHT AND THE DISEASED CITY

The changing moral climate of the downtown and the concentration of impoverished, disease-ridden slums were becoming increasingly difficult to ignore even among the most genteel of Nashville's families. The response among those with wealth and political power varied. Some organized new humanitarian efforts to ameliorate the conditions of the poor and reform the conditions of society that produced poverty. Others sought more repressive measures in an expanded police force and new legislation intended to stamp out intemperance, prostitution, gambling, and crime of all sorts. Ultimately, the social tensions that heightened during the depression of the 1890s were resolved by an accelerated movement of middle-class and wealthy families away from the old central city to the new suburbs. From this time forward, the suburban frontier became a kind of safety valve releasing pressures that built up within the city.

The expansion of the city into its suburban fringe began immediately after the Civil War and accelerated steadily before the 1890s, when it was slowed by the depression. Then, as the depression lifted in the late 1890s, an explosion of residential migration away from the older city center created in Nashville the modern urban form most American cities live with today. Suburban growth was far more than just the outward flow of a growing population. It involved segregation by race and class that was unknown to the older, more heterogeneous city of earlier days. It involved, also, a separation of home and work that wrought profound cultural as well as physical effects upon urban life. Modern suburbs that grew up around the streetcars in the late nineteenth and early twentieth centuries embodied a whole cluster of new values embraced by the city's newly arrived upper class and the prosperous middle class. At the heart of this common suburban culture was a new concern for health and child nurture. Suburban domestic life was celebrated as a wholesome, moral refuge from the city.

This new consciousness of health was a product both of deteriorating conditions in the city and the acceptance of the germ theory of disease by the 1880s. Dr. J. Berrien Lindsley, city health officer in 1877, complained that Nashville led the nation with its high death rate and was fifth among cities in the world.[26] The growth of the city in the 1880s brought severe crowding to the city and strained the already poor defenses of public health.

Nashville's limestone base, lying just a few feet below the soil, made modern sewer and water systems extraordinarily expensive and difficult to construct. When modern sewers were extended through most streets in the central city by the early 1880s, the cost of installing a "water closet" and connecting it to the main line was well beyond the financial resources of most families. By 1898 the city's population of over 80,000 could count no more than 682 toilets, 212 bathtubs, and 52 urinals.[27] Most families continued to use outdoor privies, the contents of which saturated the thin soil, contaminated nearby wells, and created a constant threat from diseases like typhoid. Purer water was supplied by a new city water works, completed in 1889. A filtration plant on an island upriver from the city pumped water to a new reservoir atop Kirkpatrick Hill. Still, most poor families could not afford hooking up to the main water lines, and the supply of city water was inadequate for more than a fraction of the total population, in any case. The poor continued to rely on springs and shallow wells that were highly vulnerable to contamination.

Garbage, ashes, and kitchen slop were piled in back alleys and yards or, too often, thrown into the streets until they were picked up by an overworked scavenger hired by the city. The scavenger hauled the refuse by wagon to the river, loaded it on "dump boats," and threw it into the Cumberland. Horses and mules, the main source of transportation, produced enormous quantities of manure, and with their hooves and wagon wheels pounded it into the brick and crushed stone pavement, where it was then soaked with thousands of gallons of urine each day. This, joined by the garbage, privy fumes, and the contributions of assorted dogs, chickens, and hogs, created an abominable stench on hot summer days. Dead animals were left in the streets for days before being dragged by the city scavenger to the river to be dumped. "These carcasses," one public health officer complained, "float upon the surface of the river, presenting a loathsome appearance and exhaling offensive odors that are calculated to excite apprehension."[28]

The air was no less polluted than the ground. The streets, mostly paved with crushed limestone, produced choking dust in the dry months and slimy mud after rains. During the winter soft coal used in stoves and furnaces produced a dense pall of black smoke over the city. Dust and smoke were continually blamed for the high incidence of lung disease in Nashville, but solutions to all these nuisances remained beyond the will and power of city government to control.

As the population crowded into low-lying slums, and as slum landlords rented more damp basement rooms, the telltale signs appeared in rising rates of tuberculosis and pneumonia, which remained the leading and most constant killers of this period. Other more dramatic epidemics swept through the slum periodically: diphtheria, diarrhea, smallpox, measles, scarlet fever, typhoid, and malaria. The proximity of rich and poor and the democratic nature of germs meant that many diseases would quickly spread beyond the boundaries of the slums.[29]

In 1873, in the wake of a cholera scourge, the city government organized a small, poorly budgeted department of health. It was limited to inspecting homes, wells, and suppliers of meat and milk. It recommended sanitary reform laws to City Council and each year compiled tallies of death and disease. The department also supervised street cleaning and managed a small dispensary. Even these meager efforts had a radical impact on the city's public health before the 1890s. The death rate per 1,000 people dropped precipitously from 34.55 in 1875 to 25.53 by 1880, and 17.81 by 1890. Then, with the worsening of social conditions in the 1890s, the death rates rose again to 20.69 by 1895 and 21.96 by 1900.[30] The full impact of Nashville's squalid health conditions is seen more dramatically in statistics selected by race, age, and neighborhood. Black death rates remained consistently about twice those for the white population. Thus in 1890, when 13.52 per thousand whites died, the rate for blacks was 25.03, rising to 30.03 in 1900. The sixth ward, which in 1890 included Black Bottom, claimed the highest death rate in the city, 24.34, with blacks alone experiencing 41.19 deaths per thousand in this ward.

The same health officers who sought to educate the City Council and citizens about the links among poverty, poor sanitation, and disease fell back on racial explanations for the high black death rates. They "demonstrate most forcibly the terrible penalties incurred by their habits and mode of life," the health department reported in 1887.[31] "The high death rate among the colored people is due to . . . improvidence, ignorance, lamentable neglect of personal cleanliness . . . and above all, the negro has to contend with this marked racial susceptibility to all forms of tubercular disease."[32]

Figure 34. Tuberculosis nurse inspecting a basement laundry, 1912. *Annual Reports of the Departments of the City of Nashville, 1912* (Nashville, 1913).

Figure 35. Russell Street, Edgefield, c. 1900. *Art Work of Nashville, Tennessee* (Chicago, 1901).

These racist explanations, of course, shifted the onus to the victims of disease, but more important, they linked the growing dread of disease with blacks and the slums they inhabited in the old central city. When wealthy whites left for the clean, wholesome refuge of the suburbs, they also left behind the black population that had lived close to whites for generations.

Racial prejudice combined in the late nineteenth century with a callous disdain for the plight of the poor to discourage any massive public solution to the growing threat of disease. Yet the germ theory told wealthy whites of the democracy of disease and pushed many to seek a private solution to the public problems that festered in the city. The answer was to leave the city behind, to remove the family and especially young children to a clean, spacious semirural suburban home. When James E. Caldwell, a rising entrepreneur, first married, he built a fine home on Stevenson Street, in South Nashville beyond Black Bottom. There he was able to raise vegetables in a kitchen garden, to keep a cow, and to stable horses for his buggy. But when he and his wife started a family, he considered the health dangers of the city. "The visible force that precipitated the movement to the country was the conviction that we could not hope to bring up our two babies in the city."[33]

Suburban real estate promoters skillfully played on the growing awareness of the dangers of urban life. In an advertisement for the Nashville Realty Company, for example, an illustration showed the damaging effects of insufficient sunlight on urban residents. On one side of a crowded city street, where houses had a northern exposure, were crippled invalids and enfeebled consumptives living in dark, stuffy apartments. Opposite, those with a wholesome, sunny southern exposure danced and played merrily. Suburban life offered every home a place in the sun.[34] The capacity to act on this new consciousness of suburban health was enhanced tremendously by new developments in urban transportation.

THE SEGMENTED CITY

As the expansion of the central business district and the teeming slums bordering it pushed wealthy families from the city center, new and spacious suburban developments pulled them to the urban periphery. The ability of the middle class to join wealthier families in the suburbs was conditioned by major developments in transportation technology and real estate promotion, which coincided in the 1890s. The role of the city in annexing huge suburban districts, beginning in 1880 and climaxing in 1905, played a decisive role in stimulating the suburban trend. The breakup of several old estates on the rim of the city also provided large plots of land for a new scale of suburban development in this period.

THE MULE-CAR SUBURBS

The first streetcars appeared in Nashville immediately after the Civil War. Pulled by mules over iron tracks in the center of the street, they quickly opened a new frontier of suburban life by allowing relatively smooth, fast, and reliable commuting service within two miles or so of the city center. In 1865 the South Nashville Railway constructed a line up the gentle slope of Cherry Street (Fourth Avenue) past the old City Cemetery to Chestnut, returning to the square along College (Third Avenue). This line served a prosperous suburban neighborhood atop Rutledge Hill, which was favored by high ground and proximity to the downtown. The University of Nashville, later to divide its interests and be absorbed principally by Peabody Normal College, occupied the top of the hill and served as a magnet for numerous wealthy families, who built fine brick homes around the campus. Captain Tom Ryman's elegant mansion on Lea Avenue gave a special stature to the neighborhood. A number of churches, Howard School, and the Medical Department of Vanderbilt University all contributed to the tone of this early middle-class streetcar suburb.[1]

Another mule-drawn streetcar line, the McGavock and Mount Vernon built in 1865, extended north from the downtown along College (Third Avenue) and Cherry (Fourth Avenue), eventually all the way out to Saint Cecelia Academy, a Catholic school for girls patronized by many of the city's well-to-do Protestant and Catholic families. An open field of crops and fruit trees, owned by John H. Buddeke, became settled largely by Nashville's growing German population. Germantown, as it came to be known, centered on a retail section on Monroe Street, and a number of fine brick homes, churches, fraternal lodges, and schools soon emerged to define this subcommunity.[2] The most elegant of the early streetcar suburbs was across the river in Edgefield. The Nashville and Edgefield Street Railroad Company built a line across the river in 1872. Later, in 1881, the Fatherland Street Railroad Company improved service to Edgefield with a second line. Along Russell Street a row of large brick mansions went up, many of them custom designed and elaborately ornamented to display the wealth of the rich young merchants and manufacturers who flocked to Edgefield in the 1870s and 1880s. Congregations of Methodists, Presbyterians, Baptists, and Episcopalians all built splendid new churches along Woodland and Russell. With its spacious lots, tree-lined streets, and its proximity to the country, Edgefield nurtured a special quality of genteel, suburban refinement. The river served as a moral buffer against the saloons, gambling dens, and brothels of the city as well as a barrier to fire.[3]

Expansion to the west was inhibited by the deep gulch beyond Walnut (Tenth Avenue), which the mules had difficulty traversing. In the 1880s the McGavock and Mount Vernon Company erected a wood viaduct and extended a line out West End all the way to Vanderbilt University. Residential settlement strung out along Broadway to Belmont (Sixteenth Avenue) and on the gentle hill to the south known as Belmont Terrace. By the late 1880s this neighborhood, with its fine brick town homes and several new churches, was showing all the promise Edgefield had a few years earlier.

These suburban outposts were available only to a small portion of the population because of the daily cost of commuting and the limitations of animal-powered transportation. They gave a growing number of people, generally well-off young families with children, a taste for the amenities of suburban life and the habit of commuting daily to work and shop. These tastes would be shared more broadly with the electrification and consolidation of the city's rapid transit system between 1888 and 1903.

THE TROLLEY-CAR SUBURBS

It was southern cities, less restricted by established urban transportation monopolies and eager to show their progressive New South spirit, that pioneered in the development of the electric trolley. Montgomery, Alabama, in 1886 claimed the first successful application of an all-electric system; Richmond and Atlanta followed quickly in the same year.[4] In February 1888 Nashville's McGavock and Mount Vernon Company introduced the first electric powered service on its long Broadway-Vanderbilt line. Within the following year the company extended electric power to its entire system. Soon the newly organized City Electric Railway ran new lines into South Nashville and out to Mount Olivet Cemetery. The South Nashville and Edgefield companies quickly converted to electricity, bringing a total of fifty miles of track under electric power.[5]

The technology of electric trolleys, requiring costly steam-driven generating plants, naturally invited consolidation of the various small neighborhood lines that cropped up during the reign of the mule. Consolidation, in turn, introduced new economies of scale that stimulated the rapid invasion of trolley tracks into the suburbs. The expansion of a centralized electric trolley system was integrally connected, therefore, to the promotion of suburban real estate; the two frequently involved the same entrepreneurs. The integration of the transit system would increase passenger volume by keeping down fares and reducing or eliminating transfer fees. Consolidation came quickly after electrification, with the organization of the United Electric Railway headed by Thomas W. Wrenne, a lawyer and banker, and Isaac T. Rhea, the steamboat and grain elevator magnate. The company was capitalized with $1 million in stock (one of the largest private enterprises in the city up to this time), and it was authorized to raise $2.5 million more through bond issues. The Panic of 1893, however, forced the company to default on the bonded debt, and it was sold under federal court order.

Local stockholders, led by General William Harding Jackson of Belle Meade, reorganized the company only to sell out to Colonel Charles McGhee of Knoxville and Nathaniel Baxter in 1896. As the depression of the 1890s dragged on and suburban growth slowed, the transit business remained unprofitable. Again in 1899 the company was sold, this time to Edward T. Hambleton, a financier from Baltimore with extensive holdings in streetcar and electric light companies across the country. Hambleton and his associates also bought controlling interest in the West Nashville and Glendale Park steam dummy lines (locomotives disguised with false sides to avoid frightening horses) and the Cumberland Light and Power Company. The local manager was Thomas J. Felder, a young businessman who rose rapidly in Nashville society.[6]

Hambleton's plans to consolidate the trolley and steam dummy

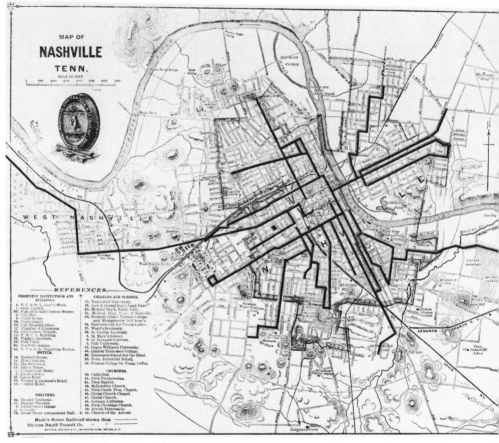

Figure 36. Map: Streetcar lines, 1897.

lines was stalled by a court injunction and strong resistance from Mayor James M. Head, a stalwart defender of public interests against corporate monopolies. The courts finally allowed the consolidation in 1900, and a new company, the Nashville Street Railway Company, was set up with James C. Bradford as president. The city government then brought new suits challenging the company's claim to earlier streetcar franchises and declaring the company responsible for paving the strip between and alongside the tracks.

In the face of these legal obstacles the company was forced into receivership in 1901, and Percy Warner, son of wealthy iron manufacturer James C. Warner, and Eugene C. Lewis of the L&N took control. Finally, in 1902 the Tennessee Supreme Court decided in favor of the company, but in consideration of the city's franchise to the company, it was to purchase and deed to the city the land that became Centennial Park. The next year the company was reorganized once again as the Nashville Railway and Light Company, with Percy Warner as president. Cumberland Light and Power Company was merged later with it during the same year, and its generating capacity was doubled. Finally, a fully integrated electric transit system with its own electric light and power company was on a firm financial footing under a single management.[7]

THE WESTWARD TREND

The major thrust of suburban expansion in the electric trolley car era was to the west. This was owing in part to the deterioration of the older, more settled mule-car suburbs. South Nashville and Rutledge Hill were adjacent to Black Bottom, through which pedestrians and streetcar commuters had to travel to get downtown. Also, farther to the south the industrial plants and flour mills that centered on the NC&StL South Yards spawned a large working-class neighborhood, Trimble Bottom, consisting of black and white workers. By 1914 Peabody Normal College, a successor of the University of Nashville, removed its campus from Rutledge Hill to a new site adjacent to Vanderbilt on Hillsboro Pike. Some families who built substantial homes on Rutledge Hill in the 1870s and 1880s lived out their lives there, but the area failed to hold and attract young families who would fill those homes in the next generation.[8]

North Nashville's Germantown also drew industrial activities that undermined its semirural repose of earlier years. Along the railroad tracks the meat-slaughtering and -packing industry produced a foul smell. The waste was dumped into the Cumberland, where it rotted, along with city garbage and animal carcasses, all adding to the stench of North Nashville. A large cotton mill, the Tennessee Manufacturing Company, began operations in 1872.[9] Around this factory emerged a growing working-class neighborhood of cheap cottages that intruded on the rows of more substantial brick homes built by the prosperous German burghers. Along Criddle Street, near the old L&N depot and the factories, a thriving red light district also tainted the middle-class aura of respectability Germantown once claimed. The coming of World War I and the rise of anti-German sentiment in America acted to accelerate the flight of the middle class from this early suburb.[10]

Edgefield, the most opulent of the early suburbs, declined just as rapidly as the others. It too suffered from being too close to a thriving industrial sector of lumber mills and the furniture and bucket manufacturing plants that grew up along the eastern river bank. In a low drainage area north of Main Street called "Crappy Shoot" emerged a black shanty town filled with laborers from the lumber mills.

The prevailing eastward winds blew much of the industrial smoke, coal soot, street dust, and garbage odors into the pristine suburban neighborhoods that were intended as a refuge from those ills. When a fire broke out in Crappy Shoot the morning of March 22, 1916, these same winds whipped a tremendous blaze through the heart of Edgefield, leaving a wide swath of charred ruins where the mansions of the 1870s and 1880s had been built, supposedly safe from the threat of fire that prevailed in the city. The rubble and empty lots remained through the building slump of World War I, thus accelerating the deterioration of this once grand suburb.[11]

To the west, the railroad gulch that inhibited dense suburban growth before the trolley era and discouraged industrial development left open a wide expanse of largely unsettled rural land. In this area a new style of extensive, highly aggressive suburban promotion would quickly replace the earlier pattern of ad hoc lot and house sales through individuals or small realty companies. The day of the trolley brought with it a new era of heavily capitalized real estate syndicates, often financed by the same capitalists who owned the transit system. New techniques of mass advertising and innovative sales and financing were also an integral part of the new suburban trend.

As early as the spring of 1890 these promotional techniques were skillfully displayed in a large public auction of suburban lots sponsored by the Nashville Real Estate Exchange. On the evening before the sale a "rousing meeting" at exchange headquarters downtown whipped up enthusiasm for the auction. A hall packed with local businessmen and speculators "brought to the city from the North and West" listened to the "eloquent presentation[s]" from Nashville's boosters predicting the "grand destiny" of the city.[12] The next afternoon at three o'clock a good crowd gathered at lot number one in Waverly Place, the former estate of A.W. Putnam, organized as a suburban real estate venture by Percy

Figure 37. West End Avenue, c. 1900. The trolley car opened a vast suburban frontier, particularly on the western side of the city. Nashville Land Improvement Company, West Nashville (Nashville, 1900).

Figure 38. Belmont Avenue, c. 1900. A bucolic scene of spaciousness and healthfulness in the new suburbs. *Art Work of Nashville, Tennessee* (Chicago, 1901).

and James C. Warner and several others in the 1880s. For the next four hours the auctioneer moved from one lot to the next selling them off to the highest bidder. The next day the "monster sale" moved over to the old Maney Estate in East Nashville, then downtown, where inner-city lots were sold.[13]

Suburban real estate companies now used aggressive advertising in full-page newspaper advertisements, handbills passed out on trolleys and busy street corners, posters, and outdoor billboards. A newspaper advertisement for Belmont Park and Belmont Annex (a subdivision of the late Adelicia Acklen's estate) lured hesitant buyers with hyperbolic claims for suburban life in 1891: "The prettiest and most desirable residence property in the South. . . . It overlooks the entire city. Its location cannot be equaled; its scenery cannot be approached; its healthfulness cannot be questioned." Transportation preceded housing in most of these suburban developments. The open lots in Belmont Park were accessible by "Electric Car Service" and served by two 80-foot-wide boulevards macadamized and "rolled as smooth as a dancing floor" with the "best stone curbing and sidewalks."[14]

These and other early experiments in large-scale suburban real estate promotion were to change the shape of Nashville. But the depression that came in 1893 ruined the real estate market, and it was not until after the turn of the century that it resumed full tilt. Coinciding with the consolidation of the electric transit system in 1902, Nashville experienced a boom on its western frontier.

The connection between the trolley and the suburban trend was nowhere better illustrated than in the opening of the Murphy Addition. Samuel Murphy, a whiskey distiller, came to Nashville from Cincinnati in 1870 and built one of the city's largest personal fortunes. Murphy invested in several pieces of country property to the west of town and built a magnificent mansion surrounded by 66 acres of beautiful woodland (where Baptist Hospital now stands). Murphy became an eccentric millionaire in his old age and was known to enjoy the source of his wealth in long afternoons of drinking with friends. When Thomas Felder came to Nashville in 1898 to take over the streetcar system for Hambleton & Company of Baltimore, he provided Murphy not only a prosperous business association (Murphy was director of the new transit company), but an ideal drinking partner, Felder being one of the few men reputed to be capable of drinking Murphy under the table.[15] Felder was a young, ambitious man who knew an opportunity when he saw it. He already had married well (to the daughter of Milton H. Smith, president of the L&N), and the Felders quickly became accepted in Nashville society. Murphy and his wife had no children, and they became extraordinarily fond of the young Felder couple. During a summer vacation together at Narragansett, Rhode Island (perhaps after another afternoon of whiskey drinking), the Murphys decided to adopt the Felders, putting them in line to inherit one of Nashville's largest fortunes. Murphy fell ill and died in December 1900, just before Christmas when the adoption papers were to be filed. Mrs. Murphy proceeded with the adoption, much to the chagrin of other distant kin, and Thomas Felder, at age thirty-one, now laid claim to an estate of $1.5 million dollars.[16]

After a respectable period of mourning, Felder set out to consolidate Murphy's estate with other western suburban real estate, construct a trolley line, and engineer what was to be a booming real estate development in Nashville's suburbs. In January 1902 Felder organized the Murphy Land Company with John and William Vertrees, Mrs. Murphy, and Thomas Taylor. Two other real estate syndicates controlling almost 600 acres on the city's west side joined interests with Felder as well. At the same time, Felder, in league with several other local capitalists, including Daniel C. Buntin, organized the Suburban Street Railway. This company extended trolley service far past the city limits, from Centennial Park about two miles out Harding Pike.

With a broad boulevard on either side of the track, this line would open hundreds of acres of "splendid suburban property." The line would fork at the intersection of Murphy Road and go all the way to West Nashville. This area, the petition for right of way explained, "is in pressing need of facilities to reach the City of Nashville; and it is hoped, by building this line of road, to develop all that property and afford facilities for property holders and others contemplating locating in that vicinity, in getting to and from their homes rapidly and conveniently."[17]

To stimulate development at the eastern head of his new suburban empire, Felder offered to sell the entire 66 acres of the Murphy homestead to the city at a liberal price, under the condition that it be used as a public park. The "wilderness of beauty" would "materially enhance the value of property in that vicinity," the *Daily News* observed.[18] Felder's offer was turned down by the city in favor of nearby Centennial Park, given to the city by the Nashville Railway and Light Company in October 1902.[19] In Nashville, like many other cities, public parks would now replace cemeteries in stimulating midday and weekend passenger fares. In this capacity Centennial Park, the grandest of an expanding system of parks after 1902, would act as a powerful magnet pulling the suburban frontier to the west and beyond.

Lots sold briskly in the Murphy addition east of the park. New financial terms allowed buyers to put 25 percent down, the balance in monthly installments over ten years at 5 percent interest. Relatively small lots, 50 to 60 feet wide, sold at $20 to $45 a front foot, "popular prices that put in the power of every person to pick a prize lot. . . ."[20]

On the hilly land adjacent to the west side of Centennial Park, West End Park offered a stylish suburban plan with large blocks and curving streets conforming to the hill. By 1905 the western suburban frontier

Figure 39. Centennial Park and West End Avenue, looking northwest from Kirkland Hall tower, 1925. The park became a magnet for suburban residents and trolley car patrons after 1897. Leopold Scholz album, Vanderbilt University Photographic Archive.

Figure 40. Alabama Avenue, West Nashville, looking east, c. 1900. Nashville Land Improvement Company, *West Nashville* (Nashville, 1900).

leapfrogged across a wide expanse of mostly undeveloped property between Centennial Park and the Tennessee Central Railroad. The Richland-West End neighborhood was served by the new West End trolley line.[21] In February 1905 the Richland Realty Company was organized and bought out the Murphy property north of Harding Pike. At the company's expense, the West End trolley line was completed to Wilson Boulevard. An area of 260 acres was divided into small, affordable lots. The streets were macadamized, and granitoid curbs and sidewalks were installed. Landscaped center park strips for shade trees, "similar to Saint Charles Street in New Orleans," gave Richland a "beautiful park-like appearance."[22]

Along West End to Wilson Boulevard, where Benjamin F. Wilson's magnificent estate stood, and along Richland and Central avenues to the north, a good number of fine brick mansions went up after 1905. They were occupied by several of the wealthiest young families in Nashville. Many of these families contributed to the Nashville Golf and Country Club, which built a clubhouse and laid out a course across Harding Pike on the former Whitworth estate.[23] Golf, imported from Great Britain, had become highly fashionable among wealthy suburban Americans everywhere in this period. The club gave Richland-West End a special claim as a new enclave of the city's upper class. By 1912–13 the Richland-West End neighborhood reached its zenith. These years witnessed banner sales of lots. At this point, the John S. Bransford Realty Company, a major force in Nashville's suburban growth, took over sales. After the front line of houses along West End and Richland Avenue was sold, Bransford adopted a strategy of lowering prices and promoting cheaper, bungalow-style housing.[24]

No sooner did this neighborhood begin to take shape in Richland-West End than a new suburb, Belle Meade, eclipsed it. Belle Meade, the former plantation of the Harding family, was symbolic of the decline of the old landed gentry of antebellum times—and of the rise of a new upper class of commerce, finance, and manufacturing, a class that would transform Belle Meade into its own suburban showcase of the wealth and power generated in the city since the Civil War. By the turn of the century Belle Meade, the "Queen of Tennessee Plantations," survived under the management of General William Hicks Jackson, son-in-law of William Giles Harding, founder of the estate. General Jackson lived up to the old standards of hospitality with lavish parties at the mansion, and he indulged in cavalier betting at the race track. But the economic base of this once flourishing thoroughbred horse farm could no longer sustain that style of life, especially in the prolonged depression of the 1890s. General Jackson placed the estate in the hands of his son and two daughters. One daughter, Eunice, died in 1901, leaving her share of the estate to her husband, Albert Marks. Marks, acting as his father-in-law's lawyer, had secretly borrowed against the estate and pilfered funds. When these facts came to light in 1902 Marks shot himself in the head and died.[25] The other daughter, Selene, was divorced in 1901 from William Robert Elliston, who had fled to England after a drunken shooting affray with his brother-in-law. General Jackson, profoundly depressed by the demise of his family, died in March 1903. In July his son, William Harding Jackson, died of typhoid.[26]

The estate went into receivership, the horses and furnishings were sold at auction, and the land divided into suburban lots and sold to the moneyed families of Nashville. The Belle Meade Land Company, organized in 1904, was led by Jesse M. Overton, president, and Goodloe Lindsley, secretary, representatives of two venerable Nashville families. In 1909 the company, with aid from Chicago planners, laid out the former Deer Park into forty-six large lots for "country homes" arranged on winding roads cut in from Harding Pike across the Richland Creek.[27] Jacob McGavock Dickinson, another scion of old Nashville, bought the mansion and 400 acres along Harding Pike. He used it as a summer home and tried to keep up the old standards of opulence, especially when entertaining President Taft and other visiting dignitaries. But in 1909 he sold his holdings to James O. Leake. A new company was formed in 1910, with Wirt S.H. Armistead, a professional real estate promoter, at its head and Luke Lea, the omnipresent newspaper publisher, politician, and entrepreneur-at-large, acting as the major stockholder and promoter. Lea persuaded the Nashville Golf and Country Club to relocate on a 145-acre plot he donated to the club in the heart of Belle Meade. By 1916 the Belle Meade Country Club, as it was now known, opened with a lavish new clubhouse, which was to become the social center of this nascent upper-class suburb as it blossomed after World War I.[28]

WEST NASHVILLE: AN INDUSTRIAL SUBURB

West End was only the most prominent of several long, fingerlike projections that penetrated Nashville's western suburbs along the trolley-car lines. Charlotte Avenue owned most of its traffic to the growth of West Nashville, which lay over three miles from the city center beyond a wide swath of undeveloped hilly land west of Centennial Park. West Nashville was laid out on the old Cockrill, Pilcher, Clare, and Irwin farms in 1887 as an industrial satellite community. It offered sites for the new large-scale factories that required cheap land outside the central city and access to the river. The West Nashville Land Improvement Company deserves recognition as the first of the great suburban real estate promotional schemes in the 1880s. Dr. Henry M. Pierce of Buffalo, New York, came to Nashville in 1887 and joined with local capitalists in organizing the company. To attract new industry the company needed a sizable pool of workers within easy reach of the factories. In order to draw working-class families to the area, the company laid out small home-size lots and two public parks (Clifton and Richland parks) on a modern grid plan, with east-west streets named after the states of the Union and the north-south streets numbered. Lots were sold in what was simply called "New Town" at a huge three-day land sale in May 1887. That fall the company built a spur railroad to the NC&StL, then deeded it to the railroad on the condition it would be used as a steam dummy commuter line for workers. The spur also would serve the factory sites along the river.

All the necessary ingredients were there, it seemed, to make good West Nashville's claim as the "Manufacturing Metropolis of the South." But most workers could not afford suburban lots, and train fare, even at five cents, took a big bite out of a daily wage of one to two dollars. The risks of investing in a large industrial plant so far from the pool of labor were well understood by manufacturers, and as late as 1893 there was not a single factory constructed in West Nashville.[29]

Dr. Pierce, described as a "Northerner of Southern inclinations," enjoyed his new wealth, entertained lavishly, and left Nashville a poor man after a few years of high living.[30] The company languished with the hard times following 1893. Then, during the depths of the depression in 1896, West Nashville benefited from a phosphate strike in Maury and Hickman counties to the south. West Nashville soon became a national center for phosphate fertilizer manufacturing. By 1908 there were fifteen fertilizer plants in Nashville, many owned by local capitalists. The noxious fumes these plants produced made West Nashville's remote location a distinct advantage.[31] The lumber industry, by this time overcrowded at its location on the east bank of the Cumberland opposite the downtown, also found room to expand in West Nashville. The labor problem was partially solved in the 1890s by the erection of the new state prison, which provided convict labor within the prison walls under contract to nearby manufacturers. Nashville firms now used convict labor to produce shoes, hosiery, stoves, and a variety of other manufactured goods.[32] Electric trolleys also were introduced out Charlotte Avenue to bring the "ever growing army of workmen" to their jobs in West Nashville, now within a twenty- or thirty-minute journey from the central city.[33]

As the industrial base expanded, and as new real estate promoters emerged after the turn of the century, West Nashville was ready for residential development. By 1903 a new syndicate, the Nashville Realty Company, superseded the old West Nashville Land Improvement Company and combined its 675 acres to two adjacent tracts controlled by the Charlotte Park Company, with 183 acres south of Richland Park, and the Fogg syndicate, with 180 acres farther south in the Sylvan Park area. This merger created "one progressive wide-awake company" controlling ultimately 1,200 acres and led by experienced financiers and real estate promoters, including Daniel C. Buntin, president, and Lewis T. Baxter, vice president.[34] In May 1903 the Nashville Realty Company staged a huge three-day sale in the Charlotte Park and Sylvan Park areas south of Charlotte Pike. This neighborhood, served by the Sylvan Park trolley (a branch off the main line along Charlotte) provided ideal housing for workers and supervisors in the nearby plants. The lots, sold at auction, went for relatively low prices, about $5.50 to $6.00 a front foot. Most appear to have been purchased by speculators who erected inexpensive cottages to rent to workers and their families.[35]

West Nashville's promoters began to advertise the semirural qualities of their community and its sharp contrasts with the city. One pamphlet described the "homelike and comfortable" cottages, surrounded by lowing cattle and clucking hens, "the view from any of them extends to blue hills, grassy slopes, and meadow lands not far away, and not a suggestion of the hot stone pavements and smoke-begrimed city is visible."[36] West Nashville claimed 4,000 inhabitants in 1901 and by 1908 boasted almost 10,000.[37] Churches and schools were built to serve the growing number of families. Developers planted shade trees along the streets, put in concrete sidewalks, street lamps, sewers, and improved Richland Park, to produce what one booster publication described as "the most desirable resident sections." It was an "ideal 'home' town" that could brag it had "no saloons or gambling places."[38] In every way this industrial suburb offered to working-class families the same kind of semirural refuge from the city that their more wealthy counterparts were seeking in West End, Belle Meade, and Belmont.

THE ETHNIC SUBCOMMUNITIES: LITTLE IRELAND

The evolution of Nashville's urban form was shaped also by the multitude of ethnic subcommunities that sought identity and insulation from adversaries by withdrawing to their own tribal neighborhoods and institutions. By 1880 about 17 percent, or one in six of Nashville's 80,000 citizens, either had been born in a foreign country or had at least one parent born in a foreign country.[39] This was nothing, of course, when compared with the teeming immigrant ghettos of the northern cities where 80 percent and more were immigrants or children of immigrants. But it was enough to bring to Nashville the kind of rich cultural diversity—and ethnic conflict—that was typical of American urban life during the nineteenth and early twentieth centuries.

The first immigrant wave to come to Nashville in the mid-nineteenth century was also the largest. These were the Irish, the "Green" or Catholic Irish (as opposed to the Protestant Scotch-Irish who had migrated earlier). The Catholic Irish came after 1845 when the potato famine pushed millions of impoverished tenant farmers into an exodus of desperation. In Nashville many of the Irish found their niche toward the bottom of the occupational ladder doing the work that required strong backs and little skill — peasant life in Ireland had prepared them for little more. Many found work on the riverfront loading and unloading the steamboats that plied the waters of the Cumberland. Others worked in construction gangs, grading and paving new streets, digging sewers, and erecting buildings for the growing city of Nashville.

Before the 1870s most Irish lived close to their primary source of employment, the river and the Public Square, where unskilled day laborers gathered early in the morning six days a week to sell their labor to a foreman, typically for a dollar a day, ten hours — or more — a day. The Irish crowded into the rough-and-tumble shanties and tenement apartments clustered in the low-lying areas next to the river south of Broad and near the city's lower wharf, north and downhill from the Public Square. Here, the squalid homes of the Irish competed with grog shops, tippling houses, and cheap brothels in a notorious district known simply as "the Jungle." Indeed, it was in some of these seedy retail services that some more enterprising Irish men and women began to climb into their own middle class. In the same manner, Irish contractors climbed atop the brawny shoulders of Irish construction workers.[40]

The initial wave of young males from Ireland was followed by a more balanced stream of men and women, so that as early as 1860 the census showed a fairly even ratio between the sexes in Nashville. As these young migrants matured, they married mostly within their own ethnic and religious group, a function of their preferences but also of the strong Protestant taboo against Catholics. As the Irish formed typically prolific families, they rapidly produced a first-generation Irish-American population, which by 1880 had outstripped the Irish-born population. At this point, in 1880, the foreign and American-born Irish together claimed more than one in every eight persons in the city.[41]

As the Irish-American population grew, and as the Irish began to generate their own modestly prosperous middle class, they began moving away from the grimy slums of the Jungle and Lower Broad (which became "Black Bottom" as the Negro took the place of the Irish), many of them to an area west of the railroad gulch that by the 1880s came to be known as "Little Ireland." This neighborhood, filled with many substantial brick homes and apartments, was ideally located close to the railroads, one of the major sources of employment for the Irish in the late nineteenth century. Saint Joseph's Church, located on McLemore (now Twelfth Avenue) and Cedar (now Charlotte), served as the nucleus for this neighborhood from its inception in 1887. Here, a church-sponsored school served the growing population of Catholic children, whose parents were suspicious of public school education.[42]

Another Irish neighborhood hovered around Saint Patrick's Church, founded in 1890, on what is now Second Avenue in South Nashville.[43] It was in this neighborhood that a fascinating colony of Irish gypsies, or Tinkers as they are known in the old country, gathered each year. These Irish nomads, consisting of four large family clans, wandered the South trading horses and mules. They rendezvoused in Nashville every May Day to attend Mass for their dead at Saint Patrick's and follow a solemn procession to the Catholic burial ground at Calvary Cemetery.[44]

As Nashville's Irish community matured in the late nineteenth century it spawned a number of voluntary associations, some of which spun off the church, others being purely secular. The Ancient Order of Hibernians, the Hibernian Benevolence Society, the Parnell Branch of the Irish National League, the Catholic Knights and Ladies of America, the Young Men's and Young Women's Institutes, the Knights of Columbus, and the Saint Joseph Total Abstinence Society were among the organizations that reinforced Irish identity in Nashville. By the late nineteenth century these and other organizations could be seen in elaborate processions on Saint Patrick's Day, winding through the streets of the city from the Public Square out to Saint Patrick's in South Nashville. The *Catholic Herald*, a weekly newspaper, gave the Irish their own means of publicizing events and encouraging businesses within their own subcommunity. It also served as a watchdog against anti-Catholic attacks from Protestants and helped mobilize the Irish for political action.[45]

It was in the political arena that the Irish found the most powerful levers for upward social mobility and the means to protect themselves against Protestant discrimination. From the start, the Democratic party cultivated the Irish vote, and the Irish learned to trade their loyalty to the party for places on the ticket and for patronage jobs. Irish residential concentration gave them an advantage in ward-level politics. Despite efforts to dilute the ward-based strength of ethnic blocs, the Irish politico began to gain a foothold in Nashville city politics. Several identified as Irish began to win seats on the City Council during the 1880s and 1890s; Michael Nestor, John L. Kennedy, and William Smith were appointed to the Board of Public Works; Thomas Tyne was elected Davidson County representative to the state legislature. Soon the Irish were a growing presence on the police force, and other patronage appointments were thrown their way by grateful politicians.

As Irish political power grew, conflict with the dominant white Protestant culture intensified. In 1887 a state referendum on prohibition was defeated, thanks in part to Little Ireland, where the vote was heavily against what was interpreted as an assault on personal liberty and

Irish culture. By 1895 the anti-Catholic backlash found a political vehicle in a new party called the American Protective Association (APA).
It advocated "good government," prohibition, restrictions on foreign immigration, and actively denounced the influence of the Catholic church.
Despite strong opposition in the Irish wards, the APA swept city elections in 1895 and brought William McCarthy—an avowed anti-Catholic
—into power as mayor. In the next election, in 1897, the Irish backed
Richard Houston Dudley, who defeated McCarthy's bid for reelection
and all but finished the APA as a viable political force in Nashville.

"From a city of bigots," the *Catholic Herald* proclaimed in 1899,
"Nashville has become a city of progressive, tolerant people who . . .
see that Catholics endeavor as faithfully, or even more so, than others
to make our city what it is, the Athens of the South."[46] But strong anti-
Catholic feeling in Nashville had not been buried. The rising reform
movement during the early twentieth century continued to decry the
Irish influence in city government, particularly in the police department, which was headed by two Irish chiefs, Thomas Kerrigan and Owen
Fitzgerald. The reformers also continued to press relentlessly for prohibition, which finally triumphed in 1909.[47]

By this date the ethnic solidarity of the Irish community was already beginning to dissipate, not so much from nativist persecution
as from the upward social mobility of the Irish themselves. Many began to migrate out of Little Ireland toward more congenial suburbs along
West End. The new Cathedral, completed in 1908 (and located disturb-
ingly close to Vanderbilt, still a Methodist stronghold), was sympto-
matic of the dispersion of the old Irish neighborhood. After World War I
there was comparatively little left of the residential and political solidarity the Irish once displayed in the city.[48]

THE ETHNIC SUBCOMMUNITIES: GERMANTOWN

World War I also witnessed the demise of Nashville's German-
American community as a compact residential and political subcul-
ture within the city. The Germans had arrived in Nashville about the
same time as the Irish, many of them fleeing their mother country after
the abortive Revolution of 1848.[49] Others, mainly Catholics from southern Germany, were fleeing (like the Irish) grinding poverty, religious
persecution, and potato famine. As a group, the Germans entered the
occupational ladder a rung or two above the Irish. More of them brought
skills, capital, and prior urban experience with them to the New World.
Those in positions to employ others tended to hire fellow Germans,
thus accelerating the process of upward social mobility. The census
of 1860 showed only 10 percent of the Germans in unskilled labor or

domestic service, compared with 80 percent of the Irish work force. The Germans were also religiously diverse; they included Catholics and Jews, who suffered the prejudice of native Protestants, but many were Lutheran and Methodist. This religious diversity, along with their relative prosperity, helps explain why Germans from the outset tended to intermarry with native Americans or with other ethnic groups. One result of this flexibility was the rapid creation of an American-born German population, which as early as 1870 outnumbered the German-born in Nashville.[50]

Nor did the Germans imitate the residential patterns of the Irish, who began in densely packed inner-city ghettos and migrated out to the periphery. Before the 1870s the Germans were scattered in South Nashville, where many found employment in the Gerst brewery and other food-processing establishments, and elsewhere in the city away from the low-rent waterfront districts of the Irish and blacks. Later, as the German community became more prosperous, it became more cohesive residentially, the reverse of the local Irish pattern. What came to be called Germantown in North Nashville emerged in the 1870s as a generally middle-class suburb of "handsome cottages and villages surrounded by tastefully laid out grounds," which had grown up along one of the new mule-drawn streetcars. By 1880 about 60 percent of the city's German community could be located here.[51]

One of the magnets drawing Germans to North Nashville was the Church of the Assumption for Catholic Germans. Alienated from the Irish in Saint Mary's, the Germans at first worshiped in the basement of John Buddeke's spacious mansion. Buddeke, a wealthy German baker, owned a large plot of land, which he sold to fellow Germans for churches, homes, and stores. The Church of the Assumption went up in 1859, and the German Methodist Church was organized in 1865 not far away. First Lutheran Church, organized in 1866, remained centrally located downtown. The Germans, too, quickly generated a host of voluntary associations that reinforced their solidarity as a subcommunity. The German Relief Society, the Turnerverein, the Shutzenverein, a German Masonic lodge, and German Odd Fellows lodge were among the several that brought Germans together in organizations that at once imitated those of the dominant native culture and kept Germans apart from that culture.[52]

Many Germans rose to positions of extraordinary wealth, such as Edward Bushrod Stahlman, a railroad man and later publisher of the *Banner*; Henry Neuhoff, an enterprising butcher who built a prosperous meat-packing business; George Jacobs, another meat packer; William Gerst, a wealthy brewer; Charles Nelson, Victor Emmanuel Shwab, and George Dickel, all prosperous German distillers of fine Tennessee whiskey. These were among the dozens of astute, wealthy German businessmen whose capital and prestige in the community did much to

Figure 41. Germantown in its early years, c. 1880–85. John Buddeke's home and the Church of the Assumption are on the left, the Capitol is in the background. Tennessee State Library and Archives.

help their compatriots move up the social ladder. Some of their capital began to move into banking. Charles Nelson, alarmed by the rising prohibition movement and by the antiforeign sentiment linked to it, joined a young German friend, Herman Justi, in founding the Nashville Trust Company in 1889. Henry Neuhoff, Joe Werthan, Lee J. Loventhal, and other German-Americans backed A.E. "Ed" Potter, Jr., in 1916 to found the German American Bank. German influence in these institutions opened the paths to credit for other Germans to begin new business ventures. Tony Sudekum, a young German-American, for example, began his chain of movie theaters before World War I with capital generated within the German business community.[53]

Whatever power and goodwill German business leaders and craftsmen had earned for their people was lost with the rage of anti-German sentiment during World War I. These flames were fanned by Luke Lea's feud with Edward B. Stahlman, which turned Lea's *Tennessean* into a rabid anti-German organ. As war fever mounted, the German community in Nashville and across America was forced to display its patriotism by spurning its heritage. The German American Bank changed its name to Farmers and Merchants (later Commerce Union); the German Methodist Church became Barth Memorial, and German language courses were dropped from several schools. Mrs. Bertha Benz recalled from her childhood in Germantown: "When World War I came, our father told us that we must remember 'We are loyal citizens of the United States and German is not to be spoken in our home again.' It never was."[54] An informal boycott against German businessmen in Nashville forced many into bankruptcy. Some German families changed their names, just as banks and churches were doing, to avoid anti-German discrimination. At the same time, German families began dispersing from Germantown. The slaughterhouses and stock yards in "Butchertown" had turned the air foul by this time, but the exodus was accelerated by the rising sentiment against the German enemy.[55]

THE ETHNIC SUBCOMMUNITIES: THE JEWS

Nashville, and the South in general, received very little of the great stream of immigration from southern and eastern Europe in the period from 1880 to 1915. These so-called new immigrants from Italy, Greece, Poland, Hungary, Russia, and other Slavic nations tended to concentrate in the cities of the North. But those new immigrants who did arrive in Nashville, though small in numbers, were a highly distinct group because of their religion. Jews, fleeing from the pogroms of Russia and from Hungary, joined the German-Jewish community in Nashville, which was well established by the time these newcomers arrived.[56] A religious census in 1890 showed 290 people who were members of the Jewish congregations, and by 1916 a similar census showed only 350.[57]

The eastern European Jews arrived desperately poor, for the most part. They concentrated in the waterfront district in the low, easily flooded area south of Broad, formerly the home of the Irish poor, alongside the Negroes of "Black Bottom." This was near the Orthodox synagogue on Summer Street (later Fifth Avenue), and near the wholesale and retail dry goods establishments on Market Street and the Public Square, where many of them found employment with established German-Jewish businesses. This advance guard of coreligionists was a distinct advantage for the east European Jewish immigrant, who was often hoisted into more skilled occupations by German-Jewish employers and creditors.[58]

Though sometimes subject to gentile suspicion for its insularity, the Jewish community was itself divided by ethnic and class tensions. This was most clearly reflected in religion itself. By 1900 Nashville's small Jewish population supported no less than three religious congregations. The Reform Temple, joined primarily by prosperous German Jews, occupied an elaborate temple on Vine Street (now Seventh Avenue), one of the city's finest residential streets at the time. A Conservative congregation split off in 1886 to accommodate more traditional religious practices among Germans and the new eastern European immigrants in a temple at the foot of Capitol Hill. This congregation, in turn, split in 1905, and an Orthodox congregation, made up largely of poor Russian and other east European Jews, established a synagogue near their neighborhood on Fifth Avenue, above Lower Broad.[59]

Whatever divided the Nashville Jewish community from within was less significant than the religious gulf that separated all Jews to some degree from the Christian majority. With Jews, as well as Irish and Germans, it was their minority role within the dominant culture that provided the strongest reinforcement to their identity as a group.

THE AGE OF SEGREGATION

Nashville's largest ethnic subcommunity, the Afro-Americans, also had the largest impact on the social geography of the city. Coinciding with the suburban trend was a growing pattern of racial segregation in neighborhoods, institutions, and politics. When these traditions of segregation were challenged during the civil rights movement of the 1950s and 1960s, many white southerners would defend them as deeply embedded regional folkways that no meddling reformers could alter. In truth, race relations in cities like Nashville had been quite change-

Figure 42. Vine Street Synagogue, c. 1900. *Art Work of Nashville, Tennessee* (Chicago, 1901).

able in the decades after the Civil War.[60] Segregation was an invention
of the late nineteenth century, the curious product of white hostility
and white paternalism on the one hand, and black accommodation on
the other. Between the 1880s and the 1900s the races were pulled apart
in ways that were unprecedented in Nashville's history.

Beginning with Federal occupation during the Civil War, a surge
of runaway and abandoned slaves swelled the city's population. Beginning with less than a quarter (23 percent) of the population in 1860,
blacks claimed 38 percent of Nashville's population by 1870. This level
held reasonably steady through the coming decades and by 1910 it stood
at 33 percent (see Appendix A). The black stream of migration into the
city continued as freedmen sought new job opportunities offered by
Nashville's expanding economy. They left behind the harsh conditions
of tenancy and sharecropping for jobs as wage-earning day laborers, servants, and factory workers. They came to Nashville also for the personal freedom and dignity the city seemed to promise. Blacks achieved
a measure of economic security and freedom in Nashville. By 1890
among black male workers, over half (52 percent) were in unskilled
jobs, 5 percent in semiskilled jobs, and another 15 percent in domestic
and personal service. But one-fifth claimed skilled jobs, and a small
but highly visible 6 percent were in professional, business, and clerical
jobs. About 45 percent of all black women in Nashville were gainfully
employed (three times the rate for white women), and most all (90 percent) worked as housemaids, laundresses, cooks, and nurses in the
homes of wealthy whites for as little as five dollars a week. At almost
every level of the occupational ladder blacks could be found in segregated work forces, or in what were exclusively "Negro jobs" within a
mixed work force. In Nashville black laborers found employment in
the lumber mills, iron foundries, flour mills, fertilizer plants, and wherever hard labor and relatively low wages required black labor.[61]

Table 3. NASHVILLE BLACKS: OCCUPATIONS BY SEX, 1890.

Occupation	Males	Percentage of Total	Females	Percentage of Total
Professional	169	22	99	21
Proprietary	219	8	33	18
Clerical	60	2	8	3
Skilled	1,590	28	2	2
Semiskilled	351	26	428	22
Unskilled	3,811	78	53	76
Domestic or personal service	1,112	90	5,849	92

SOURCES: Adapted from Howard N. Rabinowitz, *Race Relations in the Urban South, 1865–1890* (New York, 1978), 64–65; and Department of the Interior, Census Office, *Report on Population of the United States at the Eleventh Census: 1890* pt. 2 (Washington, D.C., 1897), 696.

The growth of this black wage-earning class, however meager its income, helped to spawn a new black middle class of businessmen, lawyers, doctors, undertakers, and clergy, which usually catered exclusively to a black clientele. Nashville already had a core of relatively prosperous, respected black leaders who descended from the antebellum free black community, many of whom were actually light-skinned, or "blue-vein," mulattoes.[62] Whites, for their part, were accustomed to dealing with this cadre of the black middle class, if not as full equals, at least as respected spokesmen for an aspiring minority.[63]

By the 1880s a prosperous, educated black bourgeoisie had emerged, some with roots in the antebellum free black community, but several were "new men" of wealth and status who came from outside the city. James C. Napier was born near Nashville to free black parents in 1845. He was educated at Wilberforce University and Oberlin College, served in the War Department in Washington, D.C., and graduated from Howard Law School. He returned to Nashville as the city's most prominent black lawyer, a Republican party stalwart, and a successful real estate investor.[64] Preston Taylor, born to Louisiana slave parents in 1849, worked as a stone cutter and a railroad laborer, and then joined the ministry of the Christian Church. He came to Nashville as pastor of the black Christian Church on Gay Street and later built the Lee Street Christian Church. He opened an undertaking business on the side and soon became an influential leader in the business as well as spiritual affairs of black Nashville. He opened Greenwood Cemetery for blacks just beyond Mount Olivet Cemetery. By 1910 he added an amusement park adjacent to the cemetery, catering to black Sunday picnickers.[65] Robert Fulton Boyd, born in Giles County, Tennessee, came to Nashville as a youth after the Civil War and attended evening classes at Fisk School. In 1872 he hired himself out to a white real estate agent as collector and bookkeeper in exchange for room and board while he continued his education. He taught school in country towns for a few years, then entered Meharry Medical Department of Central Tennessee College. Boyd later received postgraduate training in Chicago, taught at Meharry, and carried on a flourishing medical practice in Nashville's black community.[66] Richard Henry Boyd (no relation to Robert Fulton Boyd) was born in slavery in Mississippi, entered the Baptist ministry after the Civil War, and came to Nashville after a successful career in Texas. In 1896 he organized the National Baptist Publishing Board, the nation's first and largest black publishing house.[67] These, and many other black leaders, emerged by the late nineteenth century as counterparts of members of the rising business and professional elites in the white community.

Following the war a cluster of black colleges appeared in Nashville as it assumed the role of black Athens of the South. Central Tennessee College (later named Walden University) was organized by the Freed-

Figure 43 (left). James C. Napier (1845–1940), attorney, member of City Council, and Registrar of U.S. Treasury. Thomas O. Fuller, *Pictorial History of the American Negro* (Memphis, 1933).

Figure 44. Dr. Robert Fulton Boyd (1858–1912). G.F. Richings, *Evidence of Progress Among Colored People* (Philadelphia, 1897).

Figure 45 (left). Richard Henry Boyd, founder of the National Baptist Publishing Board. National Baptist Publishing Board, *National Jubilee Melody Song Book* (Nashville, n.d.).

Figure 46. Henry Allen Boyd (1876–1959), cofounder of the *Globe,* Citizens Savings Bank, and secretary of the National Baptist Publishing Board. Lester C. Lamon, *Black Tennesseans, 1900–1930* (Knoxville, 1977).

men's Aid Society of the Methodist Church in 1866. The American Baptist Home Mission Society organized what became Roger Williams University in the same year. Fisk University was also brought to life by the American Missionary Association, an abolitionist society. Meharry Medical College, attached at first to Central Tennessee College, was established in 1876. In 1909 Tennessee Agricultural and Industrial State Normal School (later Tennessee State University) became yet another important institution for black Nashville. The history of these black schools is discussed elsewhere (see chapter eight), but their development was important to the emerging patterns of residential segregation during the late nineteenth century. Both Fisk and Tennessee A&I reinforced the concentration of blacks in North Nashville. Later, Meharry would leave its campus in South Nashville to locate adjacent to Fisk. Though dominated by white faculty and administrators in the early years, all these schools contributed a steady stream of new teachers, ministers, doctors, and businessmen, many of whom joined Nashville's black middle class.[68]

In the decades preceding World War I, Nashville's educated, ambitious black middle class developed a proud voice with which to protest white discrimination where necessary and articulate the aspirations of black Nashville. But it did so within a climate of rapidly deteriorating race relations, beginning in the 1880s. The very growth of the black population, which resulted from the migration of the rural poor during the prosperous 1880s, strained race relations. Whites were experiencing increased competition for jobs and were afraid that black labor would undermine the wage scale. The concentration of poor blacks in squalid slums, like Black Bottom and Hell's Half Acre, and the identification of those slums as pervasive threats to public health also contributed to the deterioration of race relations in the city. In addition, there was growing competition in the political arena as blacks learned to use their voting power to win political favors. During the 1870s and 1880s Thomas Kercheval, a Republican, had been elected repeatedly as mayor and as a member of the powerful Board of Public Works, largely on the strength of the black vote. His opponents turned to racial discrimination as a political tool to oust him from power (see chapter six). Jobs, poverty, disease, and politics all worked to reshape the patterns of race relations in Nashville in the late nineteenth and early twentieth centuries.

One sign of the trend toward rigid segregation was in residential patterns. The index of dissimilarity is a statistical measure of the percentage of a minority that would have to move from one ward or census tract to another in order to have proportional representation in all wards. It ignores clustering within each ward, but it provides a rough measure of segregation over time. In 1890 the index for Nashville blacks and whites stood at 29 percent, suggesting limited clustering in places like Black Bottom. By 1900 it rose to almost 34 percent and by 1910 stood at 38 percent. This was still a long way from the level of segregation that would appear in the mid-twentieth century (when indices of over 80 percent were common), but it was an indication of the trend toward residential separation.[69]

This pattern was due largely to white suburban flight, leaving the central city to blacks. There was also a black suburban migration in this period. The Fisk University campus became the western salient of a rapidly expanding black settlement along Jefferson Street. Fisk became the counterpart of Vanderbilt, which drew settlement out West End in the same period. In 1873, after several years in a ramshackle old Union soldier's hospital on Church Street near the railroad gulch, Fisk broke ground on its new campus, a gentle hill one and a half miles northwest of the downtown on the former site of Fort Gillem. The first building, Jubilee Hall, was built with money from the highly successful tours of Fisk's Jubilee Singers, who treated northern and English audiences to Negro spirituals. A magnificent Victorian limestone structure, Jubilee Hall with its tall spires on the western skyline were symbols of the pride and aspirations of Nashville's black community. As streetcar service extended out Jefferson Street in the 1880s, the campus became the center of a cluster of fine homes built for the rising black middle class.

By 1910 the concentration of blacks on the north side of Nashville made this area the largest and most important black neighborhood in the city.[70] The pattern of residential segregation was, however, by no means as clear and concentrated as it would become after World War I. Blacks lived in every ward of the city. Live-in house servants occupied basement or attic apartments of suburban mansions, or back-alley shacks or carriage house apartments for black servants behind the homes of whites. There were also large and small pockets of densely black settlements scattered about the periphery of the central city next to the large industrial plants that gave blacks employment: Trimble Bottom in South Nashville, Crappy Shoot in East Nashville, Rock Quarry Bottom in North Nashville. Indeed, the vagueness of the boundaries between black and white neighborhoods brought forth several appeals to real estate agents to avoid mixing of the races when selling or renting property.[71]

The segregation of public institutions was a clearer mark of the status whites wished to assign to blacks. An 1866 state school statute required that the races be taught separately. Northern teachers came south after the war to staff the black schools that were established and to prepare the ex-slaves for freedom. There were some protests against segregation, but most black leaders pursued a more pragmatic strategy of improving the number and quality of black public schools. They also shrewdly used segregation to their own advantage by insisting that black teachers and administrators be hired to staff the black schools. James C.

Napier, a member of the City Council, led the battle for black teachers.[72] The white school board was persuaded by the argument that black teachers could be hired far more cheaply than whites. In 1887 Pearl School, then in the vicinity of Black Bottom, became the last school for Negroes to be given over to black teachers.[73] Thus, segregated schools put a new rung on the occupational ladder for blacks, and the school now became subject to more direct influence from within the black community.

Other public institutions generally included separate, but rarely equal, accommodations for blacks. The Municipal Hospital (now General Hospital) opened in 1890 with segregated wards. The Davidson County Poorhouse and Asylum, the Tennessee Industrial School, established in 1888, the Tennessee School for the Blind, established in 1881, all included provisions for separate "colored departments." Voluntary welfare agencies imitated the pattern of segregation. When the Nashville Ladies Relief Society decided "to let the colored people manage the taking care of their own people," black women organized the Colored Ladies Relief Society in December 1886.[74] By the 1880s segregation was apparent in a wide range of public facilities. For example, Nashville had a separate fairgounds and separate grandstands for blacks at the racetrack. Black baseball teams played only against teams of their own race. Railroad stations had separate waiting rooms. Some saloons accepted only white customers, and even brothels catered to black customers in separate basement-level rooms. Watkins and Glendale parks were open to whites and blacks, but segregation was maintained informally within these facilities. Glendale Park, for example, had a separate area for blacks with a large tent for their entertainment. Mount Ararat Cemetery and Greenwood Cemetery opened next to Mount Olivet Cemetery to assure segregation even after death.[75]

Before the late 1880s, however, the pattern of segregation was incomplete and its purpose was ambiguous. As historian Howard Rabinowitz has demonstrated, the creation of new all-black schools and welfare agencies after the Civil War was an effort to extend services that were formerly denied blacks altogether. Segregated institutions were championed by white liberals and embraced by black leaders because both were willing to accept "half a loaf" at a time when full integration and social equality seemed a hopeless, self-defeating goal. Moreover, a segregated world opened new opportunities for black teachers, doctors, and businessmen.

If the tendency toward segregation in housing and public facilities was ambiguous in its meaning before the late 1880s, race relations in Nashville took a decided turn for the worse at this juncture. The most important sign of the shift was the move to drive blacks from the political arena by restricting their right to vote. The reduction in black political power opened the door to a harsh regime of white discrimination and segregation in the 1890s. At the same time, a rising national tide of racism, filled with fears of interracial "mongrelization" and black rapacity, had its effect on local conditions. Within the city the new mood coincided with growing concerns about communicable disease and with the rapid expansion of the suburban frontier in the trolley-car era.

In the face of increasing white hostility during the 1890s, blacks pondered alternatives by two leading spokesmen for the race. Booker T. Washington and W.E.B. DuBois both had connections with Fisk, and their ideas made a deep impression on Nashville's local black leadership. Booker T. Washington was born in slavery. After the war he worked his way through Hampton Institute in Virginia and became a leading advocate of industrial training for blacks in the New South. In 1881 he founded Tuskegee Institute in Alabama as a showcase for his vision of black industrial education and self-help. His strategy of accommodation with white racism was most clearly articulated in his famous address at the Atlanta Exposition in 1895, discredited by DuBois as the "Atlanta Compromise." Blacks, Washington assured his largely white audience, did not insist on immediate equality or full civil rights. They would gradually achieve both by making themselves economically essential to the New South. He envisioned far more than black craftsmen and manual laborers; he also encouraged the rise of an urban black middle class of businessmen, bankers, and professionals. In 1900 he organized the National Negro Business League to foster black enterprise. Two years later James C. Napier organized a large chapter in Nashville, and the league's annual convention was sponsored by Nashville the following year. This organization served, like the all-white Commercial Club, to encourage black enterprise and unite black businessmen to promote the interests they shared.[76]

In Nashville the success of Washington's self-help philosophy was manifest in a number of new businesses organized by black entrepreneurs. The One Cent Savings Bank and Trust Company opened in 1904 "to encourage frugality . . . among our people." It was the first black-owned bank in the city since the collapse of the Freedman's Bank in 1873. By 1909 this was joined by the Peoples Saving Bank and Trust Company, organized by younger black businessmen to pursue a more aggressive investment strategy. These local banks gathered the pennies and dollars of Nashville's black community, and with that capital, dozens of new black enterprises could now look to their own community for financing.[77]

The response of black entrepreneurs to the opportunities for credit and enterprise within the black subcommunity was encouraging. Moses McKissack, an architect, and Searcy Scales, a contractor, bought the Capitol Planning Mill in 1907 and began a flourishing business in manufacturing lumber and in designing and building houses.[78] Two black newspapers sprang up: the *Clarion*, sponsored by Richard H. Boyd's National Baptist Publishing Board, and the *Globe*, established in 1905 by Richard H. Boyd, Joseph O. Battle, Henry Allen Boyd, and Dock A. Hart.[79] These, and dozens of other ventures in black capitalism, were applauded by the National Negro Business League as prime examples of what black self-help could accomplish, confirming Booker T. Washington's program. Instead of assaulting white racism and fighting for black civil rights as the first priority, these men turned segregation to the advantage of black entrepreneurs by appealing to race pride and working within markets white businessmen often shunned.

W.E.B. DuBois was raised in Massachusetts after the Civil War. He came to speak for a new generation of blacks with no personal memory of slavery and white paternalism, a generation impatient for full citizenship and less willing to accommodate to white racism. When DuBois first came to Nashville as a student at Fisk, he was appalled at the treatment southern whites accorded him. While gawking at the sights downtown, he accidentally bumped into a well-dressed white woman who, despite the young man's apology, became furious with his effrontery and made him sense her "scorn and hate." After leaving Fisk, DuBois was educated at Harvard and the University of Berlin. He went on to a brilliant career as a scholar and spokesman for black America. His answer to Washington's Negro Business League was the National Association for the Advancement of Colored People, organized in 1910. This was an interracial effort to end discrimination against blacks, and through it DuBois attacked Washington's whole program of black accommodation. Instead of industrial education for the masses, DuBois urged academic education for the "talented tenth" at colleges like Fisk. It was the talented tenth, DuBois hoped, that would serve as the opening wedge breaking apart the barriers to equality for the black masses.[80]

Most of Nashville's black leaders leaned toward Washington's program of economic self-help, but they often combined it with the racial pride and militancy of DuBois. Nothing better illustrated their ability to link the two ideologies than the streetcar boycott of 1905–1906. Growing pressure from whites to segregate the trolley cars was resisted by the streetcar company for a time, in part because of the enormous expense involved. The first concession to Jim Crow came in 1903 when the West Nashville Line added an extra car for black workers en route to and from the fertilizer plants. The rationale here was the foul smell of the fertilizer workers rather than their color. But the next year the City Council began debating legislation that would segregate the trolley lines on the basis of race alone. By January 1905 the state legislature enacted a Jim Crow streetcar law for all Tennessee cities. The law was to go into effect on July 5, one day after blacks and whites would celebrate Independence Day.[81]

"The self-respecting, intelligent colored citizens of Nashville will not stand for Jim-crowism on the street car line in this city," announced

Figure 47. "Nashville's Manly Protest Against Jim Crowism." The Reverend Preston Taylor leads the boycott against the "Jim Crow Car Co." and raises the black-owned Union Transportation Company. *The Voice of the Negro* 2(Dec. 1905).

the Reverend James A. Jones of the African Methodist Episcopal (AME) Church.[82] A mass meeting, attended by approximately two thousand blacks, passed resolutions to boycott the streetcars. The *Clarion* recommended "those of the race who are able to buy buggies, and others to trim their corns, darn their socks, wear solid shoes and walk."[83] The boycott began July 5 with the aim of forcing whites to rescind the segregation law. By the end of the summer Nashville's black leaders had moved well beyond this goal.

Segregation and the boycott opened an unusual opportunity for black enterprise. Richard H. Boyd, James C. Napier, and Preston Taylor, with backing from the National Negro Business League, organized the Union Transportation Company and purchased five steam-driven "auto buses." Rallies were held in black neighborhoods across the city to sell stock and build solidarity behind the boycott. Lapel buttons with pictures of the steam buses were worn with pride by boycotters, and maids were urged to "stay off the [Jim Crow] cars by all means . . . the motor cars will arrive in a few days . . . we can afford to walk a little longer."[84]

By October 1905 the new steam-driven vehicles were in operation along the main thoroughfares of Nashville. Black Nashville seemed on the verge of both a magnificent triumph over white racism and a powerful demonstration of black enterprise. But in a way that was symbolic of the whole struggle for black dignity in the New South, the Union Transportation Company quickly disintegrated. The steam-driven buses were not powerful enough to climb Nashville's hilly terrain. Fourteen electric buses, each with capacity for twenty passengers, were brought in to replace the steamers. Confidence in the venture among blacks already began to sag, and stock subscriptions slowed. Undaunted, the Union Transportation Company put the buses into operation in January 1906. Rather than purchase electric power from the Nashville Railway and Light Company and risk having batteries ruined by overcharging, the company installed its own dynamo and generator in the basement of Boyd's National Baptist Publishing House.[85]

Failure was imminent, however. In April the city announced its intention to levy a privilege tax of $42 annually on the electric buses, to add further to the expenses of the operation. The buses were unreliable and often not powerful enough to pull a full load of passengers up Nashville's steep hills. The limited fleet of vehicles was strained also by the dispersion of Nashville's blacks, who lived or worked in all parts of the city. Ridership slumped as scheduled routes proved impossible to meet, and by July 1906 operations ceased. Within a few months the company collapsed. The boycott had already been abandoned by many blacks, who lost confidence in the Union Transportation Company and had to depend on the Jim Crow streetcars to carry them to work.

A venture that began as an experiment in black militancy and

shrewd exploitation of white segregationism became yet another lesson in the power of the dominant white race. Those who could not
avoid it rode in silence in the Jim Crow cars; others refused to patronize the streetcars. "There are hundreds of Negroes in Nashville," proclaimed the *Globe,* a black-owned newspaper born during the boycott,
"who have never 'bowed their knees to Baal.'"[86] The Nashville boycott
was part of a larger black protest among militant blacks in cities across
the South in this period.[87] The lessons of the boycott were ambiguous,
and a later generation would resume the same tactics barely conscious
of the historical precedent they followed.

In the modern city that emerged between 1880 and 1915 the lines
that separated the wealthy, the poor, the Irish, Germans, Jews, and blacks
were defined partly by voluntary withdrawal into satisfying subcommunities, each with its own institutions and ways of life, and partly by
hostile rejection on both sides of the lines. Those lines, defined by human values, joined new transportation technology and business practices to radically transform the social geography of Nashville.

REVIVAL, REFORM, AND RACE

The segmentation of the city was one way of reducing the increasing social tensions that attended growth and change in Nashville. Some Nashvillians sought to resolve the problems of their community in other ways, with a variety of reform measures. Many of these had their origins in the electrifying revivals of Sam Jones in the 1880s. The religious impulse to reform through conversion of individuals rapidly flowed into organized philanthropy to alleviate the misery of the poor and, from there, to governmental coercion to enforce moral standards for the community.

REVIVALISM AND SOCIAL REFORM

Amid the prophecies of material wealth in a New South of burgeoning cities, factories, and business houses were unsettling symptoms of social disorder in Nashville. The tremendous growth of the city in the decades following the Civil War came largely from the stream of country folk who arrived from Middle Tennessee and other parts of the South. Some were ex-slaves whose ties to the land and to their former masters had been sundered; others were white farmers pushed off the land and out of small towns by the strains of postwar agricultural readjustment. Mostly young and poor, they drifted into the strange new environment of the city, some to thrive on the opportunities it offered to ambitious newcomers, others to flounder in the absence of family, church, and community ties that had guided them in the country. These rural migrants were the southern counterpart of the "dangerous classes" of foreign immigrants and native poor that worried reformers in larger northern cities at this time.

James E. Caldwell, a pious youth who left his widowed mother in Franklin, Tennessee, to make his way in the city, looked out on the moral chaos of cheap theaters, saloons, and prostitution that teemed outside his small room on Cherry Street: "The city had the appearance of a human sewer, the stream came in fresh from the country, meandered through the immoral shoals and eddies and disappeared in oblivion and early death."[1] Many young people, like Caldwell, came into the city and resisted the sinful life by using the strength of their resolute religious piety ingrained in them by their families and churches back home. But those most concerned with the moral order of the city realized how rare and insufficient these restraints were amid the transient new population of Nashville. They understood religion would have to reach beyond the conventional realm of established congregations to bring moral discipline to the unchurched. In the process of reaching out to the poor and destitute, these religious reformers understood also that these people needed more than simple faith; they needed help through organized, sustained social welfare programs. As this new, liberal consciousness of Christianity evolved, primarily in the large cities of the North, it came to be known as the "social gospel." This movement made limited headway in the rural fundamentalist South, but in Nashville and other southern cities it made an important mark.[2]

Nashville had a strong, articulate cadre of clergy and laymen who were responsive to the new trends in "social Christianity." Table Four shows the changing religious configuration of the city as revealed in the religious censuses of 1890, 1906, and 1916. As the membership data suggest, the Methodists made the largest imprint on the religious life of the city in the late nineteenth century. The federal census of 1890 showed the Methodists had over 10,000 adherents in the city, rising to over 17,000 by 1916. Most were white Southern Methodists, and the rest were with the African Methodist Church or the Methodist Episcopal Church. Southern Methodists in Nashville were more numerous than in any other city and had nearly three times the membership of any other Protestant denomination.[3] McKendree Methodist Church was a leading religious force in the city and the region. "What they do at McKendree Church, in Nashville," one observer claimed in 1887, "is felt to a greater or lesser extent to the borders of Southern Methodism."[4] Bishop Holland McTyeire and Vanderbilt University, the Methodist Publishing House and its journal *The Christian Advocate*, were also strong voices for Methodist influence in Nashville. Methodist ministers John B. McFerrin, David C. Kelly, Warren A. Candler, Oscar P. Fitzgerald, along with many wealthy and prominent laymen, including Edmund W. Cole, were among the most influential Methodists in the city during the 1880s and 1890s.[5]

The Southern Presbyterians were another important religious force

Table 4. NASHVILLE'S RELIGIOUS AFFILIATIONS, 1890, 1906, 1916.

Denomination	1890	1906	1916
Baptists:			
Regular	5,722	—	—
Southern	—	4,417	5,814
National (Black)	—	6,408	14,146
Other	440	706	140
Methodists:			
Methodist Episcopal	1,143	1,305	1,245
Methodist, Southern	7,094	8,413	11,216
Black Methodist Bodies	1,926	3,401	4,650
Other Methodists	41	—	—
Presbyterians:			
(U.S.) Southern	2,496	3,259	4,133
(U.S.A.) Northern	—	—	1,064
Cumberland	—	1,989	929
Other	1,123	—	—
Church/Disciples of Christ:			
Disciples	2,400	1,438	2,070
Church of Christ	—	2,662	3,946
Episcopal:	953	1,574	1,789
Other Protestants:	567	2,336	3,169
Roman Catholic:	6,000	5,865	5,845
Greek Orthodox:	—	150	—
Jewish:	290	275*	350
Total:	30,195	44,198	60,506

SOURCES: U.S. Census Office, Department of Interior, *Report on Statistics of Churches in the United States at the 11th Census, 1890* (Washington, D.C., 1894), 112–13; U.S. Bureau of the Census, Department of Commerce and Labor, *Religious Bodies: 1906*, pt. I (Washington, D.C., 1910), 374–405; and idem., *Religious Bodies, 1916*, pt. I (Washington, D.C., 1919), 442–44.
*Jews in 1906 include "heads of families only" according to the census.

in the city, with close to 2,500 members in 1890 and rising to over 6,000 by 1916. The First Presbyterian, with its magnificent Egyptian revival edifice on Church Street, claimed 1,000 members in 1890. Its minister, James I. Vance (from 1894 to about 1901, resuming after 1910) was among the most powerful religious figures in the city and remained so until his death in 1939.[6] As with the Methodists, several prosperous suburban Presbyterian churches spun off the downtown congregation as their wealthy followers migrated from the central city. Both denominations appealed to a disproportionate number of wealthy business and professional men and their wives.[7]

Two other denominations, the Cumberland Presbyterian and the Christians, or Church of Christ (the two names were often used indiscriminately before their formal split in 1906), were small in numbers but usually committed to social reform in the city. David Lipscomb, editor of the *Gospel Advocate*, was an influential spokesman for the

Church of Christ. The *Cumberland Presbyterian*, edited by Ira Landrith, was another influential religious journal guiding church members on social issues.[8]

Other denominations were less receptive to the secular activism
and liberal premises of the social gospel. The Baptists were numerous,
with over 6,000 members in 1890, but highly fragmented, particularly
in contrast to the centrally organized Methodists and Presbyterians.
They were divided racially into two distinct organizations, with the
black Baptist church members claiming about half the total. Doctrinal
schisms further divided the Baptists into Southern Baptists, Primitive
Baptists, and Free Will Baptists. Opposed to any supra-congregational
hierarchy and inclined to stress personal salvation through faith rather
than good works, the Baptists were less influential as a denominational
organization in social reform.[9] However, the Baptist stress on personal
piety made many individual followers sympathetic to reforms, especially to the prohibition of liquor. The First Baptist Church, with its
impressive new building on Broad and Vine, completed in 1886, was
an imposing presence in the religious life of Nashville and the spiritual home of many of the city's prominent families. Dozens of smaller
congregations sprang up in all parts of the city, typically appealing to
working-class people, black and white.[10] The Episcopalians, centered
at Christ Church on Broadway, included more families of wealth and
social status but were disinclined by doctrinal persuasion to pursue social reform through the church.[11]

Outside the Protestant denominations, the largest church following in Nashville was Catholic, with about 6,000 souls in 1890. The
Catholic church reacted against most of the Protestant social reformers, not least because reform, temperance in particular, was so often
linked to anti-Catholic and antiforeign sentiment. The Catholics, too,
stressed the salvation of individual souls through faith rather than the
reformation of social evils in this world. They also preferred to keep
organized charity and education within the confines of the church and
resisted the kind of ecumenical organization favored by the Protestant
reformers.[12]

In the spring of 1885 the religious community of Nashville was
suddenly jolted by a young evangelist who, more than any other individual, was responsible for bringing "social Christianity" alive in Nashville. No one was better able to adapt the social gospel to the southern
environment than Sam Jones, whose Nashville revivals beginning in
1885 left an indelible impact on the city and its social consciousness.
Jones, who grew up in rural Georgia, became an itinerant Methodist
preacher after being saved from a life of drunkenness. By 1880 Jones
was head of a Methodist orphange in Decatur, Georgia, and in raising
funds for the orphans Jones fashioned his message stressing the moral
sins of the city and the needs of the urban poor.

Figure 48. Sam P. Jones (1847–1906), evangelist and advocate of temperance and reform. Laura McElwain Jones, with assistance of Walt Holcomb, *The Life and Sayings of Sam P. Jones* (Atlanta, 1907).

Jones, a gifted orator, soon became a legendary revivalist in demand across the South. He delivered his message to the people in plain speech and told them bluntly of the wages of sin and their obligations to the needy. In a brief visit to Nashville in March 1885 Jones left the city "buzzing" with religious enthusiasm, and an interdenominational committee of clergy and laymen invited him to return in May for a twenty-day revival. The lot at Spruce (now Eighth Avenue) and Broad (former site of the 1880 Centennial Exposition) was cleared, and a huge Gospel Tent erected with seats for 7,000 souls.[13]

The religious leaders of Nashville eagerly anticipated the Jones revival. It would give the chief rival denominations, the Methodists, Presbyterians, and Baptists, a rare occasion to join in common cause and to extend their collective influence within the community. The religious community was not disappointed. Within four days of Jones's arrival the *Banner* announced, "a religious movement is underway which promises to be the deepest and [most] far reaching ever witnessed in the city."[14]

Jones's sermons gave cold comfort to the city's Christians, however. He launched a vigorous attack on the moral apathy of the church-going, respectable families of the city who ignored the sin and misery in the community about them and indulged themselves in social frivolity. "I will say something to you rich men of Nashville," he began one such attack in 1885. "If I had your money I would do something with it that would redound to my credit in eternity." "Selfishness! Selfishness!" he exhorted at a later sermon. "Hell is selfishness on fire, and the great wonder to me is that some of you don't catch on fire and go straight to hell by spontaneous combustion. . . . you love money more than your souls."[15]

The impact of Jones's message on the rich was dramatically demonstrated in the conversion of steamboat captain Tom Ryman. Ryman, who had a thriving liquor concession on his riverboats and owned a large saloon on the waterfront, was an unlikely candidate for conversion, even at the hands of Sam Jones. But Tom Ryman came to the Gospel Tent to scoff in May 1885 and he stayed to pray. He was seized by a powerful religious experience, and Jones made the most of his exemplary new convert. With great publicity, Ryman ended liquor service on his riverboats. Legend has it that he dumped the liquor in the river, but the evidence indicates he allowed the contracts with liquor concessions to lapse. The results were the same in any event, and Ryman's bold reform, against his best financial interests, was a sterling example for Jones to hold before the wealthy church-going families of Nashville.

Ryman converted his waterfront saloon, the largest of 170 in the city, into "Sam Jones Hall," a meeting place for religious temperance meetings.[16] Ryman became a devoted proponent of Jones's religious message and began to campaign for a large tabernacle to house the annual

Figure 49. Sam Jones conducts a ladies' meeting at the Union Gospel Tabernacle, c. 1895. Byrd Douglas Papers, Tennessee State Library and Archives.

Figure 50. The Union Gospel Tabernacle, c. 1900, later renamed Ryman Auditorium after Tom Ryman, its principal founder. Tennessee State Library and Archives.

revivals Jones led in Nashville. In 1888 Ryman and other followers contributed the money to begin construction, and in 1891 the Union Gospel Tabernacle witnessed its first Sam Jones revival. It was Jones who suggested that the building be renamed after its principal benefactor, and it was, after Ryman's death in 1904.[17] Ryman Auditorium, on Fifth Avenue near Broad, remained a permanent reminder of the religious power Sam Jones had tapped in Nashville.

There were other monuments left in the wake of religious enthusiasm Jones helped inspire. Organized philanthropy in Nashville before the mid-1880s was sporadic, poorly funded, and staffed by part-time volunteers. Churches dispensed occasional relief through ladies' aid societies, and the county government sponsored a poor house that offered a harsh form of charity to the desperately poor and disabled. There were few effective private charities that cut across rival denominational lines to provide sustained charity on the scale required in a growing city. The Protestant Orphans Asylum, founded in 1845, and the Nashville Protestant School of Industry, founded in 1854, both owing their existence to the leadership of Francis B. Fogg, were the most enduring examples of interdenominational philanthropy. Blacks, who were frequently excluded from white-sponsored charities, organized the Nashville Provident Association in 1865 to dispense relief to their poor. The Colored Ladies House of Industry of Nashville, formed in 1873, became another black counterpart of white charitable institutions.[18]

All these philanthropic efforts struggled against an antagonistic disposition among the wealthy who worried that charity would only encourage vice and sloth. Jones's major contribution was to discredit this point of view and to define a corporate moral community. He told the rich it was their Christian duty to aid the less fortunate and that the sins of the poor, intemperate, and vicious were the sins of the community — all must share in their salvation, just as all would surely suffer their damnation. It was Jones's ability to ridicule the moral apathy and selfishness of Nashville's rich families that helped open their coffers to philanthropy in the city.

Few exemplified the practical applications of the social gospel to philanthropic work better than Fannie Battle and her United Charities. Mary Frances Battle was born near Nolensville, Tennessee, in 1842. As a girl she attended Nashville Female Academy and seemed headed toward the comfortable life of a well-born woman whose place would be at home as wife and mother. The Civil War brought tragedy to her family; her two brothers were killed, and her father was imprisoned. She also was sent to federal prison, accused of espionage against the Union troops occupying Nashville. After the war her fiancé was killed in a train accident on their wedding day. Fannie Battle became a schoolteacher in 1870 and gave her spare time to volunteer work for the McKendree Methodist Church.

At Thanksgiving in 1881 Battle and her friends organized an informal food drive for the poor. Impressed by the great numbers that lined up to receive the donations, they took down names and began laying plans for a sustained relief program in Nashville.[19] Within a month this small band of dedicated volunteers found an unexpected opportunity to demonstrate the need for organized relief in Nashville. A massive flood of the Cumberland River swamped low-lying, poor neighborhoods in the city and left over a thousand people homeless. Fannie Battle quickly rose to the challenge and became the leading force behind organizing the relief effort. She, Mayor Thomas Kercheval, and others formally organized the Nashville Relief Society and enlisted the aid of "gentlemen of responsible stature and business in the community" to supervise the dispensing of food, clothing, and coal to the destitute.[20] The *American* applauded their efforts as "practical Christianity in eloquent action."[21]

The Nashville Relief Society continued as a permanent organization after the flood, but the humanitarian spirit that buoyed its flood relief program in the winter of 1882 soon ebbed, and the society faced extinction by 1886. It was then that Fannie Battle gave up her job as schoolteacher and devoted her life to social work, serving as secretary of the Relief Society.[22]

Battle was one of several women in late nineteenth-century America to become a pioneer in professional social work. She understood the need for sustained, centralized charity in place of sporadic disaster relief and alms giving.[23] She reorganized the Relief Society as United Charities in 1901 and made this serve as the center of a number of related social service organizations. Battle also worked tirelessly to educate political leaders about welfare problems in Nashville and Tennessee, and she raised money from local business leaders. At the same time she recruited the wives and daughters of these wealthy men for volunteer work in behalf of United Charities.[24] In 1891 she opened the Addison Avenue Day Home in North Nashville for factory workers' children, who otherwise were left at home or sent to work in the textile mills with their parents. Two kindergartens, named after Bertha Fensterwald and A.B. Ransom, and the John Thomas Fresh Air Camp in Craggie Hope, Tennessee, were later added to the United Charities of Fannie Battle's day.[25]

The Woman's Mission Home for prostitutes, unwed mothers, and other "fallen women" was another organized charity inspired by the religious fervor of the 1880s. The Mission Home received an important endorsement from Sam Jones when he held a benefit for it in May 1885. Nellie Jackson, a local prostitute, was saved at one of Jones's revivals that year and was taken into the home. In a short time she abandoned her addiction to liquor and opium and served as a widely publicized example of the home's value to the city and of the capacity for even the most depraved women to be redeemed by Christian charity.[26] By 1892 the home, boosted by a steady flow of contributions, was able to build an enlarged facility. Later, it became part of the Florence Crittenton Mission Home Corporation, a national organization, and it continued its service to unwed mothers into the 1980s.[27]

The Randal Cole School, an industrial training institute for homeless boys founded in 1885, was another product of local philanthropy spurred by Jones's evangelism County Judge John C. Ferris had been lobbying for county and state support of such a facility since the early 1870s. Frustrated by the lack of interest among political leaders, Ferris turned to private charity in 1885. Sam Jones gave another of his benefit lectures for the cause, which elicited some funds but not enough to launch Ferris's school. Not long afterward, Edmund W. Cole, a wealthy railroad entrepreneur and devout Methodist layman, mourned the sudden death of his son and decided to memorialize him by donating his son's intended inheritance to an industrial school for less fortunate boys. He bought over 100 acres of land for the school and carried its expenses for the first two years of operations. When it was given to a reluctant state legislature in 1887, it was renamed the Tennessee Industrial School, and it continues as a visible reminder of the evangelical roots of social reform in Nashville.[28]

The Nashville Colored Ladies Relief Society, founded in December 1886, was one of several expressions of the social gospel in the black community. Shunned by many white charities, these women raised money, gathered food and fuel primarily through the black churches, and dispensed the donations to needy blacks. By 1890 they were administering relief to almost a thousand people and continued doing so until the depression of the 1890s overwhelmed their efforts.[29]

The Young Men's Christian Association (YMCA), founded in 1855, had gone through several reorganizations, the last one in 1873. It was designed to reach out to young men in the city and provide wholesome recreation and fellowship, but it struggled along with little support and no permanent facilities before Jones's visit in 1885. Tom Ryman led a successful fund-raising drive to build a large facility for the YMCA on Church Street. Sam Jones gave a benefit lecture to kick off the campaign and soon $70,000 was raised. The building was complete in 1888, and the YMCA became one of the most visible arms of social Christianity in the city.[30]

Watkins Institute was another lasting manifestation of organized philanthropy in the 1880s. Samuel Watkins was a self-made man who made a substantial fortune as a brick manufacturer and real estate speculator in Nashville. He became a notable philanthropist in his final years. He donated his first home to the city, which became Watkins Park in North Nashville. He also grew concerned with the education of the poor. An uneducated man, Watkins wanted to establish a school modeled after the Cooper Union in New York City. It would be a tuition-free night school for working adults and children, devoted, as his will specified, to "such useful subjects as will be beneficial in the business of life." At Watkins's death in 1880 the trustees of his bequest controlled his homesite on Church Street and $100,000 as an endowment. The plan was to build a large three-story building (completed in 1882), rent out the ground floor for income, and use the upper floors for a library and lecture halls. Watkins Institute was formally organized in 1885, and the night school started offering classes in 1889 with over four hundred students. The school was immediately popular among working-class adults and youths, who learned rudimentary reading and writing, mathematics, and business skills. For many students these classes opened doors to jobs in banks and offices. One grateful student, Ann Webber, a German-born immigrant who learned English at Watkins, became a prosperous businesswoman and donated valuable real estate to the institute at her death in 1902. Watkins's legacy became a durable example of the many private philanthropic efforts that were inspired by the reform sentiment of the 1880s.[31]

These and many other private philanthropic institutions had their roots in the religious impulse of the social gospel that Jones and local supporters helped awaken in the 1880s. Their work helped alleviate the strains of a fast-growing urban community and reduce some of the distress of the 1890s depression. These private charities came at a time when the sense of public responsibility to help the destitute was weak or nonexistent and the scope of government welfare was extremely limited. Many survived into the twentieth century, long after the federal welfare state had all but eclipsed private charities as the major benefactor of the unfortunate.

THE TEMPERANCE CRUSADE

The other stream of social reform that flowed from the religious enthusiasm of the 1880s was the temperance crusade. This, too, had gained some momentum before Sam Jones galvanized moral reformers in Nashville. The Four-Mile Law, passed in 1877 by the state legislature, prohibited any saloons within four miles of a school but only in areas outside incorporated towns. This law, upheld by the courts as constitutional, became the main weapon temperance forces used in their mission to dry up the entire state of Tennessee.[32]

Statewide temperance conventions in 1884 and 1885 resulted in the coordination of the Women's Christian Temperance Union, the Prohibition Party, and other temperance organizations under the Tennessee Temperance Alliance, which held annual meetings in Nashville and became a political force to be reckoned with in the coming battle. The *Issue,* published in Nashville beginning in 1885, became the voice of temperance in Tennessee.[33] The temperance organizations and journals were front organizations for the major Protestant churches, particularly the Methodists, Baptists, and northern Presbyterians, who now actively embraced political action on this issue.

Temperance was also a major concern of women reformers, many of whom entered the political arena for the first time to lobby for a reform they saw closely connected to the protection of the home and children. Nashville's liquor interests and their "wet" allies tried to dismiss the whole movement as a silly expression of meddling preachers, women, and their henpecked husbands, but the temperance movement became a powerful political force in Nashville and Tennessee politics in the coming decades.

The temperance crusade drew on the same logic that inspired organized philanthropy in the 1880s: sin was a community concern. It was not enough for individuals to live correct, temperate lives; they must help save their fellow man. Among all the sins reformers wished to eradicate, intemperance took on a singular, obsessive importance in the nineteenth century. Drunkenness was seen as the root cause of so many other evils, its eradication seemed to promise deliverance to a radically improved moral order. "Christian Rum is the king of crime," the minister of Nashville's Spruce Street Methodist Church told his congregation in 1886. Liquor was

> the great anaconda, which wraps its coils around home altars to cripple them, to make room for Bacchus. The vampire which fans sanity to sleep while it sucks away the lifeblood. The vulture, which preys upon the vials [sic] of the nations. It defies God, despises Jesus Christ, sins against the Holy Ghost, which is sinning against light and knowledge. Above all it murders humanity. . . . No festering pest-house — not even the Chinese opium den is more deadly to virtue than the Christian rum hole.[34]

This kind of hyperbolic rhetoric was standard fare among temperance advocates, and it left little room for compromise with the "whiskey devil."

The goal was total prohibition through a state constitutional amendment. The legislative election of 1886 became the first major political test of the movement. At issue was the question as to whether a referendum on the constitutional amendment would be submitted to the voters, and almost every candidate was forced to make a stand.

As the temperance forces coalesced, the liquor interests followed suit. Whiskey distilling was a significant industry in Middle Tennessee, and some of Nashville's leading men of wealth depended on it. Victor Emmanuel (Manny) Shwab, of George A. Dickel & Company, was among the wealthiest men in town and a major contributor to the antiprohibition battle. Charles Nelson of the Greenbrier Distillery and William Gerst of Gerst Brewery were also leading Nashville citizens with a strong stake in the battle. The liquor interests organized the State Protective Association in 1886 with George S. Kinney, a Nashville wholesale liquor dealer, as president.[35] *Bonforts Wine and Spirit Circular*, a New York trade journal, became a propaganda organ for the antiprohibition struggle.

Nashville, the headquarters for the Tennessee Temperance Alliance and the State Protective Association, became a hotly contested battleground by the time of the election in November 1886. Prohibitionists were scandalized when the Davidson County Democratic convention, which had nominally endorsed the prohibition amendment, nominated men who—at best—were soft on prohibition, including T.J. Slowey, a saloon keeper recently arrested for selling liquor on the Sabbath.[36] Arthur S. Colyar, a Democrat and ardent prohibitionist, used his newspaper, the Nashville *Union*, to attack the Democratic slate, focusing on Slowey as the puppet of the liquor interests. "On one side stands all that makes life worth living—God, morality, peace and good order; on the other side the saloons, with their record of crime, insolently dictating to every man." The opponents were "enemies of religion, morality, purity, and innocence."[37]

The night before the election the liquor poured freely for voters sympathetic to the antiprohibition stand. During the night a man named William Owen was killed in a barroom fight. His murderer was arrested later that night in T.J. Slowey's saloon. The temperance crusaders were quick to take advantage. Tom Ryman drove Owen's widow and children around town to polling sites. A large placard on the side of his buggy explained: "The only support of this family was murdered last night in T.J. Winfrey's saloon, one of T.J. Slowey's friends, by William Gallagher who was afterwards arrested in T.J. Slowey's saloon." Temperance women broke tradition by showing up at the polls that day. They passed out free coffee (a sobering device doubtlessly welcomed by some citizens who had overindulged the previous night) and pressed the men to vote for temperance. Slowey and the Democratic slate went down in defeat, and the Republican party savored a rare victory in Davidson County. Across the state prohibitionist candidates carried the day.

Now the question could be put directly to the people in a referendum on a prohibition amendment to the state constitution. The election day was set for September 29, 1887, and both sides prepared for a decisive battle. The Tennessee Temperance Alliance staged a magnificent state convention in Nashville that February, and a kick-off rally followed in Nashville in April.[38] Sam Jones toured the state for a month that summer, calling on Christians to join the crusade and chiding clergymen afraid of political action. In Nashville the temperance movement worked hard to arouse its followers before the election. The WCTU organized a series of lectures in different neighborhoods of the city, many of them in "temperance tents" set up in vacant lots. The organization formed ward committees that sponsored nightly meetings in some neighborhoods.[39] The local clergy, led by Methodist ministers Warren A. Candler, David C. Kelly, T.J. Duncan, and Oscar P. Fitzgerald, joined, of course, by Sam Jones, addressed their congregations and interdenominational rallies to preach for prohibition.[40] Colyar's Nashville *Union* and the Nashville *Banner,* along with religious and temperance periodicals, the Methodist *Christian Advocate* and the *Issue,* filled their columns with articles on prohibition and letters from sympathetic readers.[41]

Serious efforts were made to enlist black Nashville in the temperance crusade. The WCTU organized a "colored" branch in North Nashville, and a black was appointed to the Davidson County prohibition committee of the Tennessee Temperance Alliance.[42] Blacks were invited to attend integrated temperance rallies, where the Excelsior Jubilee Singers, a Negro spiritual chorus, were the featured entertainment. Their music, one white speaker hoped, would "sing the colored people into prohibition."[43]

The antiprohibitionists also organized and met the temperance crusade with their own propaganda and popular rallies. Nashville lawyer and politician John J. Vertrees became the point man for the liquor interests. In a lengthy article in the *American,* Vertrees gave the fullest statement of the antiprohibition position. In addition to the traditional defenses of personal liberty and difficulty of enforcement, Vertrees warned that the temperance crusade portended a massive upset of the whole political system in Tennessee. Under the guise of a nonpartisan moral reform movement, a coalition of "well-meaning but sentimental women" and Methodist "rabbis" were attempting to undo Democratic control in Tennessee. This would reopen the door to Republicans, out of power since Reconstruction and ambitious to regain it by way of this new issue. Along with sincere prohibitionists and "political Methodist priests," Vertrees argued, were "the Republican, the ambitious place hunter, the woman's rights shrieker, the fanatic. . . ." "While they are rolling their eyes to heaven and singing psalms set to non-party music, they know that the work in hand is to *super annuate* the Democratic party in Tennessee."[44]

The other weapon used effectively by the antiprohibitionist was ridicule of the women and clergy on the other side. The *National Review,* a Republican newspaper opposed to prohibition, mocked the Tennessee Temperance Alliance convention by putting out a bogus call for all "ugly women, henpecked husbands, chronic dyspeptics and $3 preachers . . . to meet Sunday night at Crank's Hall. . . ."[45]

The evening before the election huge rallies were held on the Public Square, the prohibitionists with between 5,000 and 6,000 people on the west side of the square, and the antiprohibitionists on the east side. The supporters of temperance met in their churches afterward, and "all night long the women of the First Presbyterian church prayed and had the bell rung every hour."[46] The opposition sent kegs of beer to neighborhood gatherings throughout the city. The next day they fitted up a wagon with a large transparency of a mug of beer and a banner announcing "Ryman's Jubilee Singers," a raucous chorus of "singing antis" who paraded behind the beer mug mocking the piety of their opponents.

Women temperance crusaders and their children went to the polls to serve free lunches and coffee and to stand witness to the male voters. They wore white badges and pinned the same on their supporters. (The "antis" had their own blue badges.) Choruses of women and children sang hymns at the polls. Mrs. Turnbull's "Prohibition Belles" from South Nashville and Mrs. J.D. Allen's "Loyal Temperance Legion" from North Nashville were brought by wagon to the polls to sing temperance songs and wave banners: "KING ALCOHOL MUST DIE!" "VOTE FOR YOUR BOYS. VOTE FOR YOUR GIRLS. VOTE FOR YOUR WIVES. VOTE FOR YOUR HOMES. VOTE TO EMPTY THE POOR HOUSE AND PRISON."[47]

But the amendment failed to win in Nashville and across Tennessee, despite strong support in East Tennessee and in many rural counties. In defeat, the temperance forces expressed profound pessimism about the political system that had denied them reform. Mrs. J.D. Allen of Nashville's WCTU admitted she was unprepared for the "woeful ignorance of some human creatures who are bent upon their own and others' ruin." She recalled the "depraved, debauched creatures" voting against prohibition and asked, "are these the guardians and makers of laws to govern the intelligent, educated and refined women of our land?"[48]

Black voters were singled out for special blame because their strong vote against the amendment presumably swung the election. The Nashville *American* estimated that of the 145,000 statewide votes against prohibition, about 90,000 were cast by black voters.[49] Mrs. Allen alluded to the antiprohibition voters who "marched to the polls shackled slaves, nothing more," the black voters "under the lash of the liquor traffic." She gave credit to those "colored men" who supported her cause but regretted there were "not more to redeem their race."[50]

Women who entered politics for the first time to fight for temperance would soon demand direct political power in the right to vote. Their entry into the political arena coincided with the movement to push blacks out of that arena.[51]

POLITICAL REFORM AND DISFRANCHISEMENT

The disillusionment that followed the 1887 failure of the temperance crusade was quickly seized by Democrats, who led to an all-out

assault against the political power of blacks and against Republicans
in general. During the 1880s sincere motives of moral reform and political "purification" joined the most partisan and racist sentiments to
define the goals of the Democratic party.

Before this attack began Nashville and the state of Tennessee had
a viable two-party system, the most "consistently competitive" in all
the former Confederate states, according to historian J. Morgan Kousser.[52] From their stronghold among anti-Confederate whites of East Tennessee, Republicans had built a large following among black voters in
Middle and West Tennessee, and among whites (many of them former
Whigs) who favored Republican tariff and economic policy. In Nashville, where the black population was 38 percent in 1880, the power
of the Republicans was enough to elect Augustus E. Alden as mayor
during the Reconstruction era in Tennessee and Thomas A. Kercheval
as mayor twelve times between 1872 and 1887. Kercheval, a major force
in Nashville politics in this period, has remained an obscure historical
figure. Born in 1837 in the country town of Fayetteville, Tennessee,
Kercheval came to Nashville during the Civil War. He worked as clerk
to the Federal provost marshall and remained a steadfast Union man.
Kercheval read law and practiced on the side, but his love was politics.
He jumped into the embattled Republican party's leadership during the
tumultous years of Reconstruction. A generous, well-met man with a
natural flair for popular politics, Kercheval rose quickly in the young
party and managed to survive the quick end to Reconstruction in Tennessee. He ran successfully for the state Senate twice, beginning in 1867,
then was elected to the City Council from the Fourth Ward. He went
on to win the office of mayor in 1872 and 1873. The following year
he lost to Morton B. Howell but came back to run successfully every
year from 1875 through 1882. Defeated again in 1883, Kercheval refused
to die. He won the mayor's race in 1885 and again in 1887.[53]

During this long period of Republican ascendance, Nashville blacks
used their political power to elect their own to the City Council on
a regular basis, and they traded their support for jobs and contracts with
city government. Historian Howard Rabinowitz described Nashville's
black political leaders as "the most successful and sophisticated" among
those he examined in the cities of the postwar South. Their followers,
he argues, "demonstrated the most active and sustained interest in
casting their votes selectively."[54] Thus, James C. Napier, an eminent
black Republican lawyer, represented the voters of the predominantly
black Fourth Ward in North Nashville beginning in 1878 and became
a powerful spokesman for all of black Nashville.[55] In dozens of other
ways the Republicans under Kercheval had fashioned a kind of urban
political machine with "Boss Kercheval" and a host of black and white
ward-level politicos exchanging political favors in the form of patronage, jobs, and contracts for votes on election day.

Beginning in 1881 reform Democrats pushed for a new city charter. Their leader was Arthur S. Colyar, New South industrialist and publisher of the *Daily American.* The goal was to make the structure of city government more centralized, efficient, and businesslike, and to enable businessmen—the "best people," as Colyar called them—to run the city.[56] When Colyar sponsored Edward B. Stahlman's bid for mayor on this kind of platform in October 1881, the reformers met a resounding defeat at the hands of Kercheval's machine.[57] In December 1882 the Citizens Reform Association was organized with Colyar as president and about four hundred members, mostly from among the city's businessmen.[58] An ostensibly bipartisan alliance in favor of government reform, it was a political movement to destroy Kercheval's "ring." "The change proposed is a business change . . . ," the *American* announced, "an effort to abandon the semi-political ward system for a government run on business principles."[59]

The obstacle to this efficient, businesslike government was Kercheval's confederation of ward-based political leaders and his power to award jobs and contracts to supporters. The Citizens Reform Association, with the aid of lawyer Jacob McGavock Dickinson, designed a new city charter, the key features of which were to reduce the City Council from a bicameral system with forty-two representatives to a single body with ten representatives, who were to be elected by the citizens at large instead of by the voters of each ward. The council, in turn, would appoint a three-man Board of Public Works, with total power over hiring city employees and awarding contracts. This arrangement would favor Colyar's businessmen, whose wealth and reputation would generally triumph in a citywide election over the ward-level politician whose constituency was narrowly circumscribed in the neighborhoods. By the same principle, the concentration of blacks in certain neighborhoods, which now allowed them to elect their own representatives, would give them no advantage in at-large elections because citywide, blacks were in the minority. The elected council would then appoint the three members of the Board of Public Works, each for staggered six-year terms. The board would enjoy control over some of the most vital functions of government, but its members would not be responsible to the electorate.

This charter reform, intended to debilitate Kercheval's Republican organization, was to be decided not in the local political process but in the state legislature, which Democrats controlled in 1883. As the bill worked its way through the General Assembly, efforts to amend it and retain ward-based elections were fought off successfully by the reform Democrats. Colyar's *American* stated the case plainly when it said, "The fight is between the better class of citizens and the rabble, who wish to have control of the Common Council." The people, the *American* went on, must have "relief from an evil greater than came upon us by the Alden crowd" (a reminder of Reconstruction-era Mayor Augustus Alden).[60] "Office-hunters are not the men we want to manage our affairs. We want business men and we must have them."[61] Compromises in the final bill allowed no more than one councilman be elected from any of Nashville's fourteen wards, but the basic principles of the Citizen's Reform Association charter were approved.[62]

In October 1883 the first election under the new charter was held. The reformers, still using the nonpartisan front of the Citizens Reform Association, put forth a slate headed by C. Hooper Phillips, a merchant, for mayor, and eight other prominent businessmen for council. In a strategy to split the black vote, the reform ticket included two blacks, James C. Napier and Charles C. Gowdy. Both had served Kercheval's organization, Napier as councilman, Gowdy as constable, but were now drawn to the reform ticket by the promise their support would "make everlasting friends among the better class of white people."[63] William H. Young, another popular black political leader, joined Napier and Gowdy in their campaign to alienate blacks from Kercheval's machine. They reminded blacks of recent acts of police brutality against Negroes and promised jobs, schools, and equal justice for black Nashville if it supported reform.[64]

Most blacks jeered these defectors and rejected the patronizing appeals of white reformers, but enough deserted Kercheval to end his long reign. The reform ticket swept the election, and the *American* proclaimed the "era of business government" had begun.[65] Colyar and Mayor-elect Phillips addressed a large postelection crowd on the Public Square. A red fox, an allusion to Kercheval's nickname, was presented to them. Colyar, standing on top of a cotton bale, expressed his gratitude to the blacks who abandoned Kercheval: "In the name of the suffering taxpayers of this city, I . . . thank the colored men who in such large numbers came to their relief. . . . The colored voters, realizing this is no arty contest . . . stood by the right with a courage that is gratifying."[66]

White reformers demonstrated their gratitude in more concrete ways during the next two years. Under Councilman James C. Napier's constant prodding, the reform regime allowed the establishment of a black fire company in East Nashville, the hiring of more black workers on the city payroll, the award of several contracts to black bidders, and improvements to black schools. It was Napier, also, who insisted that if black school children were to be taught in separate schools, they should be taught by black teachers and supervised by black principals.[67]

When Napier tried to claim fuller social justice for his race, he learned just how uneasy was his alliance with white reformers. Napier's resolution requesting the Board of Public Works "to make no discriminations on account of political affiliation, religious inclination, race, color, or previous condition" was adopted by the council but later vetoed by Mayor Phillips, who explained such practice "would be contrary to the best interests of the colored people."[68] In trying to override the mayor's veto, Napier and his fellow black councilman, Charles Gowdy, stood alone.[69] Later, Napier put forward a resolution that the Board of Education arrange for the city to pay tuition for black high school-age students (who were denied access to the city-owned high school) to local universities that admitted blacks (namely, Fisk and Central Tennessee College). This too, passed in council and was vetoed by the mayor, who saw it as a violation of the city charter.[70]

The reformers were caught in the difficult position of trying to award sufficient political favors to maintain black support without alienating Democrats who, out of racism and partisan antipathy, resented a close alliance with black Republicans. In the city election of 1885 black leaders again advocated the reform ticket and pointed to the benefits blacks had received during the previous two years.[71] Once more, James C. Napier was placed on the reform ticket, though he was now the only black candidate. Gowdy, a black reform candidate in 1883, had been appointed captain of the black fire company in East Nashville and was replaced on the council, and on the 1885 ticket, by a white man. Though the four other council nominees were white Democrats, the reformers made a fatal error by putting forward a Republican, Major Andrew W. Wills, for mayor. Kercheval's slate included one black, the Reverend Luke Mason, one of Napier's political enemies.[72] Black voters apparently split their vote in 1885, as they had two years earlier. But this time many white Democrats stayed home, alienated by the interracial and interparty alliance, or by other policies of the reformers. There was outright election fraud and bribery on both sides, but Kercheval's Republicans—except for black candidate Luke Mason—were returned to power.[73]

That evening Kercheval's jubilant supporters swarmed around his Cherry Street campaign headquarters and lit a huge bonfire on the street. Kercheval, elected to his eleventh term as mayor of Nashville, was presented with his own red fox, "which he kissed several times." His followers formed a large procession, headed by a brass band, that paraded through the streets late into the night, pausing in front of Colyar's *American* offices to play the "Dead March."[74]

Reform, it seemed, was dead in Nashville, at least in the form of a nonpartisan interracial alliance. Kercheval won the 1887 mayoral election with no opposition, and his slate of councilmen defeated Colyar's "Citizens Ticket," which included one black candidate, John Bosely, and several white businessmen.[75].

At this juncture Nashville reform Democrats abandoned their experiment in nonpartisan biracial reform. The failure of the prohibition referendum that same year, and the role black voters played in that defeat, compounded white disillusionment. Rather than try to appeal to the "better sort" of Negro voter, reformers now turned to "purifying" the electorate by means of restrictive registration and voting laws. This new tactic coincided with a blatantly partisan Democratic strategy of reducing Republican strength in Nashville and across the state.[76]

The 1888 state elections — rife with fraud and intimidation — gave Democrats a solid majority in the General Assembly, and the voting laws they passed in the next two years assured that Republicans would never again threaten their dominance.[77] The Meyers Registration Law required voters in districts or towns with at least five hundred voters in the last election to register at least twenty days before each election and to bring their registration certificate to the poll. The Lea Law provided separate ballot boxes for simultaneous state and federal elections in order to circumvent federal supervision of elections (as proposed in the Republican-sponsored Lodge election bill before Congress). The Dortch Law requiring the Australian, or secret, ballot had a more devastating impact on Republican voting strength. Before the Dortch Law came into effect, each party or local faction printed its own ballots with only its candidates listed, often on colored paper with pictures or symbols to identify the ticket. The illiterate party loyalist had only to pick up one of these ballots at a party rally, or local saloon perhaps, and drop it in the ballot box. Under the Dortch Law, ballots had to be printed by election officials, and candidates for each office had to be listed alphabetically and with no party identification of any kind. This amounted to a kind of literacy test and effectively eliminated more black than white voters, since most blacks had been denied education under slavery and had only limited educational opportunities since emancipation.[78] As a concession to illiterate rural whites, the Dortch Law initially applied solely to the four urban areas of Tennessee, including all of Davidson County.[79] In a special session in 1890 Democratic legislators added the poll-tax requirement, one more nail in the Republican coffin, since it would eliminate more impoverished black voters, along with many poor whites.[80]

These laws, constituting radical changes in the rules of the political game, were at once dressed in the sanctimonious clothing of reform and the coarser garb of partisanship and racism. Edward Ward Carmack, editor of the *American*, articulated all three motives in straightforward language. The Republicans, he accused, "sought to give over as prey to negro barbarism the land which our fathers wrested from the Indian savage." The African race, Carmack argued on another occasion, never had "a gleam of light across its dark history and . . . had within itself no promises or possibility of progress. It was a race without history, without ideas and without hope."[81]

Whatever hope black Nashville had left was dimming quickly in 1889. The city election of that year demonstrated the "magical effect" of the new voting laws on local politics. The Republicans worked hard to register black voters and help them surmount the new obstacles to the franchise. In some wards illiterate voters used tin templates—guides with holes cut so that when placed over the ballot only their party's candidates would show. But these tactics failed to overcome the new rules, and the Republican mayoral candidate, James Trimble, won only 1,142 votes, about one-quarter of the average Republican vote in the four previous city mayoral contests.[82] Kercheval had already stepped aside as mayor to accept a paid six-year term on the Board of Public Works. But even his presence on the ticket could not have reversed the tide. Republican rule in Nashville's city government, for all practical purposes, ended in October 1889. Nearly a century later, the Republican party in Nashville had not fully recovered.

The black presence in Nashville politics also went into a long, dismal period of repression. The impact of voting restrictions was demonstrated more forcefully in the county elections of August 1890. Though blacks claimed 35 percent of the voting-age males, in Davidson County they constituted only 21 percent of the registered voters, and it was estimated that far fewer than half of these men actually voted in the 1890 county elections.[83]

James C. Napier, who had allied with Democratic reformers and was so full of hope back in 1883, was badly trounced in his bid for circuit court clerk in the August 1890 poll. Now quite useless to his former white allies and alienated from his Republican constituency, Napier failed to get more than 280 votes and won only 38 from his Fourth Ward constituents.[84] With one notable exception (Councilman Solomon Parker Harris, elected in 1911), there would be no black officeholders in city government from 1885 until 1951. "The election laws in Tennessee . . . have effectively disposed of the negro vote" and thereby "solve the race problem," the *Banner* observed with only partial accuracy in 1890.[85] Edward Ward Carmack of the *American* approved the new suffrage laws for having "dignified and rendered decent" the polls, ridding them of the "old crowd of negroes and ruffians . . . with their reeking smells and coarse profanity."[86]

Now that the black vote was impotent, many white Republicans abandoned their former allies and moved to cut off the large black wing of their party in order to attract white support. These "lily white" Republicans, as they were known, eliminated blacks from their nomination slates and from party conventions that made up the slates. In the 1893 city elections white Republicans organized as the Comanchee Club and met secretly to draw up a lily-white ticket. Black Republicans were furious and ran their own candidate for mayor, Dr. Robert Fulton Boyd. The election showed only 135 votes for Boyd and 213 for the lily-white candidate, a lesson in futility for white and black Republicans in Nashville.[87]

In 1893 the Democrats adopted the all-white primary, which simply banished nonwhite voters from party primary elections. This device guaranteed no recurrence of interracial alliances and eliminated the need for any Democratic candidate to curry favor with black voters. In a one-party system the winner of the Democratic primary election was guaranteed victory in the general election.[88] Many in Nashville's black community continued against all odds to exercise the franchise as a sacred right of citizenship, but others resigned themselves to the new era of repression and gave up voting.[89]

During the 1890s there were other signs of the new harshness of white supremacy. By denying black voters their basic political rights, white political leaders and editors had, in effect, given white southerners "permission to hate" at the same time they took from blacks the most important weapon they had to protect themselves against such hate.[90] The symptoms were evident in a wave of brutal lynchings that swept the South in the 1890s.

Nashville had its own spectacle of racial hatred in April 1892. Eph Grizzard, a black man, had been arrested with others on suspicion of raping two white girls in Goodlettsville, a country town north of Nashville. One of the men confessed and was hanged by a mob, led by that town's "best citizens," according to one report. Grizzard, whose guilt was uncertain, was brought to the Davidson County jail for safety. But incriminating evidence pointing to Grizzard's involvement was revealed, and a huge mob of several thousand, "mostly men from the country," gathered in Nashville's Public Square. The police repulsed one attack on the jail and tried to disperse the crowd, but after it organized another assault on the jail, the police gave way without firing a shot.

Grizzard was hauled from his jail cell in terror, a rope was put around his neck, and he was pushed out on the Cumberland River Bridge. There the rope was tied to the rail and Grizzard was flung over the side. As he hung there, members of the mob pumped at least fifty bullets into his head and body and jerked the rope up and down to watch the bloody corpse snap. Grizzard's half-nude body hung from the bridge all afternoon; a placard pinned to his breast warned against removing it. This lynching was the deed of outsiders, and it did not portend a reign of violent terror for Nashville blacks in the 1890s. The restrictions of blacks in the job market and their effective exclusion from real political power now guaranteed they would not compete seriously with whites, thus reducing whites' need for violent repression. Still, it was a grisly omen of the new state of race relations, which just a few years earlier seemed to hold such promise as reformers sought black votes. Without a strong political voice, blacks were more vulnerable than ever to the injustice that now was unleashed upon them.[91] The road from religious revivals and philanthropic reform to political "reforms" that disfranchised many blacks and opened the door to racial repression was a strange journey that Nashville followed with much of the South during this period.

PROGRESSIVE NASHVILLE
AND THE RISE OF BOSS HOWSE

The modern potential for reform was fully realized during the Tennessee Centennial Exposition, sponsored by Nashville in 1897. This event served as an object lesson in the power of business and civic leaders to promote social progress through expert planning and institutional reform. The triumph of Centennial City as an experiment in social planning signaled the beginning of Nashville's own progressive era. It was a period of concentrated reform effort dedicated to the efficient restructuring of city government with the modern business corporation as the model. In parallel reform movements, altruistic women, social welfare and public health workers, clergymen, and black leaders sought to rescue and rehabilitate those they saw in need of benevolent reform. Whatever specific objects of reform these people pursued, they shared a modern faith in the inevitability of progress through enlightened planning by trained experts.

At odds with these progressive ideals were the stubborn ways of the common folk who preferred their own devices for coping with the stresses of city life. In the poorer neighborhoods of the city these people found solace in the saloons and brothels, or—in different ways—in the many small fundamentalist churches that continued to deal with sin in more traditional fashion. These people distrusted the vision of a secular, progressive future, and they distrusted the reformers who planned to deliver them into that world.

They found their champion in Hilary Howse, a pragmatic politician who gave his followers what they wanted, and not what the reformers thought they needed. Howse used city government to grant the poor thousands of small favors, from groceries and coal in winter, to jobs and police protection for bootleggers, saloon owners, and their patrons. He was the counterpart of the more famous Boss Ed Crump of

Memphis, who built a similar political machine based on rural migrants and the black and white poor.[1] Boss Howse served his people
over thirty years (off and on) beginning in the early twentieth century,
but his place in the city's history has never been memorialized; no
street, school, or hospital was ever named after him.[2] During his time
he was one of the most durable political forces in the city, and in his
own way he did as much as the more respectable reformers to ease the
people of Nashville through the often difficult passage to modern urban life.

THE CENTENNIAL EXPOSITION OF 1897

The growing strains in Nashville's race relations and the lingering effects of the depression that began in 1893 were put aside for a few
months in 1897. On May 1 of that year the Tennessee Centennial Exposition celebrated the opening day of an extraordinary collection of
industrial exhibits, school and art displays, parades, conventions, and
speeches. Before it closed six months later, approximately 1.8 million
visitors would pour through its gates.[3] It would be the grandest of a
series of southern expositions and an experience that would leave an
imprint on the lives of Nashvillians for years.

At the opening ceremonies a message was sent to President Mc-
Kinley in Washington, D.C. On signal, the president pushed a but-
ton, and an electric impulse traveled instantaneously by wire over 700
miles to Nashville, setting off simultaneously a cannon and an electric dynamo. Nothing could have demonstrated quite so dramatically
the new age of progress Tennessee set out to celebrate that day.

Following the Philadelphia Centennial Exposition in 1876, a flurry
of similar extravaganzas served as showcases for America's rapidly growing cities. These expositions took on special meaning within the South,
where a rising urban middle class was eager to convince the North that
a "New South" had been born, striving for industrial and social progress, and devoted to restoring interracial peace. Nashville's rival, Atlanta,
sponsored three highly successful expositions in 1881, 1887, and 1895;
others were held in Louisville, 1883, and New Orleans, 1885. By the
time Nashville came to its industrial extravaganza, a new standard had
been set by the Columbian Exposition of 1893, in Chicago, the city
that had become the epitome of industrial progress in the Gilded Age.[4]

The one-hundredth anniversary of Tennessee's entry into the Union
seemed an ideal occasion to emulate the standards of Atlanta and Chicago with a grand industrial exposition. Plans for the centennial had
been discussed vaguely since 1890; then Nashville's Commercial Club
took the lead in the fall of 1893 by calling a state convention. A com-

bination of personal friction and state sectional jealousies over Nashville's favored role in the planning undermined the initial effort. Plans were in complete disarray by the summer of 1895, when Nashville's commercial leaders called a public meeting to decide the fate of the Centennial. The meeting was about to adjourn, demoralized, when Tully Brown, a Nashville lawyer and gifted orator, gave an inspired extemporaneous speech that swept away the despair of the crowd. A series of mass meetings held in Nashville that summer drew so many people that only the Union Gospel Tabernacle could hold them. The setting seemed appropriate to the zeal Nashville demonstrated in support of the "patriotic duty" of Tennesseans to honor their past.[5]

The exposition was to be a Nashville show, and the company was quickly reorganized to reflect the dominant role of the capital city. The officers and directors included many of the city's eminent lawyers, bankers, wholesale merchants, and manufacturers, but the key leadership came from the railroads. John W. Thomas, president of the NC&StL), was elected president of the Exposition Company. Eugene C. Lewis, chairman of the board of the NCStL, was named by Thomas as the director general of the Centennial.

Railroad leaders were troubled by the bitter popular antagonism brought on by the depression of the 1890s and the resentment in Nashville against the L&N monopoly.[6] The prospect of an industrial exposition in Nashville excited visions of a commercial revival, a surge of railroad passenger fares, and other short-term opportunities for profit during a demoralizing depression. The exposition would demonstrate also the practical application of efficient organization and technological expertise. At the heart of this progressive faith was the idea that a planned, orderly, wholesome physical environment could be designed to improve its inhabitants. The exposition grounds were an experiment in planning and a model for Nashville to emulate. Already, the White City at Chicago's 1893 Columbian Exposition had stirred enthusiasm for the nascent profession of urban planning, and it sparked the City Beautiful movement, which left its mark on American cities everywhere in grand civic centers, radial boulevards, and neoclassical, or Beaux-Arts, architecture. Indeed, the Tennessee Centennial Exposition organizers began referring to their own "Fair White City of the South," and its neoclassical buildings, the curvilinear avenues, radial boulevards, the landscaping, and the lagoons, all bore strong resemblance to the Chicago model.

The exposition grounds were laid out on the former state fairgrounds, which had been recently renovated and named West Side Park, a spacious suburban resort for horse racing. The exposition was to be held near Vanderbilt University, which was growing into an increasingly prestigious university with an attractive campus drawing many of Nashville's young, wealthy families out to new mansions along West

End Avenue. The trolley lines that served this neighborhood would be extended to the main gate of the exposition, allowing visitors to use downtown hotels and restaurants. On the North side of the exposition grounds the NCStL occupied large machine shops to which was added a fine depot to bring visitors directly to the exposition from outside the city.[7]

The exposition organizers decided to incorporate their own city out in this suburban refuge rather than extend urban services through annexation to Nashville. The Centennial City charter granted by the state legislature in 1894 provided for its own police and fire protection, and several ordinances established strict moral regulations banning liquor, gambling, and prostitution—all vices that flourished in the gamey city center two miles away. The exposition gave progressive social reformers an ideal opportunity to demonstrate the practical value of moral legislation on a social tabula rasa, a city conveniently without opposition from the lower classes, Catholics, or blacks—a city without inhabitants.[8]

The progressive vision of social improvement was revealed not simply in efforts to control the moral behavior of the masses. The more positive expressions of this vision came in the exhibits that aimed at inspiring and educating the people. A central belief of the day was the notion that true progress depended on the efficient development of human and natural resources. This idea was demonstrated most vividly in the special attention given to women, children, and blacks in the exposition. To progressive minds these three components of society shared in different ways a common history of neglect and unfulfilled potential. The exposition would show forward-looking visitors the special role each would play in the future of the South.

The southern lady had been such an important point of regional pride since antebellum times, it was no simple task to accommodate the new feminism that awakened across America in the 1890s. The fact that most American feminists refused to repudiate traditional images of womanhood made it easier. It was woman's special qualities of moral refinement, chastity, temperance, and pacifism, they argued shrewdly, that must now extend beyond the home and into the community. "Woman's work," the ladies of the Tennessee Centennial took as their slogan, is "whatever may be necessary to preserve the sanctity of the home and the freedom of the State." In a manner that would make many modern feminists bristle, women in the 1890s began to press their claims to influence with a soft-gloved touch that reassured the men in power.[9]

Women took an early role in organizing the exposition. The Ladies Hermitage Association, the most socially prominent among several recently organized patriotic and social clubs, became a leading force in the Centennial as early as 1894. The Woman's Building was the first

Figure 51. The Tennessee Centennial Exposition, 1897, looking east from atop the giant seesaw.

Figure 52. The Woman's Building, Tennessee Centennial Exposition, 1897. Filled with displays of feminine domesticity, it also presaged a new role for women as social reformers. Tennessee State Library and Archives.

to go up on the exposition grounds. Designed by Sara Ward-Conley of Nashville, it was a modified reproduction of Andrew Jackson's Hermitage. The Woman's Building, an enormous empty hall, was transformed into a showcase of feminine domestic decoration that underlined the paradoxical nature of progressive feminism in Nashville and the South. In the central reception hall under a two-story rotunda, a sweeping staircase and floating balcony framed a rose-colored glass window with a design representing the "Apotheosis of Woman." Throughout the building women from different localities took responsibility for decorating each room with carefully selected wallpaper, stenciling, furniture, and art objects. Some represented period decor, like the Hermitage Room and Mount Vernon Room; others reflected the high Victorian taste of the day. The library was filled with books by women, the Art Room with painted china and other examples of women's decorative art. The model kitchen, equipped with the latest domestic technology, was used for practical demonstrations of the modern science of cooking. In back of the Woman's Building a crude log cabin was used to illustrate the striking contrast between the efficiency of modern domestic work and the difficulty of pioneer women's labor.[10]

Behind this deceptively conservative veil the Women's Department planned a series of events that expressed more clearly the aspirations of progressive-era feminists. Suffrage Days, College Day, the State Federation of Women's Clubs Conference, a Suffrage Convocation, Business Women's Day, and Women's Press Day were just a few of the events that signaled the new feminist consciousness of Tennessee women. At the Social Science Convocation, Jane Addams of Chicago, a leading feminist and social reformer, addressed the exposition visitors. The National Council of Women met at the exposition, bringing such national feminist leaders as Susan B. Anthony and Anna Shaw to Nashville.[11]

These feminist events were juxtaposed with homages to the more traditional image of women. Toward the end of the exposition Kate Kirkman Day paid tribute to the president of the Woman's Department and revealed the fascinating contradictions of the new woman in the South. A baby show in the morning, a floral parade in the afternoon, and a reception in the evening exemplified the "three great missions in woman's life—the mother . . . the artist . . . and the belle." The floral parade with carriages like "great moving beds of flowers" included men on spirited horses riding escort to the "choicest blossoms that spring from Southern soil." The procession, which reportedly drew "the best people of the State," circled through the exposition grounds with thousands of admiring spectators. That evening, in the Woman's Building aglow with electric lamps, Mrs. Kirkman received her admirers in a white satin gown and "dazzling gems" crowned by diamond stars. In this unlikely setting one speaker applauded women's work at the exposition, adding "as writer, inventor, scientist, and teacher, new wonders of her ability are unfolded."[12]

In many ways the progressive era revolved around the child as an object of reform. Child labor reform, educational reform, and concern for juvenile delinquency all stemmed from a common interest in "saving" and improving the child as a valuable human resource for the nation's future. The idea of a special exhibit of the "work of children" was born in the Woman's Department, which planned to set aside a corner of its building for a display. School children across the state were canvassed for small contributions and, encouraged by the success of this campaign, the exposition organizers created a separate Children's Department. The funds went into a Children's Building just to the north of the Woman's Building, a small, beautifully designed structure. Inside, displays of children's art work and handiwork from the public schools showed visitors the potential of the well-trained child. An "ideal kindergarten room" was set up in one of the wings. A trained specialist in kindergarten schooling demonstrated the value of early childhood education with children from neighboring homes, who attended during the exposition. A series of lectures from leading advocates of the kindergarten, a central goal of progressive school reformers, was sponsored by the Children's Department.[13]

The exposition also offered an ideal occasion to articulate the New South creed of racial harmony and black self-help. In the face of interracial violence and the emergence of Jim Crow laws during the 1890s, the exposition sought to show progressive-minded southerners that black and white destinies were integrally linked in the future of the New South, as they had been in the past. Black potential for "industrial education"—the slogan of the day—was displayed in separate Negro exhibits. An exposition, one approving white observer noted, "determines their industrial status." "This done, we shall be able, with each succeeding exposition, to measure their strides and determine their progress."

Here was the heart of the progressive faith: constant evolution—with the aid of education and science—would lift even the most downtrodden people to higher planes of civilization. The chief of the Negro Department, Richard Hill, a Nashville schoolteacher, for example, was the son of "Uncle Jim Hill," "long a favorite fiddler and prompter at balls and parties given by the best families of Tennessee." "The aristocratic negro of the future," the *Official History of the Exposition* assured skeptical whites, "will be descendants of men like 'Uncle Jim Hill,' 'Uncle Bob' of Belle Meade, and 'Uncle Alfred' of the Hermitage, just as the aristocratic whites of today are the descendants of the hunters, Indian fighters . . . of one hundred years ago." Black and white will both aspire to the "aristocracy of worth."[14]

The concept of a Negro exhibit was introduced at the Atlanta Exposition of 1895, where Booker T. Washington issued what his adversary, W.E.B. DuBois, dubbed the "Atlanta Compromise," an address urging blacks to forgo civil rights in favor of gradual economic progress. The Tennessee Centennial set out to improve on Atlanta's precedent. To demonstrate the "friendliness of southern whites" the exposition managers donated over $12,000 for the Negro Building. The railroads offered free transportation for the exhibitors in the building and granted "equal railroad accommodation" to black passengers, a concession to northern blacks who were unaccustomed to southern segregation.

A magnificent structure, done in "Spanish renaissance" style and stretching 250 feet along the east bank of Lake Watauga, the Negro Building was an impressive testimony to the ideal of racial harmony in the New South. Inside almost three hundred exhibits were displayed, most from the new black colleges and public schools that had come into being since the Civil War. In one wing a restaurant offered blacks separate but equal dining facilities.[15]

No less than eight special days were set aside on the exposition calendar to honor the Negro, and on these days blacks were allowed reduced admission rates. On Negro Day the building was officially opened with a ceremony and speeches that articulated the spirit of interracial understanding. A white spokesman set the tone: "We assemble today to reach the next great round in the ladder of human progress. In the midst of this display of the talent and genius of the Anglo Saxon race . . . we assemble to lay the cornerstone of a building in which the talent, genius, and inventive capacity of the negro will assume practical shape." Professor William H. Councill, a black educator from Alabama, answered graciously for his race: "Here on this spot the old master who followed Lee's tattered banners . . . sacrifices his pro-slavery ideas and builds a monument to negro fidelity and industry. . . . This opportunity given us to display what we have accomplished in our three hundred years' struggle from barbarism to industrious Christian liberty . . . is one of the bravest acts of a brave and chivalrous people." The Negro, he went on, needs "a higher industrial education" to fulfill his potential. Councill insisted that "congressional enactments can not make us a race. The race must make itself." The speech closed with a classic black rhetorical cadence of repeated pleas to "teach him" industrial skills, "teach him" respect for his own race, "teach him" respect for the law, and, alas, "teach him" Christian forbearance in the face of persecution.[16]

Away from the Negro Building and its exhibits of industrial education was Vanity Fair, a row of amusement shows and rides. Along with the Cyclorama of the Battle of Gettysburg, one of the leading attractions was the Old Plantation, an "improved" version of a similar show put on at the Atlanta Exposition two years earlier and said to be "an exact reproduction of an old plantation 'befo' de wah.'" Inside was a

Figure 53. The Negro Building, Tennessee Centennial Exposition, 1897. Its displays of black industrial skills promised a prosperous if subservient role for blacks in the New South. Tennessee State Library and Archives.

caricature of the "sunny side of olden times," for the nostalgic enjoy-
ment of older southern whites and the wonder of "those who had only
heard so much of the old ante-bellum day, but had never had an opportunity of enjoying their fun and frolic. . . ." The Negroes in the Old Plantation "were, to all appearances, genuine plantation darkies. . . . There
were pickaninnies with their woolly and white-headed grandmas, young
bucks and thick lipped African maidens, and happy as a big sunflower,
they danced the old-time breakdowns, which were joined in by all the
negroes with weird and guttural sounds to the accompaniment of the
scraping of the fiddle and the old banjo." Crap games, camp meeting
scenes, cake walks "were enjoyed by Northerners and Southerners alike."
Reporters were also amused by the "country negroes" and the elderly
blacks "from the old school," who seemed to verify the whites' image of ignorant, deliriously happy darkies who survived from the Old
South.[17]

The humorous vein of these reports was racist and condescending,
to be sure. But their purpose was quite the contrary, for these childlike
blacks were depicted as relics of a bygone era, superseded by the aspiring Negro of the New South who sought education, prosperity, and dignity. Herman Justi's *Official History of the Exposition* summarized the
promise of this New South Negro: "Here both Southern man and negro,
in the natural order of things, must always remain; and this being so,
they must work together in building up the South in wealth, power,
and influence. It is to the interest of the white race of the South that
the negro should be prosperous. . . ."[18]

The exposition seemed to promise that material progress would
ultimately be the answer to all social problems in the South, and it
sought above all to show how that progress might be achieved. In the
Commerce, Agriculture, Machinery, and Transportation buildings the
"object lessons" of progress were articulated clearly. In all these exhibits
there was an effort to show the remarkable recent strides in technology. Thus, a mule-drawn cotton press outside the Agriculture Building
could stand in "striking contrast" to the mechanized round bale cotton
press driven by steam. The Machinery Building contained a revolving
exhibit of modern devices: precision gear cutters, automatic brick
makers, telephones, electric looms, and gasoline engines. Steam boilers
and electric dynamos drove huge flywheels and belts which, in turn,
propelled the machines in the exhibit. Electric lights were strung by
the thousands on every major building and fountain, to the wonder-
ment of evening visitors.[19]

The new technology was celebrated with a naive innocence denied
to twentieth-century Americans. The exposition visitors saw machines
and energy as the new slaves of mankind. Machines would eliminate
drudgery and enhance productivity and leisure in the future. The startling progress of the past few decades was only the beginning; every

sector of the economy, every part of life itself, might be improved by science, and progress only awaited the genius of the new age to discover the necessary technology.

Alongside the displays of technological progress were exhibits of the bountiful resources that nature provided. Such exhibits had a strong appeal to New South promoters, who saw their region as one of virtually unlimited and untapped reserves of forest products, minerals, and agricultural products. A whole building was set aside for minerals and forestry exhibits. In addition, the southern railroads were particularly keen on advertising the opportunities available to northern capitalists to invest in the development of these resources in the South. Joseph Killebrew, a leading advocate for the New South idea in Tennessee, made the case emphatically in the exhibit he designed for the NC&StL. Filling 10,000 square feet of floor space in the Terminal Building were specimens of all the products, natural and man-made, that could be found in the company's territory: crops of every kind, soil samples, phosphates, and other minerals—all typical of "the marvelous undeveloped resources of the South."[20]

Nature and technology demanded the education of people who would exploit these resources and increase the material prosperity of the South. The exposition was itself a step toward educating visitors to the region's possibilities. But, it was clear, the new technology and ever-changing conditions of modern life required permanent institutions to transmit the necessary knowledge and values to the coming generations. Nashville's several colleges, along with the state's public and Catholic schools, were given their own display space in the Hygiene and Education Building. The emphasis in all was on "the practical character" of knowledge. Science, medicine, and engineering were shown for their utilitarian value in enlarging the welfare of the state and region.

Against this cult of the practical the exposition also gave a special place to art, music, and history. The Parthenon, a striking scale reproduction of the original in Athens, stood proudly in the center of the exposition grounds to serve as the Fine Arts Building. Though filled with an impressive collection of paintings and sculpture, the building itself became the chief object of admiration. It evoked a long-standing identification of the Old South with ancient Greece, a civilization built on slavery, and, of course, it embodied Nashville's aspirations as the "Athens of the South." The Parthenon was designed as the central symbol of the exposition, the standard for other architectural designs to emulate in scale and beauty. The Parthenon, in the eyes of one approving observer, proved that Nashville's and the South's traditions of art and poetry had not been swept away in the New South's tide of industrial spirit. "The Parthenon, after all, was the heart of the matter. At Nashville a splendid record of business ability centered about the most beautiful of works of art." In a fascinating comparison of the "Teutonic" North and the "Celtic" South, this theme was elaborated: "In the South, if anywhere, remains a flowering of Celticism, or romance, or poetry . . . . And seeing, therefore, how much we need such flowering, one delights to think that the exhaltation of the Parthenon at Nashville was no mere accident, rather that it is the symbol of a great recovery in American life, a reinstatement of Art at the Crown of Commerce. . . ."[21]

History, too would receive its due amid the celebration of modern technology. But here the homage to the southern past had to be carefully subordinated to the exposition's overriding purpose of furthering the reconciliation of North and South. Like all the industrial expositions in the New South, the Tennessee Centennial was designed to display to northerners the South's eagerness to catch up to northern standards of progress and to reassure capitalists that their investments would never again be threatened by secession or civil strife. The task was not to suppress or repudiate the past but to render it harmless, to embalm it with a thick "syrup of romanticism," to relegate it to the shelf with antiquities devoid of ideological force.[22]

The Department of History was assigned, appropriately enough, to Gates P. Thruston, a former Union general who had made Nashville his home after the war. The History Building, erected just south of the Parthenon, was a small but elegant replica of the Erectheum, which shared the Acropolis with the Parthenon in ancient Greece as well. Inside, the Tennessee Historical Society displayed relics and manuscripts from the state's early history. The Ladies Hermitage Association sponsored an exhibit of the Old Hero's personal effects and portraits. The "patriotic ladies" of the Colonial Dames and the Daughters of the American Revolution put up their own display of antiquities honoring national heroes. In the north wing of the History Building the Confederate Memorial Association, an organization of women devoted to raising monuments to the Lost Cause, set up an exhibit of mementos of the "late war," as it was tactfully referred to. Just opposite, in the south wing, the Grand Army of the Republic had its own display, reassuring the northern visitor "that his side of the story of the war was well and justly recognized at the Tennessee Centennial."[23]

Surely the most poignant moment of the exposition came in June with Confederate Veteran's Day. An estimated 16,000 veterans and their families came to Nashville for the eighth annual convention of southern survivors of the war. The Confederates packed the Union Gospel Tabernacle to hear stirring welcoming addresses by Tennessee dignitaries. Outside they formed a huge procession with twenty-eight divisions that moved out West End Avenue toward the exposition grounds over two miles away. The United Daughters of the Confederacy and the Sons of the Confederacy brought up the rear. The veterans, many dressed in their threadbare gray uniforms, were drenched in a sudden rain, but with "true Southern grit" they marched on. A near mutiny occurred among some of the more foot-weary old men after they had taken refreshments at Vanderbilt University, but spirits rallied with the reminder that gate receipts for the day would go to the Confederate Memorial Association. They marched on to the exposition.

The veterans crowded into the auditorium as the band played "Dixie." On the stage the Confederate stars and bars stood beside the stars and stripes. These "solemn circuses," as historian C. Vann Woodward characterized the New South expositions, were never complete without the obligatory reconciliation of the Blue and Gray. The crowd listened to maudlin speeches testifying that the Confederate veteran was now all the more an American patriot for having fought the Lost Cause. It fell to Governor Robert Love Taylor, a renowned southern orator, to cap the day with a stream of purple prose that neatly married the Lost Cause to the New South industrial spirit. "I doubt if the world will ever see another civilization as brilliant as that which perished in the South a third of a century ago. Its white-columned mansions under cool spreading groves . . . and its cotton-fields stretching away to the horizon, alive with toiling slaves . . . ; its pomp and pride and revelry; its splendid manhood and the dazzling beauty of its women, placed it as the high tide of earthly glory." The Old South, Taylor confirmed, had died in the late war, but not the southern spirit. "Look yonder at those flashing domes and glittering spires . . . . Look what Southern brains and Southern hands have wrought. See the victories of peace we have won, all represented within the white columns of our great industrial exposition, and you will receive an inspiration of the Old South, and you will catch glimpses of her future glory. . . . The hand of secession will never be lifted again."[24] In these moments the Tennessee Centennial exposition offered a revealing exhibit of the New South's struggle to make peace between the new icons of industrial progress, racial harmony, and sectional reconciliation and the old ghosts of the southern past.

The exposition had been a stirring experience for Nashville. Planned and executed by local talent, it constituted a cooperative enterprise unprecedented in its magnitude. It publicized to millions of visitors and readers of newspapers and magazines the "Nashville spirit"—the city's commitment to industrial and social progress in the New South. It showed, also, how careful planning of landscape and architecture could produce an aesthetically unified, beautiful environment (even if it was a bit garish at the extremes). Most important, the exposition experience helped the organizers understand the powers of cooperation and scientific planning and encouraged them to apply those lessons to the society outside the gates of Centennial City. For years after the exposition closed the board of directors met annually to celebrate their accomplishment and review its impact. The yearly event was but one of many less tangible signs that the exposition had changed the city's consciousness.

MAYOR HEAD AND BUSINESS PROGRESSIVISM

The exposition also coincided with the end of a long, severe depression. During the depression American businessmen, following the lead of the railroads, reorganized small local firms into large regional corporations and either merged with competitors or organized monopolies by forming holding companies or trusts. Nashville's counterparts of these national business leaders saw the large, modern corporation at once as a model for city government and as a threat to local autonomy. Their prescription for the social and political ills of the city was large-scale, hierarchical organization, rational planning, and efficient use of resources through the application of business principles to city government and social services.

"Business progressivism," as historian George Tindall labeled it, generally stressed the more conservative side of reform. These men wanted to improve the efficiency of city government and urban services by remodeling government structure in the image of the modern corporation. A corollary of this philosophy was that businessmen like themselves should run the city, either directly as officeholders or indirectly through their commercial associations and civic clubs. As they often put it, with no hint of apology, they wanted the "best people" in the city to govern it. The existing system of politics too often allowed corrupt, self-serving ward heelers and city bosses to rule by virtue of their willingness to cater to the lowest common denominator of public desire. These old-line politicos, in the eyes of the progressives, used power only to perpetuate themselves in office through patronage and protection and had no broader vision of the city's potential for progress in the modern age.

Nashville was already well along the road of government reform with the city charter of 1883 and the measures of 1889–90, which restricted black and lower-class voting. Since 1889, when these voting "reforms" went into effect, Nashville's local government, particularly the office of mayor and the Board of Public Works, had been dominated by Democratic businessmen. Mayor Charles P. McCarver, elected in 1889, was a businessman and farmer who resigned from the mayor's office in order to return to his business. William Litterer, his successor, was Nashville's first German-born mayor, a longtime member of the City Council, and a successful wholesale drug merchant, flour mill owner, and bank and telephone company director. George B. Guild, elected in 1891 and again in 1893, was a lawyer from Gallatin. William M. McCarthy, elected in 1895, was the only mayor since Kercheval (last elected in 1887) who was not a regular Democrat. McCarthy represented the American Protective Association (APA), a stridently anti-Catholic "reform" movement dedicated to "good government." McCarthy was cut from the same cloth as the other businessmen and was a successful insurance agent and former cashier at Fourth National Bank. Richard Houston Dudley retrieved the office of mayor for regular Democrats in 1897. He was the patriarch of the illustrious Dudley family and a wealthy wholesale grocer and hardware merchant, a partner in Gray-Dudley Hardware, the leading firm in its line.[25]

None of these businessmen-politicians personified the spirit of progressive reform better than James M. Head, who served from 1899 through 1903 as one of Nashville's most outstanding mayors. Born to a prominent Summer County family in 1855, Head attended school in Gallatin and came to Nashville as a young man to read law with John J. Vertrees, the unofficial kingmaker of Democratic politics in Nashville.[26] Head went on to Harvard law school, and after graduation in 1876 he returned to Gallatin to practice law. He soon entered state politics as a representative in the General Assembly (1880–83) and began to build a prosperous Nashville law practice in the firm of Champion and Head. Head married the daughter of William H. Cherry, a prominent industrialist (and Republican!) and settled into a respected position among Nashville's leading families. In 1895, after a brief stint as publisher of the *American,* Head became a major promoter of the Centennial Exposition, which he served as director.[27]

In the city election of 1899 Head seemed the ideal businessman's candidate for mayor. He was a vigorous, earnest man with all the qualifications of a progressive reformer. A new city charter enacted in 1899 gave the mayor expanded powers of appointment including members of the Board of Education, the Board of Health, and the Fire and Police commissions. It provided for popular election of the Board of Public Works and other key city officials. The new charter also returned to ward-level elections for councilmen. This tradition, abandoned in 1883, must have seemed safer to reformers now that much of the black and lower-class vote had been eliminated by restrictive voting laws. Moreover, all new franchises or amendments to existing franchises granted by the city to utility companies were to be approved by popular vote. This provision was in response to a growing fear that utility corporations and railroads were unfairly exploiting Nashville and interfering in local politics to protect their interests. The charter reforms of 1899 opened the way to a major battle with these corporations in the progressive era.[28] The *Banner* applauded the new charter and predicted: "the spirit of reform should pervade the community, and the determination should be general to place only the best men in office."[29]

The new charter provided that all incumbents were to be swept

Figure 54. James M. Head (1855–1930), mayor of Nashville, 1899–1903, an opponent of monopolies and advocate of municipal ownership of public utilities. Chamber of Commerce, *Nashville in the 20th Century* (Nashville, 1900).

from office in the coming election. In the election for mayor, Head won handily over George S. Kinney, a liquor dealer who had been active in the antiprohibition battle.[30] "I sought the office of Mayor the first time," Head later recalled, "deeply impressed with the idea that municipal government . . . is largely a business enterprise, in which the masses of the people are stockholders, . . . and the city officials are merely the directors and employes [sic] for the time being to administer its affairs."[31] Mayor Head brought to his office a conviction that his municipal corporation was suffering at the hands of railroads and utility companies, which had assumed monopolistic control over the city and were not responsible to the citizen stockholder. Nashville's water supply had been under municipal control since its inception in 1834, but gas, electricity, telephones, street railways, and other urban services were all done by contract with private companies, most of which operated totally free of competition and government regulation. In 1900 the Nashville Gas Company franchise expired, and Head immediately used the power vested in him by the 1899 charter to force the company to accept a new twenty-five-year franchise with limits set on rates, an agreement to pay the city a sales tax, a 5-percent royalty on gross receipts, and recognition of the right of the city to purchase the company any time after ten years.[32]

With this franchise as a precedent, Mayor Head now set out to renegotiate franchises with the electric, telephone, and street railway companies. At this time the trolley companies were undergoing a series of mergers which led in 1899 to the consolidation of all streetcar lines, the West Nashville and the Glendale Park steam dummy lines, and the Cumberland Light and Power Company. Head stalled the consolidation in the courts, contending that the franchises granted to the old streetcar companies could not be transferred to the new consolidated company. The city forced compromises from the company, and the court settlement, issued October 1902, allowed the city the right to purchase the streetcar system in twenty years and required the company to invest $1 million in improvements, including paving the strips between and alongside the track. As part of the settlement, the company purchased the site of the Centennial Exposition, which was about to be cut up into suburban lots, and gave it to the city as a free public park. In addition, the company agreed to pay a royalty of 2 percent of gross receipts on the first $1 million, and 3 percent thereafter, to be used in maintaining city parks. Though Samuel Watkins Park predated it, this was the real beginning of Nashville's public park system, which rapidly proliferated after 1902 and remains one of the finest monuments to the Head regime.[33]

The consolidated streetcar company now controlled the Cumberland Light and Power Company, which retained its old franchise and remained the sole supplier of electric power. The company was selling power at eighteen cents per kilowatt in 1902, far above the two cents it cost to produce that power. Mayor Head attacked this monopoly with another, equally effective strategy. He proceeded to build a municipal light plant which, after its opening in September 1902, was supplying power to all of the city's public buildings and street lamps in the central city. Head made it clear the municipal power plant would begin selling power commercially in competition with Cumberland Light and Power unless matters changed. The company quickly cut its rates to twelve cents per kilowatt and even lower for some large customers. The municipal power plant continued to operate as an experiment in municipal ownership and a threat to the private company, which now became more responsive to the public.[34]

Cumberland Telephone and Telegraph was another "natural monopoly" Mayor Head tried to make serve the public of Nashville under more favorable terms. Under the management of James E. Caldwell, Cumberland Telephone had become one of the largest telephone companies in the country outside the Bell system, but Nashville's service was prohibitively expensive and unreliable. The company paid the city no royalty for the franchise it operated under and paid only a limited tax. Furthermore, as the city had expanded, a maze of telephone poles and overhead wires had become an eyesore as well as a safety hazard, and Mayor Head urged the installation of underground conduits. To force the company to terms, the city asked the state legislature to authorize a second, municipally-owned telephone or conduit company, but the company's powerful political influence helped defeat Head's strategy this time. The issue was still alive in 1905 when Luke Lea and others organized a second private telephone company, but the legislature again denied a rival company the privilege of operating.[35]

The same drive to break monopolies or make them serve the city better led Mayor Head into his battle with the L&N. It was Head who pushed the city to invest $1 million in Jere Baxter's Tennessee Central Railroad system in 1901. It was Head also who fought the L&N Terminal Company's exclusion of Baxter's railroad from Union Station.[36]

Mayor Head took business progressivism to its logical extreme by advocating municipal ownership of basic urban services. This position, popular among the more liberal progressive-era reformers, was frightening to more conservative businessmen, who denounced it as "sewer socialism." Though Head advocated the right of municipal ownership, he used the principle most often as a threat to make private corporations with "natural monopolies" serve the community better.[37]

Head's regime serves as an important benchmark in the history of government and politics in Nashville. Before this time "reform" generally meant "throw the rascals out" and pull in the reins on extravagant spending. Head gave to reform a more positive meaning. He understood municipal government as a powerful tool to improve the community, and he abandoned the laissez faire faith of the nineteenth century to use government as a regulator—if necessary, an owner—of services vital to the public welfare. Head was reelected without opposition in 1901 and probably could have been elected to a third term (despite some controversy among more conservative elements), had it not been for the charter's proscription of more than two terms. He left Nashville not long after stepping down as mayor and went to Boston, where he was engaged with a street paving company until his death in 1930. He left behind many monuments to his regime, but none so important as his vision of progress for the city through the positive expansion of government.[38]

THE TEMPERANCE CRUSADE REVIVED

Head's brand of municipal reform was quickly eclipsed by the return of the more familiar themes of moral reform. The temperance forces, languishing since their defeat in 1887, now burst into the political arena with renewed force, determined to achieve total prohibition. The Anti-Saloon League, a national organization that entered Tennessee in 1899, joined the WCTU to extend the Four-Mile Law from rural areas to town and cities of Tennessee. In 1903 the Adams Act allowed towns of up to 5,000 people to prohibit liquor if they reincorporated after the act passed.[39] Dozens of country towns voted to recharter and "go dry," so that by the middle of 1903 saloons were legal in only eleven of the state's ninety-six counties. Now the prohibition movement began to close in on the cities. In Nashville they pressed Mayor Head, an avowed "wet," to rigorously enforce laws against "Sunday tippling" and gambling. These laws were routinely flouted by working men who enjoyed their one day of leisure in a saloon drinking and playing cards or betting on horses. Eugene C. Lewis, owner of the *American* and a foe of Mayor Head's Tennessee Central Railroad policy, exploited the issue fully. Exposés of gambling and Sunday violations in such notorious male enclaves as the Southern Turf, Climax, and Utopia saloons on Cherry Street (later Fourth Avenue North) helped rally the moral elements of the community not simply in defense of temperance but of "law and order."[40]

Ira Landrith, a Cumberland Presbyterian minister and active prohibitionist, led the organization of the Committee of One Hundred, a vehicle for moral reform opposed to Head and his allies in the regular Democratic party. In the mayoral election of 1903 this group turned its support to Albert S. Williams, a banker and former supporter of the nativist APA in the 1890s, who promised to "strictly enforce the laws against gambling and Sunday tippling."[41] Williams won the primary and swept into office in the general election with strong support from native whites, especially in East Nashville and the newer wards of the city.[42] The *American* hoped Nashville would have "an end of the covenant with hell" Mayor Head had allegedly signed with the liquor interests. Under Mayor Williams the police carried out highly publicized raids on the saloons and back rooms of the Men's Quarter.[43] More raids followed during Williams's term, proving as much about the persistence of the tipplers as that of the moral reformers.

The Committee of One Hundred abandoned Williams in the election of 1905 and turned to Theodore O. "Tom" Morris, a prominent Market Street merchant and county magistrate. Morris now denounced Williams as a tool of the machine, and the reformers urged voters to put the government in control of "the best element of citizens."[44] Morris rode the "moral wave" to victory in 1905, only to discover the same frustrations his predecessor met in trying to enforce laws and moral standards that a large segment of the population simply did not respect. Morris compromised by containing and controlling vice rather than attempting to repress it altogether. In 1906 the City Council approved a controversial plan to close all saloons outside a special saloon district bordered by Broad, Twelfth Avenue, Jo Johnston, and the river.[45]

In many ways the moral segregation that took place in 1906 underlined the growing conflict between the inner city and the suburban fringe. During the "Greater Nashville" movement, prior to the annexation of 1905, there was strong resistance from temperance advocates in West Nashville, Belmont Heights, Waverly Place, and Lockland and Eastland in East Nashville, who feared the invasion of Nashville's saloons after the city boundaries expanded.[46] Once annexation was completed in 1905, Nashville's temperance forces were bolstered by suburban voters, and it was, in large part, their pressure that led to the tight moral corridor of segregated saloons and vice in 1906.

But this pragmatic solution only annoyed those who wanted no compromise with the "whiskey devil." In 1907 the state Pendleton Act, introduced by Davidson County Senator I.L. Pendleton, extended the Four-Mile Law to cities up to 150,000 population if they voted to reincorporate under the terms of the new law. "The time is ripe," proclaimed the Nashville WCTU. "Let us . . . join the procession of free cities redeemed from the curse of rum."[47] Knoxville voted "dry" along with many smaller cities, but Nashville seemed content with its noble compromise. In 1907 the city gave an overwhelming vote to mayoral candidate James S. Brown, a former law partner of James M. Head, who promised no further changes in Nashville's liquor laws.[48]

It took a martyr's death in 1908 to shift the moral tide in favor of total prohibition in Tennessee. Edward Ward Carmack was in many ways an unlikely candidate for martyrdom to temperance. His stormy career as politician and newspaper editor began in Nashville in the

1880s, when he worked for the *American* and his own paper, the *Democrat*. Carmack was notable in these years for his opposition to the prohibition movement of 1887, and he "mercilessly ridiculed" temperance candidates.[49] He went to Memphis in 1892 and, as editor of the *Commercial Appeal,* began his gravitation to the cause by criticizing the influence of the liquor interests in state politics. He was elected congressman from Memphis in 1896 and U.S. senator in 1901. In his bid for reelection in 1906 against Robert Love Taylor, Carmack tried to turn the growing public sentiment for prohibition to his advantage. Former governor Taylor had signed the Four-Mile Law of 1887 and supported the prohibition amendment Carmack had opposed. Taylor effectively exposed Carmack's hypocrisy and beat him in the Democratic primary election, leaving Carmack to blame the liquor conspiracy for his defeat.[50]

When Carmack announced as candidate for governor against incumbent Malcolm Patterson in the election of 1908, some still had good cause to question his sincerity as a prohibitionist, but he made it the central issue of a hard-hitting campaign. In Nashville the contest was especially fervid. Luke Lea, who two years earlier had helped swing the nomination to Patterson, now turned his newspaper, the *Tennessean,* into a rabid pro-Carmack prohibitionist organ. The *American,* owned by Eugene C. Lewis, who preferred Patterson's friendly policy toward the L&N, was no less vituperative in its opposition to Carmack.[51]

The campaign reached a new low in Tennessee politics. The prohibitionists sought to link an "obscene label" on Levy's gin bottles with the alleged rape of a white girl by a black man. The Reverend H.M. DuBose, in the *Tennessean,* explained that the label depicted a scantily clad white woman with "pointed insinuations, too vile to be even thought upon." "This gin, with its label, has made more black rape fiends, and has procured the outrage of more white women in the south than all other agencies combined. It is sold with the promise that it will bring white virtue into the black brute's power."[52] The *Tennessean* followed with alarming articles warning that Nashville women were not safe so long as Levy's gin was being sold to Negroes. The "Negro problem," it went on, ". . . could never be solved without prohibition." "The negro fairly docile and industrious, becomes, when filled with liquor, turbulent and dangerous and a menace to life, property, and the repose of the community."[53] The "Negro problem," it seemed, had not been solved by taking away the right to vote; now reformers must take away the right to drink as well.

Carmack narrowly lost the primary and retired in bitterness to the editorship of Lea's *Tennessean.* His vitriolic editorials against Patterson and his close advisor, Colonel Duncan B. Cooper, descended to sharp ad hominem attacks. Carmack's personal ridicule of "Baldheaded Dunc" began during the heat of the campaign, but they only intensified after

Carmack's defeat. Colonel Duncan, a private citizen with no official connection to Governor Patterson, felt he should not be subject to such strident criticism. Besides, Cooper had been mentor to young Carmack when he came to work on the *American*. A Confederate veteran from a distinguished Tennessee family, Cooper was a southerner from the old school who could not allow his family name to be publicly dishonored without demanding satisfaction. He sent his friend Edwin B. Craig to warn Carmack that another scurrilous attack on him would be the last. Carmack answered the next day, November 9, 1908, with an editorial filled with "ugly allusions" to Cooper's role in the Patterson campaign.[54]

Both men carried pistols that day. Robin Cooper, the colonel's son, was worried that his elderly father's crippled right hand would make him an easy mark in a duel. He packed his own pistol and accompanied the old man that morning. Mutual friends tried to effect a reconciliation, and it looked as though they had succeeded until Duncan and Robin Cooper accidentally met Carmack near the corner of Union and Seventh Avenue. According to one account from a friend of the Coopers, the colonel started to cross Seventh Avenue to speak man-to-man to his adversary when Carmack drew a pistol and stepped behind a passing woman, using her as a shield. Cooper called him a coward, and the woman, seeing the pistol, fled in alarm. Carmack then ran forward behind two telephone poles and fired his gun, hitting Robin Cooper, who sprang forward to shield his father. Robin, wounded in the shoulder, charged Carmack (who fired a second shot and missed) and pumped three bullets into him at close range. Carmack fell dead instantly.

Luke Lea's *Tennessean* told the story differently. Headlines the next day announced, "SENATOR CARMACK IS SHOT DOWN IN COLD BLOOD." A "premeditated murder," "a dastardly crime without parallel," the *Tennessean* screamed. It was the Coopers who fired first, and Carmack in his dying act managed to return fire, wounding his assassin.[55] The trial dragged on for two months, and the *Tennessean* took every opportunity to turn it to the advantage of the temperance crusade.

Because his wounds were instantly fatal, it is more plausible that Carmack fired first, though he may have done so in what he perceived to be self-defense. But the facts of the case are far less important historically than the symbolic meaning attached to the Cooper-Carmack duel. The Coopers were found guilty of second-degree murder and sentenced to twenty years each in prison. After the state Supreme Court reversed Robin Cooper's conviction, Duncan Cooper was pardoned by Governor Patterson. By that time the pardon only fueled the flames of a temperance wildfire.

Carmack was instantly inducted into martyrdom in the temperance crusade. His funeral in Ryman Auditorium drew 7,000 mourners, who sang hymns, listened to temperance speeches, and resolved to vindicate their fallen hero's cause. A long eulogy by Grantland Rice in the *Tennessean* ended with a poetic flourish that signaled as well as anything the new fervor of the teetotalers:

> The Chief is Fallen! But the Flag
> In rippling roll
> Waves proudly, let no Trooper lag
> Of stalwart soul;
> Up! Boot and Saddle! To the Fray!
> And in the mad, wild charge today
> God pity him who blocks the way
> Or bars the goal!

By January 1909 the "mad, wild charge" led the state legislature to pass a statewide prohibition bill over Governor Patterson's veto. Women in the gallery sang the Doxology and afterward held a memorial service at the site of Carmack's death. Plans were laid to erect a statue to the fallen hero on the Capitol grounds.[56] Just before Nashville's saloon doors officially closed on July 1, 1909, local temperance forces held a thanksgiving service at McKendree Methodist Church. Hundreds of others, no less reverently, thronged to the saloons along Fourth Avenue North to enjoy their last legal glass of whiskey or beer for about three decades.[57] The crusade, at last, was victorious, and the infidels, along with the whiskey devil, had been routed from Nashville and all of Tennessee, or so it seemed to the reformers in the summer of 1909.

THE RISE OF HILARY HOWSE

The moral reformers, by carrying prohibition into the city, had finally created the conditions necessary to sustain a political machine organized to protect its constituents from enforcement. At the head of this political organization was Hilary Howse, a colorful city boss who was to dominate Nashville's politics for most of the next three decades beginning in 1909.

Like so many of his constituents, Howse was a country boy, born in Rutherford County in 1866. He left his father's farm in 1884, and at the age of eighteen he came to Nashville with three borrowed dimes in his pocket and little else. He began work in a furniture store for three dollars a week. Howse was big brother to three sisters and two brothers, all of whom he brought to Nashville and helped set up in jobs. About 1900 he and his brother Kai opened the Howse Brothers and Company furniture store.

Howse was a gregarious fellow who was naturally drawn to the camaraderie of politics. With his robust build, derby hat, bright red vest,

Figure 55. Hilary Howse (1866–1938), mayor of Nashville 1909–15, 1923–38, a professional political boss, opponent of prohibition, friend of the poor, black and white, and an effective social reformer. Tennessee State Library and Archives.

and black mustache, he looked every inch an urban political boss. He began as a member from the old Sixth Ward (downtown between Cherry and Vine) on the County Democratic Executive Committee. By 1900 he was elected to the County Court, where he took credit for the construction of two new bridges across the Cumberland River and the planning for the county tuberculosis hospital completed in 1910.

In 1905 he ran successfully as a Democratic regular for the state Senate and was reelected in 1909. Howse had become a popular and powerful leader of the Davidson County delegation by this time. In 1905 he led an unsuccessful fight against the repeal of the law allowing betting on horse racing, an issue dear to the hearts of the Cumberland Park crowd. In 1908 he backed Malcolm Patterson in the gubernatorial race against Carmack and became clearly identified with the anti-prohibition forces. Indeed, Howse, a young bachelor, was known as quite a carouser among his constituents in the Fourth Avenue saloons. "Protect 'em?," he once said of his friends in the saloon business, "I do better than that. I patronize 'em!"[58]

Howse ran for mayor in 1909, appealing to the widespread resentment toward prohibition, particularly among working-class people. "As for whiskey," he later claimed, "I am not a drinking man, but as long as I stay in a free country I will eat and drink as I please."[59] A three-way race in the Democratic primary pitted Howse against Dr. Isaac Newton Hyde, a physician who stressed strict-enforcement and anti-Catholicism in his campaign, and the incumbent mayor, James S. Brown. Brown also ran on a law enforcement platform, and to prove his point he directed the police in a barrage of liquor violation arrests just before the election. Brown made the choice clear to voters: "The question for you to consider is . . . are you in favor of law enforcement — or are you in favor of a wide open town?"[60]

The answer came in an avalanche of votes for Hilary Howse, who took every ward and 75 percent of the total vote.[61] In the general election Howse trounced independent candidate Charles D. Johns, former sheriff and strong advocate of enforcing prohibition. Howse took 64 percent of the vote and lost only four of twenty-five wards, all in suburban areas of East Nashville and Belmont.[62]

With a popular mandate against enforcement of prohibition, Howse allowed the saloons and gambling to continue operations. It was not truly "wide open," but patrons could enter the Fourth Avenue watering holes by way of back entrances on Printers Alley. Howse freely admitted that the liquor laws were not enforced because, he explained, the "great majority of the people" of Nashville opposed the laws.[63] There were arrests made by city police and county sheriffs, but the grand jury usually refused to indict the liquor violators.[64]

A whole underground network of liquor dealers, bootleggers, saloon keepers, and their patrons now had a vested interest in keeping Howse in power. Beneath Howse were a number of ward-level politicos who made the so-called machine work on an everyday personal level. Tom Ryan, an Irish wholesale liquor dealer, Gus Blodau, a North Nashville druggist, Ed Glennon, a saloon keeper in the Eighth Ward, Charlie Fahey, an Irish ward heeler, were some of the grassroots lieutenants in Howse's machine. Saloons, always important political centers in a masculine electorate, now took on added importance during the Howse era.[65]

The Howse machine was more than just a constellation of the "liquor interests" and the "tipplers" who patronized them. From the beginning of his political career Howse reached out to the poor, black and white. He extended new government welfare services to his people, dispensed charity and small favors with buckets of coal or boxes of groceries, and mobilized them on election day when they voiced their gratitude with their votes. Black citizens who had been shunned or excluded as voters since the late 1880s now responded to a political machine that needed their votes.

Hilary Howse is best understood as part of the tradition of urban liberalism that characterized the ethnic big city bosses of the Northeast in this period.[66] He saw government as a positive force to improve the health, education, and welfare of the poor and the ethnic and racial minorities who supported him. His policies were the product of no articulate theory of government. They were simply the response of genuine charity and shrewd politics (they were never far apart in Howse's mind) in the face of brutal conditions of poverty, disease, and discrimination in the inner city. In contrast to the business progressives who stressed efficiency and economy in government and sought to reform the structure of government in the image of the business corporation, Howse was a social reformer who expanded government liberally to meet the needs of his people and kept government in check when it interfered in the people's private behavior.[67]

Howse's 1909 platform included promises to improve public parks and playgrounds and to clean up Black Bottom. After his election he sparked a citywide voluntary clean-up campaign in 1910 and 1911. He made publicized visits to black neighborhoods in North Nashville and praised efforts to improve the homes and yards there. [68] He sponsored four free health dispensaries and several milk stations in the poor neighborhoods of the inner city and a major addition to the city hospital. He promised to improve the schools, calling for higher salaries for teachers and free textbooks for students, and he promoted the construction of the New High School (later called Hume-Fogg High School, after two of the city's eminent educators).[69]

Howse's reliance on black voters led him to extend a number of political favors that were as important for their symbolic recognition as they were for the practical improvements of conditions in the black community. Prior to 1915 Howse promoted the establishment of a

Figure 56. During Hilary Howse's early years the poor saw new efforts to alleviate their plight. Here a public health nurse poses with a slum family in 1912.

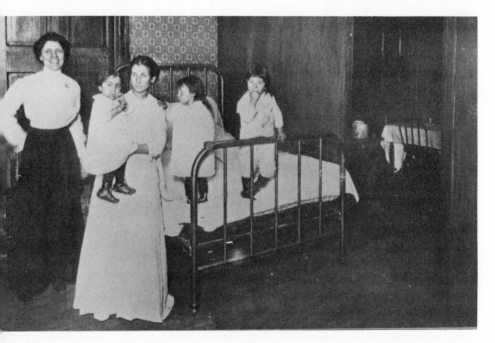

Figure 57. The same family after the nurse has sanitized the apartment.

Figure 58. Health examination day at a city–sponsored milk station, 1912.

Figure 59. Public health nurses demonstrating baby care to the Little Mother's Club, 1912. All four prints from *Annual Reports of the Departments of the City of Nashville, 1912* (Nashville, 1913).

county hospital to treat tuberculosis (a disease that afflicted blacks disproportionately), the Carnegie Branch Library for Negroes in North Nashville, Tennessee Agricultural and Industrial Normal School for Negroes (later Tennessee State University), and Hadley Park, the first public park for blacks in any American city.[70] At the Hadley Park dedication on the Fourth of July in 1912 Howse promised a "fair and square deal" for blacks and whites by his administration.[71] When Howse attended the dedication of George W. Hubbard Hospital at Meharry in 1910, Richard H. Boyd spoke of how the Negroes of Nashville "love and respect Mayor Howse for being so broad. . . . He is the Mayor of all the people, white and black."[72]

For the first time since the 1880s black political power in Nashville was being recognized, cultivated, and rewarded. In the election of 1911 the Howse ticket included Solomon Parker Harris, candidate from the heavily black Third Ward in North Nashville. Harris was the first viable black candidate for City Council since James C. Napier had been elected in 1883. Parker and the entire Howse ticket swept to victory in 1911. Howse's opponent in the mayoral race, William C. Gillespie, a dentist who ran on a strong law-and-order platform, won majorities in seven wards, all in suburban areas of East and South Nashville. But Howse piled up huge majorities in the inner-city wards, especially in the heavily black wards.[73] "But for this large negro vote cast for Mayor Howse," the *Banner* complained after the election, "Dr. Gillespie would have been elected mayor."[74]

It was true, and Howse understood his obligations. The key black wards—the Third, Fourth, and Eighth wards in North Nashville, the Twelfth Ward (Black Bottom), the Fourteenth (Trimble Bottom) and Sixteenth (Waverly) all in South Nashville, along with wards Nine, Thirteen, and Nineteen (Crappy Shoot in East Nashville)—gave him 2,122 votes in 1909, or 35 percent of his total vote. In 1911 those same wards delivered 3,172 votes for Howse, amounting to 42 percent of his total vote. The shift was not in the proportion of voters in the wards favoring Howse (about 74 percent of the voters in these wards favored Howse in 1909, 72 percent in 1911), but in the surge of additional voters turning out at the polls. Of the 12,395 males of voting age identified in these wards in the federal census of 1910, only 23 percent turned out in 1909, but in 1911 35 percent voted, enough to boost Howse's share by over 1,000 votes, approximately his margin of victory.[75]

Opponents of the machine complained about police dragging black voters from saloons to register them or take them to the polls. If these accounts exaggerated the element of coercion, they no doubt accurately portrayed a machine made up of dozens of loyal Howse appointees willing to do what was necessary to keep their man in office. Ironically, some of the very devices intended to restrict black and lower-class voting now played into the hands of Howse's machine. Preelection registra-

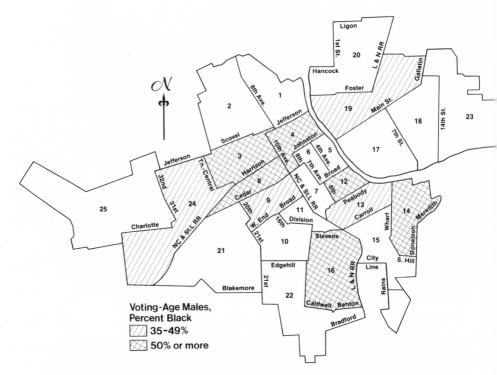

Figure 60. Nashville Wards and Racial Densities, 1910. Adapted from James F. Blumstein and Benjamin Walter, ed., *Growing Metropolis: Aspects of Development in Nashville* (Nashville, 1975), 25. Population data from U.S. Bureau of the Census, *Thirteenth Census of the United States . . . 1910; Abstract . . . Supplement for Tennessee* (Washington, D.C., 1913), 616.

tion requirements, poll taxes, and the secret ballot all required a highly organized political machine with dozens of volunteers to recruit registrants and the use of generous funds to pay the poll tax, and perhaps a little more to reward the voter's loyalty. Unlike most of Nashville's businessmen-reformers, who rotated in and out of office after a term, Howse was a career politician who was willing to invest the effort necessary to build a sustained, grassroots organization.

The reelection of Howse and the reentry of a black man into the City Council in 1911 led businessmen-reformers to devise new strategies to defeat the machine and dilute black political power. This time it was the commission form of city government. First adopted in Galveston, Texas, after a devastating hurricane in 1900, the commission plan became the ultimate model for businesslike government and was widely copied by medium-sized cities in the South and across the country. By 1913 Memphis, Knoxville, Chattanooga, and Lebanon had all adopted a version of the plan. Businessmen in the Board of Trade and the Commercial Club had been advocating commission government since 1907. They sponsored legislation in 1911 to bring it to Nashville but were unsuccessful.[76]

Their opportunity came unexpectedly slightly after midnight on November 5, 1912. It was a disaster, not unlike that which inspired commission government in Galveston, but Nashville's was man-made. The wall of the city reservoir gave way that night, and 25 million gallons of water gushed down on the homes and buildings around Eighth Avenue South. Leaks had been reported earlier but city officials had not responded, and the investigations that followed led only to a round of finger-pointing among the members of the Board of Public Works, department heads, and the mayor.[77] The business and professional leaders in the Board of Trade took full advantage of the public outrage by pointing out the lack of centralized authority and accountability in the present system of government. They brought in an expert consultant from New York, held public meetings, and drew up a new city charter implementing the commission plan.[78]

Under the commission plan Nashville would be governed by five commissioners, each with specific administrative functions: the mayor would be in charge of the Department of Public Affairs, Police and Health; another commissioner would be responsible for Finance, Lights and the Market House; another for streets, sewers, and sidewalks; another for Fire, Sprinkling, and Building Inspection; and one for Waterworks, Street Cleaning, and the Workhouse. All would have staggered four-year terms and be paid a full-time salary.[79] The City Council, with its ward-based representatives, would be altogether eliminated, for the commissioners would have legislative as well as executive powers. Citywide elections of commissioners would also reduce the likelihood that men like Solomon P. Harris, or other machine candidates, would be elected to office. "There is no odor of politics" in the commission plan, the Commercial Club *Tattler* claimed. By this plan "we are able to place our municipal affairs in the hands of responsible men—men with executive ability—not those who merely control a large number of votes."[80]

The dreams of a depoliticized, businesslike city government could be fulfilled only in the rough-and-tumble arena of politics, however. The bill fashioned by the Board of Trade was passed on the first and second readings with no major alterations. Hilary Howse, recognizing the tide of opinion in favor of charter reform, seemed to offer no resistance, and in his 1912 message he commended "the thoughtful attention of the greatest minds of the twentieth century civilization" to the search for "more efficient, economical and businesslike management" of municipal government.[81] But as senator from Davidson County in the state legislature Howse could influence the final form of the bill. At the third reading a substitute bill, apparently devised by Howse and his supporters, was passed instead of the Board of Trade bill.

During its passage through the General Assembly there was much confusion over the details of the charter bill and its various amendments, and the Board of Trade lost control over the final product. The board opposed inclusion of the Hospital Commission under Civil Service and the popular election of the city judge but chose in the end not to hold up commission government over these details. But the new charter that was approved had other provisions that were of much greater importance, though they drew little attention at the time. Under the previous charter Mayor Howse would have been ineligible for a third term, but the final version of the new charter allowed anyone to run for office. Furthermore, it allowed two members of the Board of Public Works, J. Morgan Wilkerson and J.D. Alexander, to continue their terms until 1915 and 1917. This left only three of the five commissioners to be elected in the first election under the new charter and insured at least some continuation of the "old government."[82]

The election of 1913 promised to be a major showdown between the machine and reformers. No sooner was the new charter passed than Howse and other members of the "old government" (Lyle Andrews, George Stainback, and Charles Cohn) announced for election to the Board of Commissioners.[83] Running against Howse in the primary election were two reform candidates. M. Henry Meeks, a lawyer and judge, headed the "Citizens Ticket" with the backing of Eugene C. Lewis and his newspaper, the *Democrat*. Meeks had the support of many prominent businessmen, but his candidacy was tainted by his connection with Lewis and the L&N railroad, which was highly unpopular at this time. Furthermore, Meeks's solution to the liquor question was a return to the segregated saloon district of 1906, which was both illegal under prohibition and morally untenable to the majority of reformers.[84]

Most reformers rallied around Noah Cooper, a lawyer, whose "Home

Defenders" ticket made powerful emotional appeals to protect the home and family from the vice that Howse represented. It was a campaign devoted less to ideals of businesslike efficiency than to moralistic pleas to defend the middle-class family against the saloon. "Good Business Against Bad," Cooper's campaign slogan proclaimed. "Anglo-Saxons for two thousand years have fought to protect the home. . . . Now we have a battle on as great as that against the British or the Indians. It is a battle against the devil and all his works in Nashville."[85] A cartoon published on the eve of the election showed Cooper with shield and sword in hand in front of "The Home" fending off the sinister hand of vice. "The Best Men of Nashville Will Elect Noah W. Cooper Mayor Because He Will Guard Their Homes and Children," the caption promised.[86] The *Banner* and *Tennessean* both swung their influence behind Cooper and issued a barrage of attacks against Meeks as an L&N puppet and tool of the liquor interests and against Howse as evil incarnate.

The Howse machine rose to the challenge of citywide elections and voter registration before the primary and general elections. Reformers complained about the use of police in registering black voters and the use of "saloon money" to recruit voters and pay their poll tax. The *Banner* ran an alarming story on the registration of black railroad workers with headlines that screamed, "Itinerant Negroes Will Hold Balance of Power."[87] "Throughout every negro ward in Nashville there has been a phenomenal increase in registration over that of two years ago," the *Banner* warned.[88] Howse ran campaign advertisements boasting of his accomplishments: a new high school, new parks, streets and sewers improved, and a noticeable improvement in public health—for the first time in Nashville's history births exceeded deaths.

A large advertisement in the *Globe* reminded black voters of Howse's favors to their race. It listed the new park, library, state normal school, tuberculosis hospital, along with other benefits for blacks, all credited to Howse. The mayor, it added, has "given more than his salary to the poor people" and through his administration "more than 5,000 colored people have been given relief in the way of clothes, fuel, medicine or provisions."[89]

On election day Howse took 52 percent of a record vote and thereby avoided a runoff in the general election. Lyle Andrews, with the "old government" on the Board of Public Works, easily won his bid for commissioner of finance. Of the "old government" candidates, only George Stainback, blamed for the reservoir disaster of 1912, was forced into a runoff and defeated by Citizens Ticket candidate Robert Elliott. Howse again scored heavily in the densely black and inner-city working-class wards, while Cooper and Meeks appealed to suburban wards in East and West Nashville.[90]

There were cries of fraud and bribery and threats to challenge the election. "Money won the day," Cooper accused, "but morals will win

TOMORROW IS THE DAY
BE ON GUARD

The Best Men of Nashville Will Elect
NOAH W. COOPER MAYOR, *Because*
He Will Guard Well Their Homes and Children

GOOD MEN PREFER	GOOD MEN KNOW THAT
Boys to Beer	Saloons and brothels do not help
Sobriety to Saloons	dry goods and clothing stores—nor
Virtue to Vice	jewelers, butchers, blacksmiths,
Purity to Prostitution	nor schools and churches, nor
Progress to Poverty	anybody except liquor dealers and
Grit to Graft	undertakers.

Meeks' segregation plank means his defeat.

Howse's open-town policy means his defeat.

The good men of Nashville will on Thursday, September 11, lay the corner-stone of a greater, more prosperous and a happier city.

THE HOME DEFENDERS

Figure 61. Reform candidate Noah Cooper defending the home of the respectable citizen against the Howse machine in the election of 1913. *Banner,* Sept. 10, 1913.

tomorrow."[91] The *Banner* gave grudging credit to Howse's machine with its "abundance of money" and "one of the most aggressive and compact bodies of men that ever conducted a campaign in Nashville, men thoroughly acquainted with the politics of the different wards, who knew how to work effectively." With an "army of [city] employees" and an "organization without a flaw," Howse simply beat the reformers in the business of politics he understood so well.[92] "As for Nashville," the *Banner* lamented, "unless help comes from an outside source, a power higher up, it must continue to endure the evils of vice and disorder, believing that when the uttermost depths are reached there will be reaction and keeping faith that the increasing purpose of a higher civilization must in the end bring better conditions."[93]

Howse for his part was gracious in victory and issued a magnanimous letter to his reformist adversaries in the Board of Trade. He slyly reminded them that they were "in a large measure responsible for the new commission form of government," forgave them any past political opposition, and urged them to "consult with me freely, making such suggestions as will, in your opinion, give the people of the city a progressive, enlightened administration of their affairs."[94]

THE 1915 CRISIS

Businessmen-reformers bided their time waiting for another opportunity, like the reservoir disaster of 1912, to discredit Howse and bring their own people to power. That opportunity came in the summer of 1915 in an enormous financial scandal that ultimately brought down the entire Howse regime and gave reformers full control of the commission government they had designed. The scandal was brought to light after a rapid growth in the city's public debt. The reform city charter of 1899 prohibited the budget of any given year to exceed revenue from the previous year. This conservative, pay-as-you-go standard was abandoned in 1907 (before Howse came to power) when a special act of the legislature allowed an excess expenditure of $75,000 that year only. Similar exceptions were granted in 1909 for $250,000, in 1911, 1912, 1913, and 1914 for $200,000 each year. By 1915 this deficit spending had exceeded $1 million.[95]

In the scandal that ensued few looked at the underlying causes of indebtedness. Beginning with Mayor Head's term and accelerating after Howse took office in 1909, Nashville experienced a rapid growth in expenditures for streets, sewers, and other physical improvements in the fast-growing city. At the same time, local government expanded its social services in behalf of public health, public schools, and welfare for the poor. These social services were desperately needed and were inspired by the most progressive sentiments of the day and the political imperatives of the Howse machine, which traded on its political favors to blacks and to working-class whites. Pushing in the other directions were equally strong sentiments for efficient, businesslike government and stringent laws that made it politically and legally difficult to raise taxes or float new bond issues. Business progressivism and social reform were in direct conflict, and the result was a crisis in government blamed on corrupt individuals, and not on the underlying contradictions that made such a crisis all but inevitable.

To meet the mounting deficit the commissioners suggested special legislation to allow them to issue a bond for $978,000, thus avoiding a public referendum, which the new charter required. By January 1915 a citizens committee of fourteen bankers and businessmen investigated the condition of the city's finances and recommended a thorough audit by an expert from New York City. Such an audit, the Commercial Club assured Howse, was "not to be considered . . . any reflection upon the Commissioners . . . but rather in line with the progressive business policies that have been adopted and followed to advantage by large corporations."[96] The committee agreed to support the special legislation for the bond and the commissioners agreed to open the books to an outside audit and "efficiency survey." The legislature gave permission for the bond issue to cover the deficit, and the commission quickly followed with two more bond issues, one for $450,000 for street improvements and another of $625,000 for schools. None of these bond issues was approved by popular vote, as required by the charter. At the same time, the commissioners found no provision in the charter to fund an outside audit and refused to cooperate.[97]

The Commercial Club was furious at what they saw as a broken agreement, and it finally offered to put up $10,000 to pay for the audit.[98] The commissioners relented and appointed a committee of the six national bank presidents, chaired by James E. Caldwell, to solicit bids and arrange for the audit.[99] A New York firm was hired in June, and the audit was scheduled to begin later that month. Howse and the other city commissioners defiantly refused to let the Commercial Club pay for the audit, probably for fear the businessmen would control the outcome, and they denounced the "vile and slanderous tongues [of] lifelong political enemies [who] have cast vile insinuations concerning the honesty and integrity of the mayor and other members of the board of commissioners. . . ."[100]

On the morning of June 12 Mayor Howse was forced to announce, in a more restrained tone, that certain books vital to the financial audit were missing from the revenue office. Rumors circulated they had been tossed into the river or burned. A furious round of accusations followed. Howse took the offensive and suspended City Comptroller R. Miles Burns, who was in charge of the books. Burns got a court injunction allowing him to continue in office and hired attorneys Harry S. Stokes, William C. Cherry, and J.G. Stephenson, who were to become important figures in the coming crisis. Burns accused his supervisor, Commissioner of Finance Lyle Andrews, of serious misconduct in office and implicated Mayor Howse. Howse issued warrants for the arrest of Andrews, Burns, and Johnson B. "Doc" West, assistant city treasurer, who disappeared for two months.[101] Commissioner Andrews was removed from office by the other commissioners, who then appointed Park Marshall, a prominent attorney, in his place. No such powers of dismissal and appointment were specified in the 1913 charter, and this became one of many legal tangles connected to the 1915 crisis.

In the meantime the Commercial Club, Business Men's Association, and other civic groups organized the Committee of Public Safety, made up of seventy-five or more of the city's "foremost citizens" and modeled after the vigilance committees of early San Francisco, to do its own investigations and monitor the audit. This group worked closely with the Bankers Committee, set up earlier to arrange for the audit. On July 3 the Bankers Committee stood aside, and the Committee of Public Safety took over supervision of the audit and became the major voice of reformers in pushing the crisis to its conclusion.[102]

Testimony before a special investigator appointed by the Chancery Court spread before the public a multitude of charges involving graft, corruption, and nepotism throughout city government. Burns reported that the missing books had been known to be gone as early as April Fool's Day, but Howse had kept it quiet until the audit was certain. More books were revealed to be missing and others to have pages cut out.[103] Testimony by the mayor's brother, H. Kai Howse, revealed that the Howse Brothers furniture store had numerous lucrative contracts with the city government.[104]

That summer was one of the hottest on record—it stayed above 100 degrees day after day—and for Howse and company it was getting too hot. Commissioner J. Morgan Wilkerson, commissioner of streets, sewers, and sidewalks, was accused of using city wagons to "haul negroes" working on his farm to and from town. Wilkerson resigned on July 20 under threat of an ouster suit.[105] George W. Stainback, former waterworks chief under Howse, was appointed to fill Wilkerson's seat. R. Miles Burns resigned a day earlier, on July 19.

With the Howse regime on its knees, the businessmen-reformers moved in for the coup de grace. Under the 1913 charter a petition signed by 25 percent of the voters in the last election could force a recall election. A group of young men led by attorney Laurent Brown filed such a petition on July 8. But the recall movement immediately became snarled in legal questions, as to whether it would apply to newly appointed commissioners, for example. Also, the Commercial Club and the Committee of Public Safety apparently discouraged a recall election for fear Howse would simply win any popular election and be vindicated.[106]

Another strategy utilized a recently enacted state law, the ouster law, allowing ten citizens to bring suit to remove any public official who failed to enforce the laws of the state. This law was enacted in tandem with the prohibition law, and now Howse's refusal to enforce prohibition would come home to haunt him.[107] The ouster suit, filed on July 21, called for the dismissal of Howse, Andrews (already removed), Wilkerson (already resigned), Elliott, and Treasurer Charles Myers. The plaintiffs called them "crafty, unscrupulous politicians" and listed the string of charges recently brought to light.[108] The suit, argued by Harry Stokes, William C. Cherry, and J.G. Stephenson, came before Judge T.E. Mathews of the Circuit Court. On July 27 Judge Mathews ruled in favor of the suit and temporarily suspended all four from office, pending the outcome of the ouster litigation that was to follow.[109]

On the same day Chancellor John Allison of the Chancery Court threw the city of Nashville into receivership and appointed Robert Vaughn, a prominent Nashville attorney, to take complete charge of the business affairs of the city. Within two days this order was rescinded by the Appellate Court, however.[110]

The five-man commission elected in 1913 was now reduced to J.D. Alexander (who was also to be subject to a separate ouster suit, and who resigned August 10), Park Marshall, and George Stainback, both appointed under questionable legal authority.[111] The Committee of Public Safety now pushed hard for these commissioners to fill the positions of mayor, commissioner of waterworks, and city treasurer vacated by the ouster suit. The committee issued its own list of approved candidates, with railroad executive Whitfoord R. Cole for mayor. A rival group, the Businessmen's Association, had resented the Commercial Club's assumption of authority throughout the scandal and announced its own slate, headed by R.B.C. Howell for mayor. Harry Stokes staked out a third position, arguing that no positions should be filled, especially not by the current commissioners, and that the city must be placed in the hands of a competent receiver. Though they disagreed strenuously on which nominees, if any, to appoint, these business and professional leaders seemed to share a premise that the decision should not be left to the unpredictable process of popular election.[112] A mass meeting of citizens on July 31 was addressed by representatives of the Commercial Club and the Businessmen's Association and by Harry Stokes. Stokes, one account explained, "awoke great popular enthusiasm, but met with almost unanimous opposition from the business interests of the city."[113]

Though business interests successfully asserted their claim to expertise in managing the city's affairs in 1915, the factional squabbles between the Commercial Club and the Businessmen's Association did not bode well for "businesslike efficiency" after the Nashville coup d'etat. Under pressure from both associations, the three men left on the Board of Commissioners met July 30 to elect a mayor and a commissioner of waterworks, street cleaning, and workhouse. In the election for mayor Commissioner George Stainback apparently voted for the Businessmen's Association man, R.B.C. Howell, while Commissioner Park Marshall voted for Whitfoord R. Cole, the Commercial Club favorite. Commissioner J.D. Alexander, the only one elected in 1913, withheld support from both factions and threw his vote to a series of compromise candidates (including—to the horror of reformers—Hilary Howse).

After 304 ballots the stalemate remained unbroken, and the City Hall became like a steamy oven, thanks both to politics and the weather. The next day, various business groups came before the commissioners to recommend compromise candidates and plead for a quick and orderly transition. The balloting resumed, now with Alexander joining Stainback in support of Howell and Marshall holding out stubbornly for a series of Commercial Club compromise candidates. The charter required three votes (in this unexpected case, unanimity) to elect a replacement, so the deadlock went on. It dragged on through ballot 332 on July 31, through ballot 445 on August 2, through ballot 485 on August 3, and late into the evening on August 4. By this time, Alexander and Stainback abandoned Howell and tried a number of new candidates.

Finally, on ballot number 579, Park Marshall voted for Robert E. Ewing, an elderly lawyer and former member of the original Board of Public Works in the 1880s, who had been supported by the Commercial Club. "Alexander arose and changed his vote to Ewing . . . ," an exhausted city clerk recorded, "Stainback likewise," and Nashville had a mayor. Jesse O. Tankard, a favorite of the Businessmen's Association, was elected as the fifth commissioner on the first ballot later that night.[114]

The legal suits and the audit dragged into the fall. When Howse took the stand in his defense at the ouster trial in November, he freely admitted his refusal to enforce the prohibition laws and denied any personal wrongdoing in the scandal of 1915. This bold response only intensified the moral outrage against the Howse regime, and the court concurred on November 30 with a decision to oust him from office.[115] Reform, it seemed, had finally triumphed in City Hall, just as it had against the liquor interests after Carmack's death. Now it remained to be seen if the reformers, once in power, could uphold the standards of morality, law enforcement, and efficiency they had held up to their political adversaries.

The currents of reform that surged out of the religious revivals of the 1880s had flowed into the political arena with the temperance movement. The long struggle and eventual triumph of the temperance crusade guaranteed politicians like Hilary Howse a loyal following among the whiskey interests and the public they served. Another current of reform was propelled by partisan and class interests. Conservative Democrats and business leaders wanted to take political power away from the ward-based politicians who supported Boss Kercheval and Boss Howse. For these reformers "good government" meant government modeled after the business corporation and controlled by business leaders. Their assaults on black, poor, and illiterate voters and their efforts to undermine ward-based politicians also met with piecemeal victories from the charter reform of 1883 to the advent of commission government in 1913 and the ouster of Howse two years later. But their efforts to reform moral behavior or to alter the rules of the political game only galvanized the political power of the opposition.

FLUSH TIMES IN WAR AND PEACE

World War I gave America's business leaders an opportunity to use their progressivism to organize the economy and society in a massive effort to make the world safe for democracy. In Nashville the war brought a windfall of industrial development, particularly the DuPont powder plant. Finally, it seemed, Nashville's frustrating quest for a solid industrial base would be answered. But the wartime boom ended, and the city's industrial sector quickly receded, attracting only a few important additions in the ensuing years.

The postwar years in Nashville were a time of vigorous growth, despite the city's failure to sustain an industrial boom. The population, which stood at 110,364 in the census of 1910, edged up only about 7 percent in the next ten years, then surged ahead by 30 percent in the 1920s, leaving the city population at 153,866 in 1930.[1] By this date former rivals Memphis, Birmingham, and Atlanta all exceeded Nashville's population by 100,000 or more. Nashville had settled into a middling place in the regional urban hierarchy by this time, and no amount of urban boosterism—however earnest—could change this.[2]

Nashville's economic vitality in this period derived less from the things the city produced than from the services it provided. The service economy that emerged in the 1920s looked to Nashville as a regional center in banking, insurance, and securities. Higher education and medical care may also be understood as components of the city's expanding service economy in this period. Elsewhere, in northern manufacturing cities, new methods of mass production made consumer goods, from automobiles and radios to electric household appliances and clothing, available to the average American at affordable prices at a time when real wages were rising.

THE GREAT WAR

More than any other section of the United States, the South has been shaped by war. The Civil War left a legacy of sectional antagonism while it gave Nashville an important role in shaping the New South. The "Great War," which broke out between distant European enemies in 1914, took on special meaning in the South. It pulled southerners into a conflict that united them with other Americans in a patriotic cause. It brought together masses of people from every section, and it changed the economy and society at home in several profound and irreversible ways. After the war in Europe, one southerner lamented, the world would know all Americans as Yankees.[3]

When Americans entered the war in April 1917, the *Tennessean* proclaimed: "We have cause to go to the conflict gladly, with joy in our hearts . . . as the man in any contest who knows that he extends his effort in a cause that is eternally right. . . ."[4] The irrepressible Luke Lea announced to a meeting of the Commercial Club, "We are going to fight until freedom is enthroned and civilization protected. . . . America is consecrated to its duty."[5] These were the lofty, abstract goals every citizen could stand behind. America's late entry into the war and its distance from the trenches and mustard gas meant the nation would be spared the ghastly death tolls suffered by European nations. Indeed, for most Tennesseans the war would be remembered as a grand adventure abroad. Private Alvin C. York, who killed twenty Germans and unaided took 132 prisoners, became a folk hero; in the public's eye he was the shrewd mountaineer defending American democracy on foreign soil. At the war's end Nashville's own Luke Lea, as colonel of the 114th Field Artillery, led a daring foray into Holland to kidnap "Kaiser Bill" and deliver him to President Wilson and to an American brand of justice. The scheme was foiled by Dutch guards at the castle where the kaiser had sought sanctuary, but for those back home Lea's exploits added to the sense of romantic chivalry and down-home morality they chose to attach to the war.[6]

The war effort suddenly caught up thousands of Nashvillians in an emergency military mobilization, war industries, and volunteer service on the home front. It "marked the beginning of a time," historian Jesse Burt observed, "when wider currents . . . flowed through Nashville's climate, for the first time to any degree since the War Between the States."[7] By July 1918, after the Selective Service Administration inaugurated the draft, 2,840 men in Nashville, and another 790 in Davidson County, had been recruited into the army.[8] Several thousand more recruits came to Nashville's two mobilization camps that were quickly arranged by local business leaders, who gleefully responded to what appeared to be a windfall. The Commercial Club buoyantly predicted that an estimated 18,000 men would come to Nashville and $660,000 would flow through the local economy each month.[9] Luke Lea and his Belle Meade Land Company graciously offered to the army a plot of 1,500 acres near the new country club, and this became "Camp Jackson," a tent city with several thousand Tennessee recruits. "Camp Kirkland" was set up in the West Side dormitories on the Vanderbilt campus to handle the overflow.[10] Dozens of the city's young business and professional men, Luke Lea not least among them, signed up for officer training.

Many of Nashville's blacks also went off to fight for American democracy, though in a segregated company led by Captain Charles O. Hadley, a native of Nashville and a graduate of Fisk and Meharry. To uncertain whites worried at the prospect of armed blacks in uniform, Hadley promised "Nashville's negro company will . . . bring credit to those who have shown trust in it."[11]

Thousands of other blacks took full advantage of unprecedented opportunities for relatively high-paying jobs offered to them by the boom in American war industries. The war shut off the flow of European immigrants, which had been the main supply of industrial labor in the North. Now labor recruiters from Chicago, Detroit, and other northern cities flocked south to offer blacks a day's wage that in the South took the better part of a week to earn. Nashville's excellent railroad connections to the North now served as siphons drawing away the black labor pool.

The social strains of war and the new competition for black labor aggravated race relations across the country. A new wave of lynchings and interracial violence rippled across Tennessee and the South. Black and white business leaders protested and organized a statewide Law and Order League led by Nashville's Cornelius A. Craig.[12] The league tried to calm racial tension and stem the tide of northward migration. At the same time, laws were passed to discourage northern labor recruiters from entering the state. License fees for labor recruiters were set at $500, but this only forced the activity underground.[13]

Whatever efforts were made to discourage blacks from leaving failed dramatically, for they were caught in a massive internal movement from South to North, from farm to city—a tidal flow that would later be dubbed the Great Migration. Set off initially by temporary opportunities for well-paid jobs during the war boom, the black exodus took on a momentum all its own as a chain of migration, forged by countless letters and visits back home, pulled kin and neighbors northward, mostly to the teeming ghettos of Chicago and Detroit. Black leaders in Nashville urged their people to stay in the region and work for a better life at home, but the exodus continued relentlessly.[14] Blacks constituted 31 percent of Davidson County's population in 1910; by 1930 they claimed 23 percent, and their share was still declining. The Great Migration had ended, but the black exodus would continue.[15]

The war opened new paths to women no less than to blacks. It accelerated the subtle changes in woman's place that could be detected before the war. An atmosphere of social emergency and temporary sacrifice to the cause opened the door to what would become permanent trends in the changing role of women in society, trends that were slowed, but not arrested, by the more conservative posture of the South.[16] Upper-class women used established organizations to extend their influence in a variety of wartime services. The Centennial Club organized Liberty Loan bond drives, sponsored "patriotic teas," and offered its club-house as a meeting place for other women volunteers. The Query Club sent supplies to France, and dozens of other literary and civic clubs joined forces, with the Federation of Women's Clubs as their coordinator, to advance the war effort on the home front.

New voluntary associations were mobilized as well, and many of these reached beyond the social elite for volunteers. The Surgical Dressings Committee began as early as 1914 supplying bandages to the troops. The Army Comfort league, led by Margaret Lindsley Warner, supplied books and entertainment for the recruits at Camp Jackson. The YWCA played a major role during the war, helping to train Red Cross nurses and teach women new job skills to fill the void in the work force left by the departing men. The Nashville Red Cross Chapter organized volunteer women for a variety of tasks, from producing bandages and clothing to chauffering government officials and nursing victims of the devastating Spanish influenza epidemic of 1918. Nashville's Saidee Williams Overton chaired state-level units of the National League for Woman's Service, which coordinated Liberty Loan campaigns, supervised local food conservation programs, and hosted a benefit ball at the Belle Meade Country Club, among other activities.[17] A Press Committee of Nashville women made certain that these and other activities of women's "war work" were kept before the public eye. In October 1917 a parade of women's service organizations publicized their work and urged other women to join forces. As Nashville's women demonstrated their patriotism and their capacity to serve society, suffrage advocates, led by Anne Dallas Dudley, pressed firmly for women's right to participate in the democracy they were helping to defend abroad.[18]

The war also offered women new openings in the work force as the economy boomed in the face of a shortage of male workers. Women took over many clerical and sales jobs in offices and banks, and they put on overalls and worked in factories.[19] "The mobilization of women continues," observed Lou Cretia Owen in the fall of 1918. "They are leaving their homes and for the first time the industries have found how valuable they are at the machines where only men have stood."[20] For women in business and the professions, the war created new opportunities that they readily seized. In the spring of 1917 Nashville women organized the Altrusa Club. The Business and Professional Women's

Figure 62. Members of the National League for Woman's Service on duty in the third Liberty Loan campaign, March 1918. Rose Long Gilmore, *Davidson County Women in the World War, 1914–1919* (Nashville, 1923).

Figure 63. Payday at the Old Hickory Powder Plant, 1918. About 12,500 workers lined up for their paychecks, which soon passed through Nashville's booming economy during the war. *Old Hickory News,* December 7, 1918, Tennessee State Library and Archives.

Club had been organized sometime earlier. Paralleling the several men's business associations, Altrusa was partly social and met in members' homes. Their meetings were devoted to lectures on business skills and efficiency and to creating a network for the small but growing number of women who entered the formerly male realm of business and the professions.[21]

At all levels, as citizens and as workers, women's lives would be in some way altered by the impact of what seemed at the time just a temporary dislocation. "Let us safeguard our girls," an editorial in the *Tennessean* pleaded." . . . Let us not leave them resourceless in a world that is dominated by the war god with all his attendants—Greed, Lust and Passion."[22] Already the kind of world that made this protective morality quite proper before the war was being swept aside, forever.

The single most significant economic impact of the war was the coming of the E.I. DuPont Nemours Company and the enormous powder plant it built. In its scale and the speed with which it was organized, the Old Hickory Munitions Project eclipsed everything that came before it. It occupied 5,000 acres at Hadley's Bend, ten miles northeast of the city. The plant employed 50,000 workers at its peak and included a company town, later named Old Hickory, which housed 30,000 workers. The whole plant and town was built within nine months. "War waved its red wand over a peaceful countryside," one observer noted, "and an industrial city sprang up as if by magic."[23]

Nashville's business leaders had been aggressively involved for some time in promoting a nitrate plant and dam at Muscle Shoals, Alabama, which they hoped would indirectly enrich their trading territory. Meanwhile, DuPont quietly bought up farm land at Hadley's Bend, and the announcement of its plans in December 1918 came as a surprise to Nashville.[24] Local boosters were not slow to see the importance of the project to the local economy, and they now took every opportunity to ally local patriotism with the war effort. "Watch us grow," the *Tennessean* crowed in January 1918. "Many serious questions which have perplexed and concerned us as a city will now find satisfactory solution, if one and all, with cheerful, brave spirits, now dedicate themselves anew to the support of their country and incidental to this the commercial upbuilding of the city."[25] Through the Commercial Club local businessmen worked hard to accommodate DuPont and its new powder plant. They pushed for new commuter trains for workers and a new bridge across the Cumberland, and they helped supply a whole range of services needed at the plant. The plant created a boom in real estate values and a surge of buying in downtown stores, which soon offered special hours to shoppers from Old Hickory.[26]

The impact of the powder plant was not all salutary. The sudden demand for labor and the relatively high wages offered by DuPont created a disastrous drain on Nashville's labor supply. Household servants,

day laborers, and clerks left their jobs in Nashville and came in droves
to the powder plant, where daily wages of $2.75 to $3.00 per eight-hour
day were "far in excess of the wages which had been normally paid common laborers in this city."[27] More than 5,000 blacks and 10,000 women
found new job opportunities at Old Hickory. Lou Cretia Owen, a social
worker at the plant, noted in her diary that many of the workers were
runaways who came to enjoy a temporary "joy of independence." "Men
and women," she wrote, "are taking the chance of breaking home bonds
and throwing off the social shackles in a desperate plunge for adventure."[28] They found plenty of adventure at the powder plant. The sudden influx of people brought serious problems of lawlessness and racial violence. Health problems were exacerbated by water pollution,
and a continuous round of malaria and epidemic diseases, most nota-
bly the Spanish influenza in September 1918, swept through the crowded
barracks.[29]

The adventure offered by the powder plant boom uprooted thousands of people, most of them young; the majority were encountering
the routine of industrial labor for the first time. Along with the soldiers, these factory employees created a huge pool of mobile workers
accustomed to working in large-scale, highly regimented organizations.
Though local employers bemoaned the destabilization of the labor
force at the time, the DuPont plant helped to create an indispensable
ingredient to the industrial and clerical work force that would be required by Nashville's postwar economy.[30]

When the armistice came in November 1918, the workers at the
Old Hickory plant hastily arranged a parade with trucks made up as
floats. Later, some workers and their floats went into town to join the
parade in progress there. "All of Nashville was wild with joy and they
gave us a great ovation," one plant worker noted with pride.[31] Unknow-
ingly, they were also celebrating the abrupt end of the powder plant
and the surge of prosperity it had brought to Nashville. Still, the changes
wrought by the war in Nashville's economy and its work force, and the
more subtle but very real changes in the local mind, were to have a
lasting effect in the city. The war was more than a brief adventure over-
seas. As Lou Cretia Owen recorded in her diary in the beginning of the
war, "We seem to have entered a new world."[32]

THE PURSUIT OF INDUSTRIAL GROWTH

The war galvanized the city's business leaders by setting before them
a clear agenda for mobilization and a number of tantilizing opportunities for profit that could not wait. The sudden end of the wartime boom
stimulated a new sense of urgency about getting the local economy mov-

ing. The paramount goal of the business elite was to expand Nashville's narrow industrial base. Before the war the industrial sector was limited to food processing (flour milling and meat packing in particular), lumber and furniture manufacturing, and iron stove foundries. All these lines survived the war, but many continued on a diminished scale. As related in chapter two, the Interstate Commerce Commission took away Nashville's favored position within the L&N freight rate system and dealt a severe blow to the "Minneapolis of the South." The timber supply in the Upper Cumberland Valley was also rapidly declining, while the rise of Birmingham as an iron and steel center placed limits on Nashville's iron works. The DuPont powder plant, which opened an entirely new avenue for industrial development, was now obsolete and scheduled by the federal government to be junked at the end of the war.[33]

Having enjoyed a taste of industrialization, the businessmen of Nashville now led a concerted drive to build a strong foundation for industrial growth. Earlier, it had seemed sufficient to rely on individual entrepreneurial spirit, aroused by yeasty booster rhetoric, to further the city's industrial expansion. The grand expositions of 1880 and 1897 were exceptions to a general lack of planning for Nashville's economic development. Now, laissez faire gave way to a new understanding that modern industrial enterprise required constant cooperation among local business leaders. Acting through commercial associations and local government, they could plan, finance, and mount aggressive campaigns to lure large corporations to the city.[34]

The clearest expression of this new consciousness of the need for planning came in an industrial survey report sponsored by the Commercial Club in 1919. The Goodrich Report, completed the following year by a New York consulting firm, was the result of a comprehensive scientific study of Nashville's failings and potential as an industrial and commercial center. The study provides a rare look behind the rosy optimism of the booster press and examines some hard data on the state of Nashville's economy.[35]

Goodrich showed how rival cities, particularly Memphis, Birmingham, and Louisville, successfully challenged Nashville's preeminence during the critical period between 1890 and 1910. Among the factors retarding the city's growth was its failure to expand industrially. The demise of the Cumberland River as an avenue of trade was another major element in Nashville's slow growth. The labor force, Goodrich also demonstrated, was steadily weakened by slow out-migration of blacks and by a failure to make full use of female workers. Furthermore, wages, even during the wartime boom, remained depressed compared with wage rates in rival cities, not only hurting labor recruitment but limiting consumer markets for retailers.

Pointing more directly to the business elite of Nashville, Goodrich criticized the "extremely conservative" posture of the city's bankers. In

Figure 64. "Busy Boosters Holding Nashville Up Before the World." In the 1920s the commercial–civic elite advocated cooperative planning for their city's economic development, as this cartoon depicts. *Tennessean*, April 13, 1924.

1919, for example, only a bit over 40 percent of Nashville's total bank resources were loaned out, compared with over 50 percent in comparable southern cities. Loan policies also appeared to follow rather conservative paths and to avoid the necessary risks in new or expanding enterprises. Investment of private money seemed to conform to a similar pattern. Nashville demonstrated that it was a city of extraordinary wealth in comparison with its rivals: Income tax data showed significantly fewer people earning under $5,000, and the Liberty Loan bond drives during the war produced $26 million, far more per capita than other cities. But too much of this private wealth was standing idle in savings accounts, rather than being invested in local enterprise. The "ultra conservative" tone among bankers and private investors in Nashville clearly discouraged the "spirit of enterprise" the city must enliven if it would catch up with its rivals.[36] In addition, the Goodrich Report advised Nashville leaders to promote a whole range of social improvements involving public health, education, city planning, and improved labor relations.

This generally critical report was read quietly in the confines of the Commercial Club and received very little publicity. But it was by no means ignored by the city's business elite. On the contrary, the many recommendations in the Goodrich Report became a blueprint for the strategies Nashville's leaders pursued in the 1920s.

The single most critical issue before the business leaders of Nashville was the future of the powder plant. The federal government, which had financed most of the construction, was clearly not interested in maintaining the plant, despite the best efforts of Congressman Joseph W. Byrns. Yet the plant and its machines, along with the large village for workers, provided "wonderful possibilities" for some kind of peacetime industrial development. By the spring of 1920 the government formally announced its decision to abandon the plant entirely, and the Commercial Club now looked nervously for some private enterprise to take over the site and avert the possibility that the government might scrap the whole plant. By August the Commercial Club organized a group of local capitalists, with some cooperation from New York and Denver capitalists, into the Nashville Industrial Corporation (NIC), a private company set up to take over at least a portion of the plant.[37]

The NIC bought a portion of the powder plant for $3.5 million and began to develop it as an industrial park with sites for a number of smaller firms. With the aid of aggressive publicity from the Chamber of Commerce (the Commercial Club changed its name in July 1921), Old Hickory began to attract a number of small industries. Most came from the North to take advantage of the cheap, nonunion workers, who —the chamber's publicity constantly reminded everyone—were made up of "good quality native American labor."[38] "Nashville enters into a new industrial era," the *Tennessean* boasted at the beginning of the

NIC, "which promises to make it the South's foremost manufacturing city."[39] One director of the NIC, however, cautioned against expecting "that an Aladdin's lamp can be rubbed and an immense industrial city will spring up overnight." "But it is sure to come," he added confidently, "and when it does come, the greatest advance Nashville has made in its history will have been accomplished."[40]

By July 1923 the revival of Old Hickory was assured when DuPont announced its plans to return, this time to build a $4 million plant for the manufacture of "artificial silk" or rayon, a product which, like gunpowder, utilized cellulose.[41] By 1927 after several stages of expansion DuPont Rayon had invested $12 million in Old Hickory, and the company employed over 5,000 people. In 1929 DuPont announced plans to add a cellophane plant with another $3 million. For its part, the county, under steady pressure from the Chamber of Commerce, built Old Hickory Bridge in 1929. It linked the factories and the city more directly and was symbolic of the new importance Old Hickory claimed in Nashville's economic life.[42]

The success of Old Hickory encouraged the Chamber of Commerce to redouble its efforts to attract industry to the city. With financial help from the NIC, an Industrial Committee was added to the chamber. Its role was to aggressively seek northern textile firms, shoe companies, and any other manufacturers willing to consider Nashville as a new industrial home. In 1925 the Nashville Industrial Development Company was formed by the chamber with $300,000 in capital, to be used to finance new plant construction for incoming firms, an approach that allowed companies migrating from the North to lease the plant temporarily and avoid interruption of production.[43] Techniques like these were particularly effective in luring industries from the Northeast. "There is a great movement southward of industry," the Industrial Committee reported in 1925. "It is most marked in those industries such as textiles, knit goods and shoe industries, which are suffering in their present location through adverse labor conditions and union domination. Nashville is today confronted with the biggest opportunity in its history."[44]

The chamber's success was evident in the transfer of such companies as Pioneer Braid of New York, which built a $500,000 plant to manufacture shoe laces, and Thomas Henry and Sons of Philadelphia, which built a $1-million plant in West Nashville to produce textiles.[45] Older textile firms in North Nashville also expanded in the healthy climate of the 1920s. Morgan and Hamilton Mills was bought out by Werthan Bag Company in 1928, resulting in a company worth $5 million.[46]

Shoe manufacturing also gravitated away from the unions of the North and toward the cheap labor of the South. Nashville's major catch in this line was the Jarman Shoe Company, which began in East Nash-

Figure 65. James Franklin Jarman (1867–1938), founder of General Shoe Company, later known as Genesco, one of the several northeastern industries that migrated to Nashville after World War I. Genesco.

ville in 1924 with aid from the Industrial Development Company. By 1928 James F. Jarman's much expanded enterprise had moved into a large modern factory covering a 2-acre site on Gallatin Avenue. This plant was capable of churning out 5,000 pairs of their best-selling "friendly fives" each day. An identical plant was built next to it in 1930.[47]

By 1927 Nashville boasted more than three hundred manufacturing plants producing over $100 million in goods, statistics representing significant progress since the turn of the century. Still, the massive shift to a new era of industrial development had not occurred. The 1930 census showed a little over 30 percent of the labor force employed in manufacturing, a figure that had remained remarkably steady since 1920 (32.2 percent), and even since 1910 (30.3 percent).[48] Instead of lamenting the city's industrial shortcomings, Nashville's boosters began to emphasize the virtues of steady growth and a diversified economy. "Unlike many boom towns, Nashville's industrial growth has been slow, sure and continuous. The city does not depend entirely upon its industries but has diversified business lines which serve to prevent Nashville from being affected by depressions or layoffs that are experienced in many industrial centers."[49] These reassuring claims, issued in November 1928, would be tested soon enough in the Great Depression.

THE CONSUMERS' CORNUCOPIA

Nashville's faith in industrial development as the only real basis for growth was never fulfilled. The most vital sectors of the economy after the war were in retail sales, finance, insurance, and other services like education, medicine, tourism, and entertainment. Between World War I and the Great Depression workers across America experienced real increases in their wages, and for the first time large portions of Nashville's population could extend their budgets beyond the sheer necessities of food, clothing, and shelter. Coinciding with the rise in real wages was a series of technological innovations that brought forth a whole new array of consumer luxuries. This was the age of the radio, movies, electric appliances, and—above all—this was the age of the automobile.

There was a new emphasis on skilled salesmanship, alluring advertising, and innovative marketing and financing in the age of consumerism. With their greater discretionary purchasing power, consumers now were lured to stores with elaborate advertisements and seasonal sales. Once in the showrooms, they could choose among competing brand names. The salesman of the 1920s worked relentlessly to sell consumers the symbols of modernity they wanted and to reconcile newfangled gadgets and entertainment with an older moral code.[50]

The retail shopping district, which had migrated from the Public Square over to the Arcade and Fifth Avenue before the war, now began to spread out along the level portions of Church Street. At the corner of Fifth and Church the Cain-Sloan Department Store enlarged and refurbished the building it occupied, creating an elaborate consumer's palace with modern elevators, marble floors, a woman's lounge and check room, all modeled after the fanciest stores in New York and Chicago.[51] Lebeck Brothers, nearby on Church, and Castner-Knott, at Church and Sixth, competed with similar comforts assuring the "shopping pleasure" of their feminine clientele. Along Church Street and Fifth Avenue ladies in hats and white gloves could shop and enjoy lunch unmolested by the speakeasies and vice dens bordering the retail district.

It was not enough to offer luxurious showrooms. Retailers during the 1920s used new means of credit to promote sales. Installment buying was introduced by Henry Ford to sell expensive items like automobiles; then it was quickly adapted to appliances, furniture, radios, and almost everything sold in large department stores. "Buying on time" would become an ingrained habit among American consumers, but at its inception it seemed to conflict with all the old precepts about thrift and postponement of gratification. A *Tennessean* editorial in 1926 applauded the rise of installment buying and dismissed skeptics who worried that shoppers would overextend themselves. "They overlook the fact," the editor wrote with assurance, "that there is every year a natural increase in the purchasing ability of the American consumer."[52] The public, which for generations learned to save for hard times, had to be persuaded to envision a future of endless prosperity. The same city boosters who worked tirelessly to project an image of progress to other cities worked no less earnestly to cultivate a modern consumer culture in Nashville.

They did so through organizations, in much the same way that industrial promoters pursued their goals. The Associated Retailers of Nashville had been organized in 1898, but it was during the 1920s that it broadened and intensified its efforts in promoting retail sales in Nashville.[53] The Retail Credit Bureau centralized credit records for the over 125,000 charge accounts that had been set up as early as 1924.[54] The Boosters Club, which began in 1904, was only intermittently active before 1924, when it was reorganized and began an exuberant role in promoting Nashville's fortunes. Each spring the club sponsored a boisterous trip into the hinterland to lure rural shoppers into Nashville. At every county seat and hamlet within a hundred or more miles, club members passed out free samples and sang the praises of shopping in Nashville. Special sales for out-of-town shoppers lured rural folk into the city as well. The small-town general stores were no match for the palatial department stores, busy downtown streets, and the general aura of excitement rural customers found in the city.[55]

One of the most compelling attractions of the city during the 1920s was the movies. As motion pictures became more appealing to the middle class in the 1920s, grandly decorated theaters were built to cater to downtown visitors. Tony Sudekum, with his brother Harry, opened the Dixie Theater on Fifth Avenue in 1907, and within ten years Sudekum owned a chain of 130 theaters in three states under the auspices of the Crescent Amusement Company.[56] By then, downtown Nashville claimed eight movie houses, including Sudekum's Princess, Capitol, and Knickerbocker; there were also Loews Vendome, Fifth Avenue Theater, the Strand, Rex, and Alhambra. Four suburban movie theaters sprang up in the 1920s, most on the west side of town, but movie houses, stage theaters, and other forms of popular entertainment remained concentrated downtown alongside and interdependent with the retail center.[57]

The movie craze was just beginning; in June 1928 the Knickerbocker announced Nashville's first "talkie" with "vita phone" sound, "When Man Loves," starring John Barrymore and Dolores Costello. Thousands of people of all ages gave up a nickel to see the movies, many of them two and three times each week. Moralists worried—perhaps not unduly—that the influence of Hollywood would subvert the church and family. Some wished to censor films that came to Nashville. But the movies won a strong hold on Nashville in the 1920s, and if they challenged traditional values, they also served to erode the walls of provincial culture.[58]

The radio was another technological marvel of the 1920s. It was estimated that over 28 percent of Nashville families owned a radio by the end of the decade.[59] One observer was comforted by the idea that radio brought the family together in the evening, as opposed to other modern fads, like the movies and the automobile, which drew youth away from the home.[60] Still, radio invaded the home with modern ideas and tempting advertisements. Because of the low levels of literacy and limited access to newspapers at the time, radio instantly became a powerful medium for advertising new products.

Nashville became a regional broadcasting center in the 1920s largely because local merchants and insurance executives saw the enormous potential of radio and set up their own stations. John E. Cain, Jr., of Cain-Sloan established WEBX in 1924, Dad's Auto Accessories began WDAD the next year, followed by Braid Electric's WBAW, and Luke Lea of the Tennessee Publishing Company started WTNT in 1929. The largest and most important stations in Nashville's early radio history were established by National Life, WSM ("We Shield Millions") in 1925, and Life and Casualty, WLAC in 1926. Together these local stations helped make radio one of the hallmarks of a new, wonderful age for the ordinary consumer.[61]

If there was any one symbol of the modern era that emerged in the 1920s, it was the automobile. Once a plaything for the rich, it became a luxury—indeed, even a necessity—for most of the middle class and

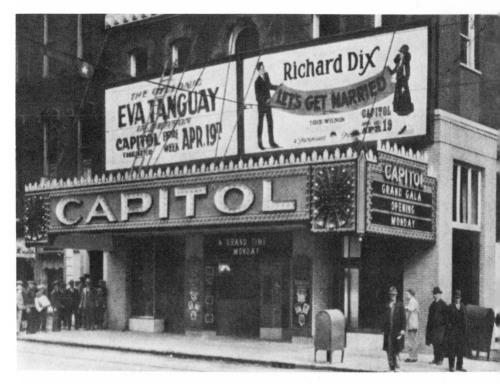

Figure 66. The Capitol, "Nashville's Magnificent Quarter–Million Dollar Theatre," 1926. *Nashville This Week,* May 10–17, 1926.

Figure 67. Automobile traffic on Union Street in the 1920s. Tennessee State Library and Archives.

a growing number of working-class families almost overnight. Earlier, Nashville had had its own small automobile manufacturer, the Marathon Auto Works, which put out a moderately expensive touring car for a few years prior to World War I.[62] With the advent of Henry Ford's techniques of mass production on the assembly line, auto manufacturing became concentrated in huge factories in the Detroit area. The automobile had a far-reaching impact on Nashville's economy nonetheless. As prices dropped, following Ford's lead, as real wages rose, and as installment buying emerged, auto sales skyrocketed. From 12,000 auto registrations in 1920, Davidson County claimed 40,300 by 1930. There was approximately one car for every six people in the county, or about two cars for every three families. Of course, automobile ownership was not distributed evenly, but over three-quarters of the automobiles owned in 1930 cost less than $1,000. By 1929 Nashville's twenty-nine automobile dealers were selling over $13 million in new and used cars, 14 percent of the total retail sales in the city. In addition, almost $2 million were spent on accessories, such as tires and batteries, and still more on gasoline and oil.[63]

Less directly, the automobile had a tremendous impact on the regional economy. Millions of dollars, for example, went into new roads. Before 1909 counties were responsible for all road construction. Most roads were unpaved, full of ruts and potholes. Under heavy pressure from groups like the Commercial Club's Good Roads Committee and the Nashville Automobile Club (organized in 1915), the state of Tennessee organized a highway department. Beginning about 1924, under the leadership of Governor Austin Peay, a massive program of road building began. Ten years and $200 million later, a system of paved roads connected every county seat and fed a network of highways into Nashville. Cities and counties added millions more dollars to the road-building program of the 1920s. Nashville's Caldwell and Company built a financial empire by selling southern municipal and county bonds, which were required in large part by the surge of road building.[64]

In Nashville new auto showrooms spread out along Broadway and West End, gravitating away from the downtown out to Sixteenth Avenue and beyond by the end of the decade.[65] Along with the showrooms, auto parts stores, tire stores, and service garages followed the expansion of "Auto Row," which pushed away the once fashionable mansions that lined West End. Some of the pioneers, like E. Gray Smith's Packard dealership and Hippodrome Motor Company, would have a long history in Nashville; many others failed to survive hard times in the 1930s. The largest dealer in the 1920s was George Cole Motor Company, claimed to be the fifth-largest Ford agency in the world in 1925. Cole came to Nashville in 1921 and at the age of twenty-seven he rapidly built an enormous business selling the affordable Model T and later the Model A.[66]

The public fascination with the automobile was carefully nurtured by auto manufacturers and dealers in the 1920s. They learned to sell cars as fashion, with the stress on two-tone colors, chrome wheels, annual model changes, and the prestige attached to particular makes. Even Henry Ford, who once offered the buyer any color he wished "so long as it was black," began to market his Model A with a choice of colors from "Arabian Sand" to "Dawn Gray."[67] Car buyers were treated to a display of each year's new models at the annual auto show in January. Usually held at the Hippodrome on West End opposite Centennial Park, the show pulled the public in with fashion shows, orchestra music by Francis Craig, and refreshments, as well as gleaming automobiles.

The consumer had to be persuaded the automobile was a necessary and sound investment, not a frivolous indulgence in modern gadgetry. "Bird Wings Not Extravagance; Car for Man Not Extravagance; Go Now and Select Your Auto," proclaimed a blurb for the auto show in 1925. "There is no such thing as a 'pleasure automobile.' You might as well talk of 'pleasure fresh air,' or of a 'pleasure beef steak.' . . . The Automobile increases length of life, increases happiness, represents above all other achievements the progress and the civilization of our age."[68]

It was also to become one of the major problems of twentieth century civilization. If the automobile was not, strictly speaking, a necessity in the age of trolleys and compact urban life, it was increasingly essential to a city that became organized around this novel form of transportation. New suburbs sprang up on the east and especially the west side of the city, well beyond, or between, the fingerlike projections of the trolley-line suburbs. Businesses, particularly groceries and furniture stores, also began catering to the motorized suburbanite by moving to the periphery of the city. "Without the motor car," an ebullient editor wrote early in the decade, "the city would not have grown so quickly, nor so solidly, and business within the corporate limits would not have been so good as it is now."[69]

This tone began to change as the decade wore on. Trolley cars could not compare with the comfort and privacy of the automobile, and shoppers jammed narrow downtown streets with cars. Merchants, at first quite delighted with the trend, were soon plagued with clogged streets, a severe shortage of parking space, and dangerous traffic that threatened their pedestrian shoppers. New garages were thrown up around the retail district and out lower Broadway, but the number of parking spaces was rapidly outstripped by the rising number of automobiles on the streets.[70] Trolley cars and automobiles now challenged one another for use of downtown streets. Both suffered as a consequence, but the number of trolley passengers declined, along with the speed and comfort of service. Illegal automobile jitneys cut further into the trolley ridership by transporting servants along West End Avenue at lower fares.[71]

All this time downtown merchants watched business gravitate away from their clogged streets and overstuffed garages. Civic leaders constantly fought to control the notorious recklessness of Nashville's drivers. The automobile, historian Blaine Brownell observed, "became a genuine symbol of modernity—representing the disruptive potential as well as the beneficient promise of new technological opportunities."[72]

THE EDUCATION INDUSTRY IN THE "ATHENS OF THE SOUTH"

The prosperity of the postwar era also generated growth in higher education. Nashville's boast as the "Athens of the South" rested before the 1920s on the rather frail foundations of several small, poorly endowed colleges, none of which had acquired national stature. By the end of the 1920s Nashville's role as a regional educational center was indisputable. The city played host to a collection of reasonably well-endowed schools with faculties and curricula equal to the task of educational leadership in the South. The reasons for this decisive improvement in Nashville's colleges involved, first of all, the concerted efforts of northern philanthropic foundations to develop quality education in the South by concentrating their money in a select number of promising schools. Nashville already had the colleges with which to work, and, for the most part, they were headed by men with a clear vision of their potential. Nashville's central geographic location was also important to funders who saw the city as the "Gateway to the South," a place to which students would be drawn and from which they would fan out and invigorate the entire region.[73]

Vanderbilt, the most prosperous of the city's colleges before World War I, had an endowment of a little over $1 million in 1915. It served fewer than one thousand students, two-thirds of whom came from within Tennessee.[74] The school was founded by the Methodists and remained nominally under control of the church for over forty years. When the authority of the church to appoint faculty was challenged in 1904, a decade-long battle ensued. The issue was finally resolved by the Tennessee Supreme Court in favor of the university, and the Methodists formally severed all connection with the school in 1914. This long ordeal arrested Vanderbilt's development at a critical juncture, but in the coming years the university was to witness a surge of growth in size, in endowment, and in the quality of education it offered.

The leading light of this movement was James H. Kirkland, who served as chancellor from 1893 to 1937. Born in South Carolina and trained at the University of Leipzig, Kirkland brought to Vanderbilt a grasp of what it meant to be a genuine university and a realistic understanding of the financial support that would require. By 1915, with the

Figure 68. James H. Kirkland (1859–1939), chancellor of Vanderbilt University, 1893–1937. Vanderbilt University Photographic Archive.

Methodist debacle behind him, Kirkland was in a position to begin his first major fund-raising drive for $1 million. By this time Vanderbilt had a body of alumni large enough and mature enough to become an important source of support. New efforts were made to organize and communicate with them. An alumni secretary was appointed and an alumni magazine published. The Nashville chapter, with its prominent connections to the local business community, was critically important to Kirkland's plans. A series of local meetings of alumni and friends in spring 1916 was climaxed by a torchlight parade and rally at the Vendome theater downtown. Kirkland proclaimed "a new day has dawned, a new era begun," and—in the words of any modern college administrator —added, *"now we must collect the money."*[75] Local alumni, the board of trustees, faculty members, and even students donated $104,000, and nonalumni in Nashville contributed $125,000 to promote Vanderbilt. This was, in fact, the first time substantial amounts of local money had gone toward supporting education in the "Athens of the South."[76] It was only the beginning of a strong alliance between the local business community and the university.

The other key source of financial aid came, as it had in the very founding of the school, from nothern philanthropy. The General Education Board (GEB) was set up in 1902 to administer portions of John D. Rockefeller's fortune. Its original goal was to improve education for blacks in the South, but the board soon broadened its mission to selected white and black colleges and medical schools.[77] It was the GEB that set off the 1915 campaign with a grant of $300,000, contingent upon private donations of $700,000. Kirkland also tapped the Vanderbilt family. William K. Vanderbilt made a conditional grant of $300,000, and Frederick W. Vanderbilt put up $100,000. The success of this first drive set the university on a new course of growth, which after the war was renewed.

The medical department was the major beneficiary of northern philanthropy in the postwar era. The Carnegie Foundation sponsored a national survey of medical schools by Abraham Flexner, which it published in 1910. The Flexner Report roundly condemned all the medical schools in Tennessee but singled out Vanderbilt and Meharry as worthy of future development. The Flexner Report marked a decisive step in the medical profession's move to simultaneously upgrade and restrict medical education in America. In 1913 Chancellor Kirkland received a $1-million gift from the Carnegie Foundation to improve the medical school. In 1919 the GEB, which Flexner had joined as secretary, granted $4 million to establish Vanderbilt as a leading institution for modern medical education in the region. The existing faculty was asked to resign. A new dean and new faculty were brought in, many of them from Johns Hopkins, which served as the model for modern research-oriented medical schools. Two years later grants of $1.5 million each from the

Figure 69. Vanderbilt University gates on West End, c. 1920. Vanderbilt University Photographic Archive.

GEB and the Carnegie Foundation brought the total to $7 million. In 1929 the GEB added $5.5 million, followed by an additional $2.5 million in 1935.[78]

Much of this money went into a massive building program. The old medical facilities in South Nashville were abandoned and a new $2-million hospital complex was erected in 1925 adjacent to the main campus. The College of Arts and Sciences, fearful for a time of being eclipsed by the Medical School, had its own $4-million fund-raising drive in 1926.[79] Alumni Memorial Hall, built with funds raised primarily in Nashville, went up behind the main building (later named Kirkland Hall). Neely Memorial Auditorium also was erected in 1925, along with other buildings, totaling close to $3.4 million by the end of 1925. "Vanderbilt," a 1926 editorial in the *Tennessean* professed, "is one of the city's greatest assets from a strictly business viewpoint."[80]

Alongside Vanderbilt's expanding campus other educational institutions built their own facilities during this period. In 1914, after a decade of planning, George Peabody College for Teachers, successor to Peabody Normal and the University of Nashville, opened its new campus across the road from Vanderbilt. Under the leadership of President Bruce R. Payne, with support from the Peabody Fund, local alumni, and the community, Peabody College began a massive building program. Nine new buildings, including the beautifully domed Social Religious Building, the Administrative Building, Library, Demonstration School, and several new dormitories, went up on the new campus before the end of 1925. In that year a five-year drive for $17 million was launched to bolster the small endowment, expand the building program, and enlarge the staff and student body.[81]

It was no accident that Peabody's growth accompanied a regional effort to upgrade the poor quality of public schooling in the South. Peabody alumni filled thousands of teaching posts throughout the South. They became administrators and faculty members in state normal schools, which produced far more teachers. Peabody's summer school program attracted hundreds of southern teachers and administrators for continuing education programs. A revamped curriculum offered training in new fields such as home economics, vocational agriculture, public school music, and school hygiene. Since Peabody's founding, no single institution has been more important to the upgrading of the South's public schools.[82]

Not far from Peabody and Vanderbilt was Scarritt College for Christian Workers. Scarritt came to Nashville in 1923 from its former home in Kansas City, Missouri. It opened in September 1925 on a small, stunningly beautiful campus of collegiate gothic buildings. Devoted to training missionaries and other lay church workers, Scarritt added a new dimension to Nashville's reputation as a center of religion as well as education.[83]

During the 1930s Vanderbilt and Peabody began to focus on graduate education. One of their major deficiencies was the lack of a high-quality library. Vanderbilt, Peabody, and Scarritt cooperated to build the Joint University Libraries, which opened in 1938. Here again the GEB and Carnegie Foundation made sizable contributions.[84]

Despite all the forces that kept them separate, the contours of development in Nashville's black colleges were remarkably similar to those of Vanderbilt, Peabody, and Scarritt. Fisk University was supported in its early years by the American Missionary Association. As this former abolitionist organization began to decline in the late nineteenth century, Fisk scrambled for annual operating expenses, relying heavily on fund-raising tours by its world-famous Jubilee Singers. At the same time, many followers of Booker T. Washington came to believe industrial vocational training should take precedence over the kind of academic education Fisk offered. Fisk stood by its faith in academic training and resisted attacks against its "elitist" or impractical education from within the black community, as well as from whites suspicious of any effort to raise blacks above "their place."[85] Ironically, it was Booker T. Washington who became one of the most effective fund raisers for Fisk in the years before World War I. After Washington joined the board of trustees, Fisk successfully raised $300,000 from the GEB, the Julius Rosenwald Fund, J.P. Morgan, and other northern philanthropists.[86]

Still, the endowment stood at only a little over a quarter of a million dollars by 1913, barely enough to support operating expenses. Like Vanderbilt, Fisk began to look to the Nashville business community for contributions. Fisk president Fayette Avery McKenzie, a white educator appointed in 1915, worked determinedly to cultivate local white support for Fisk. In 1919 he launched a $1-million fund drive with half of the projected goal pledged by the GEB, and the rest from the Carnegie Foundation, business benefactors in Nashville, and a small amount from Fisk alumni. By 1924 Fisk claimed a $1-million endowment. Under McKenzie, academic standards were upgraded, and Fisk attained genuine status as a college.

But McKenzie's close alliance with white donors, his rigid enforcement of academic standards, and his superfluous rules governing student conduct strained his relations with students and alumni. Fisk students organized a strike in 1924–25 to protest his administration. The conflict soon became a debate over white control of Fisk. Fund-raising efforts were disrupted, and previously pledged funds were jeopardized. Under persistent pressure from students and alumni, McKenzie stepped down in 1925, and Thomas E. Jones was appointed in 1926 to replace him as president.

Though Jones was also white, his administration marked a new departure, toward what many began to call the "New Fisk" in the late 1920s. Jones appointed more Ph.D.s to the faculty, and he attracted several

Figure 70. Some of the Fisk University Board of Trustees, c. 1915. *First row:* Dr. Thomas Jesse Jones, unidentified, President Fayette Avery McKenzie. *Middle row:* unidentified. *Top row:* unidentified, Paul David Cravath, James C. Napier. Fayette Avery McKenzie Papers, Tennessee State Library and Archives.

Figure 71. Chemistry class, Fisk University, c. 1920. *Glimpses of Fisk University* [n.p., 1921?], in McKenzie Papers, Tennessee State Library and Archives.

distinguished black scholars and writers, among them Charles S. Johnson in sociology, Alain Locke in philosophy, Lorenzo D. Turner and James Weldon Johnson in English, and Arna Bontemps, a writer and historian who took charge of the Fisk Library. With aid from the GEB and other foundations, a new library was built, part of which housed an important collection on black history and culture.[87]

In 1931 Meharry Medical College moved from its former home in South Nashville to a site adjacent to Fisk. Meharry, founded in 1876 as a department of Central Tennessee College and named after the Meharry family of Ohio who donated their fortune to the school, continued after 1900 as Meharry Medical College of Walden University. In 1915 Meharry split away from Walden and became an independent school. For a time a merger with Fisk was contemplated, but the two schools remained independent. They nonetheless shared facilities, had overlapping membership on their boards of trustees, and generally reinforced one another as leading black educational institutions in America.[88]

Meharry, too, benefited from the massive infusion of foundation money into Nashville. The Flexner Report identified Meharry as the only black medical school in Tennessee worthy of funding. During the 1920s and 1930s the GEB, Carnegie Foundation, and other funding agencies gave several millions of dollars to the school.[89] The new Meharry campus cost $2 million and included Hubbard Hospital. Departments for training in dentistry, pharmacy, and nursing, added to the curriculum earlier, now produced a growing number of health professionals.[90] Within a highly segregated society, where black students were denied access to white medical schools and where black patients were excluded from white hospitals, Meharry performed a vital service in training doctors to treat black patients. Its role in this period was not to advance medical research but to train doctors, dentists, nurses, and pharmacists and to prepare them to serve a black population that was denied adequate care in the segregated South.

A third black educational institution emerged in the city during this period. A state-sponsored school for blacks had been mandated in the Second Morrill Act of 1890, but Tennessee remained the only former Confederate state that failed to establish such a school. The General Assembly of Tennessee ignored the issue until 1909, when a general education bill provided for a black normal school emphasizing industrial education. Three more years passed before the legislature agreed on a site for the new school. Nashville's black community immediately put forth their claim for bringing the school to their city. They appealed to the City Council for a $25,000 bond issue to purchase a campus site, but when it was referred to the voters in 1910, the bond was defeated two to one. Chattanooga nearly won the prize by default, but early in 1911 Nashville's Mayor Hilary Howse and Governor Malcolm Patterson, two politicians indebted to black voters, successfully appealed to Davidson County to put up a $40,000 bond.[91]

Tennessee Agricultural and Industrial State Normal School for Negroes opened in 1912 with three spartan buildings on a crude, rocky farm outside the city limits. William J. Hale, a black educator from Chattanooga, was appointed head of the school. A skillful politician in his own right, Hale managed to assure white legislators of his commitment to Booker T. Washington's program of industrial education, and he managed to wheedle funds out of legislators who by instinct were distrustful of any effort to educate blacks. After the war the state gave $75,000 for more buildings on the overcrowded campus, but it was again private foundations, in league with the state, that allowed major expansion during the 1920s. Though Hale placated whites by stressing industrial education, he used the school's resources primarily for teaching training. By 1922 the school was officially designated a college, and it boasted a four-year curriculum. In 1925 nearly a third of a million dollars was allotted by the state to expand the campus and develop the faculty and curriculum. Hale successfully tapped the Tennessee Commission on Interracial Cooperation, the GEB, the Rosenwald, and Carnegie funds during the 1920s and 1930s. By 1929 the state had continued a stingy policy of granting only $12,000 each year out of almost three-quarters of a million federal dollars allocated by the Morrill Act.[92] Tennessee A&I, and William J. Hale, defied the odds and developed a successful, if meagerly funded, school dedicated to blacks who otherwise would have been denied college education in state schools.[93]

There were other smaller colleges that added to Nashville's luster as an educational center. David Lipscomb College, sponsored by the Church of Christ, was boosted by the substantial largess of Life and Casualty Insurance president Andrew M. Burton. Founded in 1891 as Nashville Bible School, the school changed its name in 1918, in honor of a founder, and at the same time removed its campus from the central city to a new site on Granny White Pike.[94] Trevecca Nazarene was another small church school that began in 1901 as the Bible and Missionary Training school. In 1910 the new name was adopted, and four years later it moved away from the central city to a new campus on Gallatin Road.[95] Roger Williams University, a Baptist school for blacks, was founded in 1882, successor to the Nashville Institute, and survived until 1905 on its campus across from Vanderbilt. The new competition from Tennessee A&I doomed the school, and it moved to Memphis in 1928.[96] Ward-Belmont School for Young Ladies, established in 1913 out of a merger of two academies, occupied the old Adelicia Acklen mansion near Vanderbilt. It was a two-year college with an outstanding regional reputation as a school not only for upper-class belles but

Figure 72. The first faculty at Tennessee Agricultural and Industrial Normal School, 1912. Principal William J. Hale is front row, center. Bureau of Public Relations, Tennessee State University.

also for academically aspiring young women, who at this time had few choices for higher education in the South.[97]

Before World War I, Nashville's epithet "The Athens of the South" rested more on the deep historical roots of its schools than it did on their eminence in the nation or region. By the 1920s education was a major asset in the local economy and a source of regional fame. Nashville's boosters took pride in the tone of cultural refinement the colleges lent to the city, but they delighted still more in reciting the figures on campus assets and payrolls. All told, the colleges had about $42 million in assets, according to a 1930 estimate. Moreover, they brought in 10,000 nonresident students who, together with faculty members, spent over $7 million each year.[98] Town and gown had become integrally connected after World War I, and neither could afford to ignore this new interdependence.

During the 1920s the frustrations some business leaders may have felt in pursuing a strong industrial base for Nashville might have been easily forgotten amid the comfortable prosperity the decade brought to their city. Instead of apologizing for the lack of industry, or becoming defensive in light of the phenomenal growth of rivals Atlanta, Birmingham, and Memphis, Nashville's local patriots seemed quite satisfied with the diversity and steady growth of its economy. "Nashville has had no sensational growth," the *Banner* conceded, "but . . . [its] growth has been based on its worth, which is not emphemeral [*sic*], but of a most lasting character." The *Tennessean* concurred in a self-serving comparison with more robust rivals: "Nashville is comparable to a man's figure, well proportioned and symmetrical, while some of the other cities resemble misshapen cripples, with dwarfed legs and herculean arms."[99] For some, these were the very symptoms of old-fashioned complacency that had hindered Nashville's quest for growth in the past. These restless strivers would find more exciting fields in the risky world of financial speculation.

ON THE WALL STREET OF THE SOUTH

The most visible sectors of Nashville's emergent service economy after World War I were insurance, banking, and securities. The insurance companies amassed large pools of capital drawn from markets that rapidly expanded throughout the South and into the North and West after the war. A new generation of bankers now competed aggressively for dominance in Middle Tennessee and solidified Nashville's position as a regional banking center. Rogers Caldwell turned the South's historical disadvantages in northern financial markets into a regional asset by marketing millions of dollars in new bonds issued to launch thousands of public improvements throughout the South in the 1920s.

On the "Wall Street of the South," along Union Street, men of vision and men of reckless ambition pursued their dreams in the heady atmosphere of prosperity of the 1920s. Nashville's financiers and small investors alike shared the buoyant confidence and speculative mania that charged the air on New York's Wall Street and across the country in this period. "We were living in a Golden Age," recalled Rogers Caldwell, "and none of us thought it would ever end."[1]

SHIFTING INSURANCE MARKETS

One of the most vital components of Nashville's economy in this period was the insurance industry. National Life and Accident's stunning growth brought total assets from $2.3 million in 1916 to $29.6 million in 1930. Life and Casualty began with under $.3 million in 1914 and by 1930 had $12.2 million in assets.[2] Both companies were firmly established prior to the war, when the rapid economic and social changes wrought by war and the 1920s forced them to adopt radically new strategies for growth. The results were not only an impressive expansion of the numbers and territory these companies served, but a decisive shift in the type of policy they sold and the type of client they insured.

Thousands of soldiers recruited into the military dropped their insurance policies, often because companies refused benefits for casualties incurred in war. Also, the federal government offered its own life insurance to soldiers to cover "war risks" for a low monthly premium which forced private insurers to compete.[3] The wartime economic boom also drew many black clients north, beyond the territory served by southern insurance companies. Then, at the end of the war in 1918, the demobilization of the troops accelerated the rapid spread of a devastating epidemic of Spanish influenza, which struck all insurance companies a severe blow but stimulated insurance sales in its wake.[4]

These disruptive episodes occasioned by the war may have been transitory, yet they produced permanent changes for Nashville's insurance companies. The continued northward migration of southern blacks during the 1920s eroded what had been a primary market both for National Life and for Life and Casualty. National Life followed the Great Migration north to Illinois, Indiana, Ohio, and even west to California, where new offices were opened between 1918 and the mid-1920s. Life and Casualty ventured into Missouri in 1923 but otherwise chose to expand within the South, moving into North Carolina, Florida, across the Deep South in 1918, and into Kentucky in 1922.[5]

More important than territorial expansion was the movement from "industrial" health and accident policies to life insurance. Though a variety of different types of life insurance policies and payment plans were introduced in these years, the major distinction was between "industrial life" (which featured low premiums and usually offered no more than $1,000 in death benefits, primarily to working-class blacks) and "ordinary life" (sold for higher annual premiums and offering higher death benefits, being geared to middle-class whites). Across the country during the 1920s, and resuming in the mid-1930s, there was a surge of life insurance sales accompanied by stagnation and decline in industrial health-and-accident insurance. New estate and income taxes made life insurance more attractive to wealthy Americans, while company- and government-sponsored plans for workmen's compensation, along with inexpensive group insurance plans, undercut the industrial insurance market.

Life insurance offered companies more dependable profits, for it involved long-term commitments, larger premiums, and far less turnover. Industrial insurance had to be sold and resold face-to-face every week. There was no significant cumulative advantage for customers to avoid letting their policies lapse. Because agents were rewarded with extra commissions on the initial weeks of a new policy, they had, in effect, an incentive to allow lapses and write new policies for customers later. Moreover, industrial insurance was sold primarily to poor, black wage earners who were prone to frequent unemployment and were always struggling to live on restricted budgets. Furthermore, Nashville's insurance companies now faced growing competition from black-owned insurance companies that cropped up in the South during the 1920s. These new companies hired black agents and appealed to racial pride in an effort to draw business away from white-owned companies and their white agents. Life and Casualty experimented for a time with a special force of black agents, but it was increasingly clear that further expansion in the black industrial insurance market was limited.[6]

Both National Life and Life and Casualty began selling a low-premium "industrial life" policy to blacks, but there were drawbacks to this strategy. Mortality rates were much higher among blacks than whites, in large part because blacks were restricted to poor, unsanitary neighborhoods and normally denied access to equal medical care. The Life and Casualty home office continually warned agents to be wary in insuring blacks, many of whom were already chronically ill. Since medical examinations were not yet routinely used to screen out high-risk clients, the company began to use blanket restrictions against insuring segments of the black population, or it set limits on the amount of insurance allowed blacks.[7]

The racial factor was more clearly defined by 1924 when Life and Casualty issued a new line of "White Industrial Life" policies, which were designed to offer working-class whites a low-premium policy with death benefits. Simultaneously, the company introduced an innovative policy for up to $1,000 on children over thirty days old that was restricted to whites. Agents accustomed to selling exclusively to blacks often felt ill at ease approaching white clients. The home office introduced a company magazine, the *Mirror*, in 1924, in part to help guide the field force in making this difficult transition. Letters from agents who had successfully moved into the white market testified to higher profits and easier working conditions. "The work is indeed more pleasant and profitable," wrote one agent, who went on to criticize the field men who "seem to be afraid to canvass white people." "They are our people," he argued. "If the agent will conduct himself becoming a gentleman, White Life business is more easily written. . . . " To underline the latter point, the *Mirror* included tips to agents on the proper grammar and grooming to adopt before approaching white customers.[8]

Life and Casualty's ultimate goal was not just to add new markets but to become a "Lily White Company," as it was announced at a 1927 sales convention. "The districts that are showing the most progress," the *Mirror* proclaimed in 1929, "are those that are expanding their energies in the production of White Life. And White Life naturally leads to Ordinary. It's White Life that is going to put the Company on the map in the future." "We have changed the color of this business," one Life and Casualty agent reported from the field.[9]

National Life appeared more intent on supplementing its largely black industrial insurance market than in abandoning it for a white clientele. The company issued no policies exclusively for one race, and agents were encouraged not to forsake their old industrial customers in pursuing new life insurance clients. Though National Life offered the same low-premium industrial life policies as Life and Casualty, it made a larger commitment to ordinary life. In 1919, upon embarking on its new life insurance venture, National Life hired a full-time actuary, organized a medical department under Dr. Rufus E. Fort, and set up a Risk Committee to review policies. By 1929 National Life claimed $101.5 million in ordinary life, almost one-third of their life insurance in force.[10]

During the 1920s both companies adopted new techniques of selling insurance. They continued to rely on field agents to sell policies, but the companies now sought to smooth the way for the canvassing agent with an intense effort to educate the public and to advertise the benefits of insurance. They used promotional publications and gave away calendars and the like, but the most important advertising instrument in this period was radio.

National Life's wsm began in October 1925. It was Edwin W. Craig, the company president's son, who first recognized the power of radio as an ally to insurance sales. The new company headquarters at Seventh Avenue and Union included plans for a thoroughly modern 1,000-watt broadcast studio on the fifth floor. The station did little direct advertising for the company before the 1930s, except to broadcast an occasional reminder of the sponsor, and of course the company slogan "We Shield Millions" was abbreviated in the station's call letters. The station's purpose was to build company identity and serve as a "door opener" for the field force. The station offered a variety of programs, most of them aimed at the more educated middle class to which agents were also pitching sales for the new life insurance policies. Programs included Francis Craig's Orchestra (live from the Hermitage Hotel), the Bedtime Story for children, Beasly Smith's Orchestra, operatic solos, and Sunday sermons by the Reverend James I. Vance of the First Presbyterian Church.

But the most famous of wsm programs was the Saturday night Barn Dance, which station director George D. Hay dubbed the "Grand Ole Opry." It featured "old time fiddlers" like "Uncle Jimmy" Thompson and Dr. Humphrey Bate and his Possum Hunters. The Grand Ole Opry's hillbilly music had an enormous appeal, not simply to rural listeners but to the thousands of city and town people who had migrated from the country. "Those old tunes carry us back to the days gone by . . . ," one fan wrote to wsm in 1926.[11]

The Opry was a great success from its beginnings. George D. Hay, nicknamed "the Solemn Old Judge," had a genius for this kind of folksy entertainment. He directed the show using an old steamship whistle as a prop and deliberately accentuated the hillbilly character of the performers. Hay used a live studio audience to add spontaneity, and it rapidly outgrew the studio. The Opry eventually moved out to the Hillsboro Theater, to the Dixie Tabernacle in East Nashville, the War Memorial Auditorium, then to the Ryman Auditorium in 1941, where it remained for thirty-three years. In 1927 the station was boosted to 5,000 watts, and in 1932 to 50,000 watts and clear-channel status. By this time the Opry was a show with a national following.[12]

Edwin Craig, who saw WSM as a means of enhancing the company's image and uplifting the region's cultural fare, may have winced at the Opry's hillbilly music, but it was remarkably effective at promoting insurance. In the minds of some listeners, it seemed, it was the Opry that sponsored the insurance company rather than the reverse. One loyal fan of the Opry's stars testified, "I love them so good that I took a 25-cent twenty year endowment policy . . . and I think everybody ought to take insurance with the WSM Company." Agents found the doors opened wide for the "Grand Ole Opry Insurance Company," and they gave away free tickets to prospective customers.[13]

Life and Casualty began its first broadcast on WDAD a year after WSM began, and it followed a similar format, with the emphasis on music from the symphonic to "old time fiddlin'." When the company moved to its new quarters on Fourth Avenue North in 1926, it too included a modern studio. In 1928, one year after WSM boosted to 5,000 watts, WLAC, as the new station was now known, followed its competitor.[14]

The companies originally intended the radio stations to promote goodwill through musical entertainment but soon became instruments with which to educate the public and advance the broad interests of insurance and southern regional progress. WLAC led the way with its "Salutes to the States," a series of addresses on public improvements and social conditions in the various southern states Life and Casualty served. WLAC mixed public-service broadcasts with lectures on health, education, and thrift.

Life and Casualty president Andrew M. Burton was a master at linking insurance to traditional religious values and regional pride. A devoutly religious man, Burton used company literature to propound a philosophy of strict Christian morality and self-help, combined with practical advice on thrift and insurance. He distributed Sunday school lesson plans, thrift booklets for children, and sponsored lectures on WLAC's "Nashville School of the Air." Burton was especially interested in reaching children with his gospel of thrift. He headed a $50-million thrift drive in 1926 to enlist 50,000 children in a one-dollar weekly savings plan.[15] Burton tied his values of thrift and Christian moral discipline to regional progress. "Within the last decade," he announced to a sales convention in 1927, "the magic hand of Thrift has touched the potent forces of the new and advancing South. . . ." WLAC, he promised, would be "devoted not simply to wholesome entertainment, but especially to the emancipation of the rising generation from the slavery of extravagance."[16]

National Life made similar efforts to link insurance with religion, family, and personal success. "We need to become evangelists, . . . alive and burning with a desire to bring into the fold every possible person that needs the wings of the National Eagle spread over their doors," exhorted the home office in 1922. In a similar vein, a preacher, quoted approvingly in 1924, insisted that life insurance was sanctioned by the Bible, and, moreover, Joseph was president of the world's first insurance company. "And from the days of the 'corn cribs of Egypt' to this good hour, the high purpose of life insurance has been one and the same — to bless humanity."[17] These sometimes strained efforts to reconcile Christian faith in the afterlife and the insurance man's concern with financial security in this world reveal something of the fascinating confluence of traditional values and the modern world in the 1920s.

ON THE WALL STREET OF THE SOUTH

Nowhere was the buoyant economic spirit of the postwar era more clearly alive than in the city's financial community. Nashville's modest status as a regional banking center in 1915 was inflated during the 1920s to the point that local boosters began calling Union Street the "Wall Street of the South." It was not an idle boast, for the power of Nashville's banks and investment houses was substantial, and when some of them crashed in 1930, a large part of the South felt the ground shake.

Annual bank clearings for all Nashville banks rose from $323 million in 1915 to $864 million in 1919, then skyrocketed up to $1.24 billion in 1929, up more than 280 percent since 1915 (see appendix B).[18] These figures reflected the general prosperity of the economy as money flowed through local banks and into new industry, homes, consumer goods, wages, and investments of all kinds. The banks enlarged their own financial base as well during this boom. Total bank resources in 1915 stood at a little over $38 million; by 1929 the figure was nearly $140 million, up 268 percent.[19] The banks were also gathering a huge volume of deposits from individuals and corporations. Total deposits stood at $25.3 million in 1915; by 1929 the banks had over $98.2 million, up 288 percent. A growing percentage of bank resources was being loaned out by the late 1920s as banks became the underwriters of new economic enterprises. Loans were only about 40 percent of total bank resources in 1920 when the Goodrich survey took place; by 1929 loans totaled over 62 percent of all bank resources.[20]

The Goodrich Report had criticized Nashville's bankers for their stodgy conservatism and blamed them in part for the city's slow growth. In the coming decade a bold new breed of young entrepreneurs appeared on the Wall Street of the South, and when they were through no one could accuse Nashville of financial conservatism. Underlying all the growth in financial institutions was the basic shift from entrepreneurial capitalism, largely dependent on family money and limited partnerships, to finance capitalism, which required huge sums of capital to underwrite new factories, to organize corporate mergers, and to control competition through holding companies. In this context financiers assumed enormous power within the economy, and the industrial or commercial entrepreneurs now took a back seat to the money men.

The first generation of Nashville bankers often consisted of former wholesale merchants, or front men for merchants. In the 1920s a second generation of young professional financiers emerged, and their vision transcended the local economy or any particular line of business. The rise of the financiers was due to the surge of new corporations that turned to the money men to raise capital through public sales of stock. An extraordinarily prosperous economic climate from 1920 to 1929 made even the riskiest speculation look smart. The new, aggressive bankers—most of whom were too young to remember the depression of the 1890s—were more willing to take the necessary risks, and their success made older, more conservative bankers seem out of touch with the times. America, many businessmen and financiers believed in the 1920s, had entered a new era of sustained economic prosperity, and the panics and depressions of the past would be no more. For a time they were right.

In 1915 Nashville had five nationally chartered banks and another five state-chartered banks. James E. Caldwell's Fourth and First National Bank, with nearly $15 million in total resources, and American National, with resources of close to $9 million, dominated the field.[21] In the coming years a few new small banks entered the field. Central Bank and Trust, headed by Watkins Crockett, was organized in 1916. Another small interloper was to become a major power in the city. The German American Bank was organized in 1916 by A.E. "Ed" Potter, Jr., the son of banker A.E. Potter, who had come from Smithville, Tennessee, ten years earlier to join Broadway National Bank. Ed Potter was only seventeen years old when he dropped out of Vanderbilt and went to work in his father's bank. Three years later he struck out to organize his own bank with backing from the wealthy businessmen in the German-American community in Nashville. Potter's father served as president of the new bank to assure its reputation and to avoid legal problems,

Figure 73 (left).   A.E. "Ed" Potter, Jr. (1896–1976), founder of Commerce Union Bank. Jesse Hill Ford, *Mr. Potter and His Bank* (Nashville, 1977), used by permission.

Figure 74.   Persis D. Houston (1874–1956), cofounder of First American National Bank. First American National Bank.

since his son was not yet old enough to sign contracts. In 1917, during the anti-German hysteria of World War I, Potter quickly changed the name of his bank to the Farmers and Merchants Bank. Potter's new bank survived the war quite well under its new name and built deposits of close to $1 million by 1919.[22]

Early in 1923, after an interlude of national financial instability, Potter was ready to launch a bold program of expansion through branch banking. Potter raised his capital stock of the bank in January, and by May 1923 he bought country banks in Spring Hill, Springfield, Lawrenceburg, Sparta, and Lebanon. This group of banks was reorganized under the name Commerce Union Bank, and subsequent branches were added in Gladeville, Gallatin, Woodbury, and Camden. In 1924 Commerce Union bought out State Bank and Trust, merged Southern Bank and Trust into it, and established it as the Broadway Branch of Commerce Union. Potter's newly acquired country branches, several of them in the rich burley tobacco areas north of Nashville, opened lucrative opportunities for crop loans. National banking laws restricted loans banks could make to any single borrower to a maximum of 10 percent of their own capital and surplus. State charters allowed 15 percent of capital, surplus, and undivided profits to be loaned to a single borrower, but this was still insufficient to allow the kind of large short-term loans needed to get big tobacco crops to market. Most country banks had to arrange cumbersome loans in cooperation with correspondent banks in the city. Now, as branches of Commerce Union, they could loan amounts based on the total resources of Commerce Union and all its branches.[23]

Unlike Tennessee's state-chartered banks, such as Potter's, national banks were prohibited from establishing branch banks outside their home county, unless expressly allowed by state law. To meet the challenge of branch banking they began to organize holding companies and to expand through them. The national banks also organized new affiliate banks under state charters to allow operations outside the stricter federal regulations.

James E. Caldwell's Fourth and First National Bank established several branch banks within Davidson County and organized a new bank under state charter, the Fourth and First Bank and Trust Company. In 1927 Fourth and First National Bank took control of Nashville Trust Company and merged its state-chartered bank into it. During the same year Fourth and First swallowed the Central National Bank of Nashville. By the end of the decade eight small country banks also became affiliates of Caldwell's empire. Together, the Caldwell bank group had about $100 million in assets.[24]

American National Bank was controlled by Pervis D. Houston and Paul Davis beginning in 1918. Houston had come to Nashville from Marshall County, Tennessee, in 1906 to help organize the First Savings

Bank and Trust Company. After Caldwell gained control of this bank in 1912 Houston continued as a vice president but resigned in 1918 when the opportunity arose to have his own bank. Paul Davis, whose father was a wealthy whiskey distiller in Tullahoma, came to Nashville after attending Stanford University and working as a banker in Cuba. He worked in the real estate division of Nashville Trust Company, tried his hand in insurance sales, and married the daughter of Victor Emmanuel Shwab, a wealthy whiskey distiller. Davis joined Houston in 1918 to purchase control of the American National and became the entrepreneur behind the scenes. Houston, with his strong statewide reputation in banking circles, served as front man in his capacity as bank president. In 1928 Davis took over as president, while Houston assumed responsibilities as chairman of the board.[25]

Houston and Davis expanded their financial empire in the 1920s. In 1921 American National took over the Cumberland Valley National Bank. A year earlier Davis and Houston set up the American Trust Company under a separate state charter. This institution became a major rival of Nashville Trust Company, which until this time enjoyed a monopoly on trust accounts. In 1925 Nashville Trust opened a stunning new building on Union Street, with fourteen stories, the tallest building with the fastest elevators in the city, according to William Nelson, then president of Nashville Trust. Paul Davis accepted this as a challenge and added eleven stories to the American Trust building at the corner of Third and Union, which made it one story higher than Nashville Trust next door. Nelson and Davis quarreled over the party wall they shared and refused to consider building common floor levels, which might have encouraged future merger of the two institutions. When the American Trust building was completed William Nelson added a parapet on his Nashville Trust building, bringing it just slightly higher than the next-door rival. When James Caldwell took over Nashville Trust in 1927, following Nelson's death, these adjacent buildings became fitting monuments to the fervid competition between the two banks.[26]

In addition to Potter's fast-rising Commerce Union Bank, one other new bank emerged in the 1920s to challenge the dominance of American National and Fourth and First National. In 1927 a group of men that had split off from the two giants organized Third National Bank. Charles A. Craig, president of National Life and Accident, was a director of Caldwell's Fourth and First National Bank until 1927, when he disputed the bank's loan policies. The bank was loaning large sums to Rogers Caldwell, James E. Caldwell's son, in order to buy insurance companies. Craig thought the loans were poor risks but objected also because the bank, in effect, was helping major competitors of National Life.[27] Craig became chairman of the board at Third National and resigned as director of Fourth and First. Watkins Crockett, president of Central National Bank until it was swallowed by Caldwell's Fourth and

Figure 75 (left).   Paul M. Davis (1882–1969), cofounder of First American National Bank. First American National Bank.

Figure 76.   Frank M. Farris (1890–1950), one of the founders of Third National Bank. Third National Bank.

First in 1927, resigned as vice president under Caldwell to take over as president of Third National. Frank Mitchell Farris, a young cashier at American National and son of a prominent Nashville lumber dealer, was a major figure in the organization of Third National Bank, which he served as executive vice president. Several other wealthy businessmen, apparently eager to support a new bank free of control by the two giant national banks, joined the board of directors and subscribed to the bank's stock. It opened at Fourth and Church with a strong show of $600,000 capital, more than the half-million dollars that had been subscribed originally. Within less than two years deposits rose from over $1 million to almost $5.2 million. Third National was off to a fast start and would meet the depression flush with new deposits and less burdened by the heavy loans that the older banks carried.[28]

During the 1920s all the major banks in Nashville plunged into security sales to attract a horde of eager investors who were shunning savings deposits for stupendous profits in stocks and bonds. The 1920s witnessed the strongest bull market that ever ran on Wall Street. The vigor of the securities market rested partly on the fundamental strength of an expanding industrial economy, but also on a speculative mania among investors, large and small, who followed hot stock tips, bought high-risk stocks on 10-percent margin, and believed fervently in the businessmen and politicians who promised endless prosperity. By law, banks could not sell securities, so they set up affiliated brokerage houses: Fourth and First Company, American National Securities Company, Commerce Union Company, and Third National Company. J.C. Bradford and Company, along with other brokerage firms, opened up along Union Street and Fourth Avenue to serve the swelling demand of the public for stocks and bonds. Whereas moneyed men in other southern cities speculated in cotton or real estate, Nashville had a well-established tradition of investing in securities, both local stocks and those on the New York Stock Exchange. Nashville mushroomed into the leading investment center of the South.[29]

THE RISE AND FALL OF THE HOUSE OF CALDWELL

The individual most responsible for Nashville's rise as an investment center was Rogers Caldwell, whose career cast a long shadow over the history of this period. Born to banker James E. Caldwell in 1890, Caldwell was raised amid the luxury of Longview, his father's estate on Franklin Pike. He attended Vanderbilt for two years but found he was a better poker player than student. His taste for gambling and business (the two became inseparable in Caldwell's career) and his indifference to studies led him to walk away from campus one day in 1910 and never to return. He went directly to his father's office and announced he was ready to go into the business world. His father sent him on a grand tour of Europe, but Rogers returned early and pressed his father for a chance to begin. The father relented and put his son in charge of a small general insurance agency he had begun back in 1876.

At age twenty Rogers Caldwell took eagerly to his new role. He sold all kinds of insurance but began to specialize in surety bonds to cover contractors in city and county construction projects. Caldwell also became active in marketing county and municipal bonds in northern money markets. Southern bonds had been stigmatized by a legacy of instability since the Reconstruction era, and southern development had been hindered by a chronic problem of poor credit and high discounts on the bonds it did sell in the North. This matter was vividly impressed on Rogers Caldwell in 1915 when, at the last minute, a Chicago bank withdrew its offer to buy some Hickman County bonds Caldwell was selling because of instability caused by the sinking of the *Lusitania.* Caldwell returned from Chicago determined to establish a municipal bond house of his own to serve the needs of the South.[30]

Caldwell split off from his father's insurance company in 1917 to found Caldwell and Company. It began with no real capital and at an unpropitious moment when federal Liberty Bonds were driving less secure local government bonds from the market. But Caldwell and Company embodied an idea whose time had come. There was no real competition for handling southern bonds, and the company emerged as the regional economy and public expenditures in particular were about to boom. "We Bank on the South," the company slogan proclaimed. Caldwell turned a regional financial stigma into an opportunity for fabulous growth. As the federal government withdrew from the bond market at the end of the war and the South began a period of rapid development of roads, schools, and other public improvements, Caldwell and Company was prepared to serve the region's needs for capital. New bond issues in the South rose from $692 million in 1919 to $1.5 billion by the end of the 1920s. Caldwell began handling bonds exclusively for Tennessee, then branched into every southern state. "Rogers Caldwell," the *Tennessean* announced, "is the Moses that will lead us out of . . . bondage and make possible for us a new freedom such as the old South has struggled for since the days of the Confederacy."[31]

The capital acquired by Caldwell and Company from sales of these bonds, by stipulation, was deposited without earning interest for the debtor in the Bank of Tennessee, which had been set up by Caldwell in 1919 solely to receive these deposits and to disburse them as public construction projects required. With access to this large pool of capital, Caldwell and Company would expand in a variety of new directions.[32]

Beginning in 1923 Caldwell began to invest in real estate mortgage bonds issued by private companies during the construction boom of

Figure 77 (left). Rogers Caldwell (1890–1968), of Caldwell and Company in his heyday during the 1920s. *Tennessean Sunday Magazine,* Oct. 20, 27, Nov. 3, 1963.

Figure 78. Luke Lea (1879–1945), U.S. senator, founder of the *Tennessean,* developer of Belle Meade, donor of Percy and Edwin Warner Parks, and behind–the–scenes political power broker in the 1920s. Morgan Blake and Stuart Towe, *Lawmakers and Public Men of Tennessee* (Nashville, 1915).

the 1920s. In Nashville alone Caldwell and Company underwrote the new Harry Nichol Building on Union Street (which became Caldwell and Company headquarters), the Andrew Jackson Hotel, the Cotton States Life Building, and several other large construction projects in the city.[33]

Starting with this minor diversion into real estate, Caldwell and Company ventured further afield into banks, insurance companies, industrial firms, newspapers, and a variety of businesses from department stores to a baseball team. From his original mission to market southern municipal bonds Caldwell had moved into the making of a gigantic financial empire which, before it fell in 1930, was worth about one-half billion dollars. The empire fed upon itself. A voracious appetite for more capital to cover obligations required new acquisitions that further overextended the business until, inevitably, it caved in like a house of cards.

Beginning in 1926, with the economy running at full steam, Caldwell began buying control of industrial firms. By 1929 the company controlled majority stock in eight textile and clothing companies worth $17.5 million; three building supply companies worth $10.3 million; six distribution and service companies, including a string of department stores, and oil companies worth $12.9 million; and two Nashville enterprises, the Nashville Volunteers baseball team and a Franklin Pike suburban development company, worth $.3 million—a grand total of over $41 million. The same year Caldwell and Company began purchasing insurance companies, including Missouri State Life and a number of smaller companies scattered across the South. These acquisitions gave Caldwell and Company control of $233 million in combined assets, but it also burdened the company with enormous new debts.[34]

Caldwell and Company's growing need for capital to support its expansion naturally led to the acquisition of banks. From its beginnings Caldwell was closely tied to Fourth and First Bank and its affiliates in Nashville, and he continued to rely on his father's banks for several large loans. However, Caldwell needed access to more capital, and in 1927 he joined Colonel Luke Lea in the purchase of controlling interest in the Holston National Bank of Knoxville. It was the first in a string of joint ventures between Lea and Caldwell, who, except for each other, had in Tennessee no match for their voracious ambition. The two men next turned to Memphis where, in 1928, with Ed Potter, Jr., they purchased control of Manhattan Savings Bank and Trust Company, then the larger Union and Planters Bank and Trust Company. Luke Lea helped launch the Liberty Bank and Trust in Nashville in 1925, and he bought control of the Central Bank and Trust Company in Asheville, North Carolina, in 1930. These banks were used by Lea to advance the expansion of his own financial-political empire and became entangled with Caldwell's affairs only to the extent the destinies of these two men had become intertwined.[35] In all, Caldwell and Company by 1929 controlled about seventy-five banks in Tennessee and Arkansas, with combined assets totaling over $213 million.

Lea and Caldwell also joined forces in 1927 to purchase two major newspapers in Tennessee, the *Memphis Commercial Appeal* and *Knoxville Journal*. Together with Lea's *Tennessean*, the papers gave the Lea-Caldwell coalition a major editorial voice in three of the state's major cities. An unsuccessful attempt to purchase the *Atlanta Constitution*, one of the South's most respected newspapers, suggested the larger ambitions Lea and Caldwell entertained.[36]

Caldwell and Lea, in different ways, embodied a dual drive for financial and political power. For Lea the effort to enlarge his fortune was subordinate to his relentless drive to reach beyond his base in Middle Tennessee and build a statewide political machine with which to promote his vision of business progressivism.[37] Caldwell, on the other hand, was driven by whatever possessed him to become the "J.P. Morgan of the South," and political power was incidental to this goal. Alone, both men might have achieved enough of their goals to have earned a respected, if controversial, place in history. Together, they were doomed to a tragic end, for the entanglement of their financial and political empires spelled ruin for both.

Lea had experienced a meteoric rise as a politician following his celebrated speech before the Democratic convention in 1906. He picked up the banner of his fallen hero, Edward Carmack, after 1908 and used the *Tennessean*, which he began the previous year, to promote his political views. In 1911, at the age of thirty-two, he was elected U.S. senator, the youngest man in that exclusive club. His defeat for reelection to the Senate in 1916, due in large measure to the opposition of the L&N, ended his career in public office. After his heroic, though controversial, episode as a colonel in World War I, he returned to an important role as behind-the-scenes leader of the Middle Tennessee Democratic party. He was now an archfoe of Boss Ed Crump of Memphis, the Hilary Howse machine in Nashville, and Edward Stahlman, publisher of the rival Nashville *Banner*.[38] With the alliance of Lea and Caldwell and their move to control newspapers and banks in West and East Tennessee, Lea's enemies became Caldwell's.

Lea's support helped elect Austin Peay governor in 1922 and to reelect him in 1924 and 1926, despite consistent opposition from Ed Crump of Memphis. Peay was an outstanding progressive governor who launched a formidable program of government reorganization, public education, and highway construction. In 1927, after Lea and Caldwell joined forces, Lea approached the state Highway Commissioner, C. Neil Bass, apparently to arrange for Kyrock, a product of Caldwell's Kentucky Rock and Asphalt Company, to be selected without competitive bidding on state highway projects. Bass refused to cooperate, but the matter was not resolved. Austin Peay died unexpectedly in October 1927, and Henry Horton, an unknown politician with no real constituency, succeeded him as governor. Horton was entirely dependent on Lea's support and proved a willing tool in the hands of Lea and Caldwell. When Horton was sworn into office, the *Banner* chided, he raised his hand toward heaven but kept his eyes on Lea and Caldwell.[39] Commissioner Bass was soon replaced by Lea's old friend Colonel Harry S. Berry, and Kyrock now found a lucrative outlet in Tennessee road construction projects.

In the election of 1928 Lea and Caldwell's influence over Horton and the Kyrock scandal became the crucial issues. The *Banner*, supporting Hill McAlister, dismissed Horton as "Governor-in-Name" and attacked Lea as "Governor-in-Fact." Hard-hitting political cartoons in the *Banner* depicted Rogers Caldwell as "Kid Kyrock," invariably loaded down with money bags and bilking the public. "Musso-LEA-ni" was satirized as a dictator unworthy of public trust. Lea used his newspapers to support Horton and launched equally vicious personal attacks on *Banner* publisher Edward Stahlman, reminding Tennesseans at every opportunity that Stahlman was German-born and not a true American. Caldwell was horrified at being dragged into the political arena but must have realized there was no turning back, for Horton's defeat now constituted a serious threat to his financial empire. As Horton's election chances appeared to dim before the August Democratic primary, Lea and Caldwell mobilized a large slush fund with donations from Caldwell-affiliated companies to help the cause. Precisely how much money was gathered and how it was used is not known, but Horton managed to squeak by McAlister, thanks also to the candidacy of Lewis S. Pope, who split Horton's opposition.[40]

Now the political entanglements of Caldwell and Company would increase. Highway Commissioner Harry S. Berry was discharged because he refused to approve road construction through the property of political cronies, including a road serving Lea's Belle Meade development. Similarly, Horton appointed as superintendent of banks a minor official in a Lea-Caldwell bank who proved helpful in protecting Caldwell and Lea from state interference. For example, when state audits were planned for Caldwell's Bank of Tennessee, word was leaked through Lea in time for the necessary funds to be shifted.[41]

The most important link between the state government and Caldwell's empire involved the custody of state funds from bond sales. In 1929 Horton pushed the State Funding Board to issue all at once nearly $29 million in bonds, mostly for new roads and bridges. Caldwell and Company, in league with the American National Company, submitted the only bid for these bonds, and the funds derived from their sale went on deposit at the Bank of Tennessee, secured only by personal surety bonds signed by Rogers Caldwell and the other officers of his company. Horton called a special session of the General Assembly in December 1929 to push through several laws that would further benefit Caldwell and Company. He urged authorization of more state bonds worth $15 million. He asked that the State Funding Board be expanded to include the commissioner of taxation and finance, Charles M. McCabe, a former Caldwell employee. Finally, Horton wanted to give the Funding Board sole power to decide on the banks in which to deposit state funds. All these measures passed, and the state government became, in effect, a Caldwell affiliate. In the middle of 1929 the state had less than $2.3 million on deposit at the Bank of Tennessee; by October 1930 those deposits increased more than $8.3 million.[42]

The deposit of state funds gave Caldwell desperately needed capital to meet his growing obligations. Too many of Caldwell's assets were tied up in nonliquid investments, particularly the large holdings of stock in affiliated companies. There was also the magnificent estate Rogers Caldwell built with company funds. Brentwood Hall was a mansion befitting a financial baron on the rise. Modeled after the Hermitage (Caldwell was an ardent admirer of Andrew Jackson), the house cost $350,000 to build in 1927. On the estate he also built Brentwood Stables, filled with some of the finest thoroughbred horseflesh in Middle Tennessee. Caldwell's expensive taste for fine antiques, lavish meals, and fox hunting exceeded his annual salary of $95,000, and his debts to Caldwell and Company rose to $380,000 by 1929.[43]

Caldwell also misjudged the direction Wall Street was headed and began selling stocks short (that is, selling in the future at current prices with the expectation that prices will fall in the interim). Caldwell sold the leading blue-chip stocks of a bull market that was to hit full stride in the two years prior to October 1929. Not only did he miss the great upward surge of prices, by selling short he suffered even greater losses of $685,000. Apparently sobered by these losses, Caldwell closed his short account in June 1929, just four months too early.[44]

By the end of 1929 only the cash deposits from the state bond sales were keeping the company alive. When the stock market crash came in October, Caldwell and Company's already weak position became desperate. Early in 1930 Caldwell approached officers of BancoKentucky, a holding company for the National Bank of Kentucky, which itself was in serious financial straits, to arrange a merger. This combination gave Caldwell and Company access to the deposits in the bank group and the use of BancoKentucky stock as collateral in other loans. In return, Rogers Caldwell gave half the stock of Caldwell and Company, which had been under his exclusive control, to BancoKentucky.[45] The merger, however, only delayed the collapse of both companies.

Throughout 1930 Caldwell madly scrambled for cash. Massive transfusions of loans from affiliated banks and from Lea's bank in Ashe-

ville kept the company alive but never cured its chronic weakness. Caldwell and Lea managed to postpone the collapse of the company until
after the November 4 gubernatorial election, which their candidate,
Henry Horton, won. The same day, the Nashville Clearing House Association called an emergency meeting to investigate rumors of Caldwell's
impending failure. With Caldwell's agreement, the association appointed a committee of leading bankers to take over the affairs of the
company and look after "conserving and protecting the interests" of
Caldwell and Company. They tried to calm the situation with brave
statements about Caldwell's solvency, but the state's examination of
the Bank of Tennessee showed it was insolvent, and the bank closed
Friday, November 7. The final collapse of the House of Caldwell was
delayed by the weekend and an Armistice Day holiday on Tuesday. On
Wednesday, November 12, the other dominoes tottered and fell. The
Holston-Union National Bank in Knoxville failed to open that morning. In Nashville panicked depositors clutching their passbooks formed
lines in front of every bank. Bankers tried to slow the run by allowing
only one person to enter their banks at a time, but public confidence
was plummeting as the day wore on.[46]

The Fourth and First had been straining under a bank run for several days when it was forced to merge with American National on Wednesday afternoon. Later to be named First American, this combination
created the South's second-largest bank. James E. Caldwell stepped aside
with the understated explanation that he "had a right to retire" after
his long service at the helm of Fourth and First.[47] It was not until Friday, November 14, that Caldwell and Company announced its insol-
vency and went into receivership.[48] Luke Lea's Liberty Bank and Trust
closed the same day. Its president, R.E. Donnell, on Thanksgiving Day
quietly left the family dining table, checked in at a local hotel, and
hanged himself.[49] On Saturday, Commerce Union took over the small
Tennessee-Hermitage National Bank before it collapsed. The People's
Savings Bank, a small black institution, also closed during the storm.
The crash echoed across the state to Caldwell and Lea's banks in Memphis, to Lea's bank in Asheville, North Carolina, and then to the Banco-
Kentucky group. When the dust settled, no less than 120 banks in seven
southern states went down with Caldwell and Company, while numerous others merged in desperation with stronger banks.[50] There was, of
course, no government safety net such as the Reconstruction Finance
Corporation to protect failing banks, just as there had been little government regulation to curb the dangerous practices that led them to ruin.

The Wall Street of the South slid into a severe depression following
the collapse of Caldwell's empire. Bank clearings, the best single indi-
cator of business and financial activity, fell from $1.2 billion in 1929
to a bottom of $460 million in 1932, only 37 percent of the 1929 figure.
As late as 1940, bank clearings were only 69 percent of what they had

been in 1929. The dollar value of building permits in 1932 was under 20 percent of what it had been in 1929 and rose to only 63 percent a decade later, despite a huge influx of federal construction dollars.[51]

The Great Depression that descended on Nashville was, of course, part of an international economic crisis, but Caldwell and Lea became obvious targets upon which to fix blame for the widespread misery. Their willingness to mix politics and financial affairs now returned to haunt them, as political enemies began arousing popular emotions and stalking the two men through the courts. Close to $7 million in state funds were lost in the collapse of Caldwell and Lea's banks. A Public Emergency Committee made up of Lea's old foes (Hill McAlister, Lewis Pope, Albert H. Roberts—all former gubernatorial opponents of Lea's men, Peay and Horton—Kinnard T. McConnico, a Howse lieutenant, and C. Neil Bass, the purged highway commissioner) organized a series of mass meetings across the state to express indignation against Lea, Caldwell, and Horton, "a scheming triumvirate which had conspired to shame the fair name of the State." The "politico-bunko-busto-banko" coalition, they insisted, must be brought to justice.[52]

Though many considered Governor Horton little more than a "misguided weakling" in the service of Lea and Caldwell, others thought he must be removed from office if only to prevent Lea and Caldwell from using him further to protect themselves. An impeachment drive, led by Lea's enemy Ed Crump, ultimately failed, and Horton was allowed to finish his term in 1932.

Luke Lea became the primary target of political enmity and of legal prosecution. Some demanded that only "stripe wearing and chain clanging" by the individuals responsible for the financial crisis would appease justice.[53] Luke Lea survived a misdemeanor indictment involving a trial in Knoxville over the Holston-Union National Bank collapse. It was in Asheville, North Carolina, that Lea and his son, Luke Lea, Jr., were brought to trial on charges of fraud in July 1931. With Governor Horton still in office, Lea could have resisted extradition, but he and his son went voluntarily to insist on their innocence. Lea was found guilty and sentenced to serve six to ten years, his son to serve two to six years. The Leas appealed the case all the way to the United States Supreme Court and, failing there, staged a desperate fight to resist extradition to North Carolina. Lea's success in postponing legal action left him in 1933 at the mercy of his political archenemy, the newly elected governor, Hill McAlister, who promptly issued a warrant for his arrest. Lea and his son fled to a number of hideaways across the state, trying desperately to buy time for additional legal appeals, but in May 1934 they gave up and began their prison sentences. After two years behind bars Luke Lea returned to Nashville, a man bereft of the wealth and political power he once commanded. He moved with his family out of Belle Meade, which he had helped build, and lived a quiet life in somewhat straitened circumstances until his death in 1945.[54]

Rogers Caldwell survived the crisis surprisingly well when one considers his role in the affairs that brought it on. Even in his ascendancy Caldwell may have been something less than the "financial genius" his friends would later claim, but in his descent he proved remarkably adroit at covering his flanks. Caldwell went to trial in Nashville and was found guilty on one count of fraudulent breach of trust, but on appeal the state Supreme Court insisted on a retrial on the logical grounds that the jury was affected by the strong public prejudice against the defendant. The Davidson County attorney general, a loyal Lea man, decided not to pursue the case further.[55]

Caldwell successfully resisted extradition to Kentucky, where state and federal prosecutors wished to try him on charges of fraud involving the BancoKentucky. He also resisted state claims against his house and personal estate, at least for a time. Brentwood Hall, it turned out, had been built on land belonging to Caldwell's father, not on the adjacent plot owned by the Bank of Tennessee, as the bank auditors had been led to believe for years. Twelve days after the bank's failure James Caldwell placed this land in a trust for the benefit of his son in order to protect it from creditors.[56] Caldwell was required to auction off some of his prized thoroughbreds and give the funds to the state, but he continued to live in his mansion with his wife and a small retinue of servants. The state, which had established a claim of $4.4 million against Caldwell, finally forced him to leave Brentwood Hall in 1957. The property was turned into Ellington Agricultural Center, and the estate that had witnessed Rogers Caldwell in his heyday reveling in financial deals and fancy fox hunts with "men in pink coats" now would be filled with bureaucrats doing the work of the state.

Caldwell retreated to an antebellum mansion in Franklin, a long way from the Wall Street of the South. There, in his declining years, a steady stream of friendly politicians, businessmen, and writers paid homage to the old financier at his dining table. "Success?" Rogers Caldwell once responded to a reporter in 1927, "who knows whether he has made a success at all until he comes to die?"[57] In ruminating over his career a few years before his death in 1968, Caldwell said that his only regret was leaving Vanderbilt early. "I should have had more schooling —and a better understanding of economics." There could be no more fitting epitaph for the man and for the era in which he rose to power.[58]

EPILOGUE

The fall of Caldwell and Company serves as a logical punctuation mark in Nashville's evolution in the New South. Over the course of a half-century the city had grown more than three and one-half times in size. The thrust of growth had been slowed by the depression of the 1890s and hampered by the lack of competitive railroad service and the lack of a strong industrial foundation, leaving Nashville lagging behind its rivals, Memphis, Birmingham, and Atlanta. Still, the dramatic developments that Nashville experienced in the course of this fifty years would have impressed the New South prophets of the 1880s.

Economically the city had grown primarily as a commercial and transportation center, collecting and distributing products within an extensive hinterland stretching south into Alabama, north into Kentucky, east into the Cumberland plateau, and west to the Tennessee River Valley. Though frustrated in its efforts to build a strong industrial base, Nashville attracted a variety of industries including food processing, textiles, clothing, and religious publishing that contributed to a diversified economic foundation. By the 1920s the Wall Street of the South could claim a regional importance as a financial center based on its aggressive banks, brokerage houses, and insurance companies. The constellation of institutions in higher education, furthermore, gave the Athens of the South added economic diversity and a tone of cultural refinement that helped to counter the materialism of the city boosters.

The prophets of the New South would have been impressed also with the dramatic physical changes evident in the city's streets, buildings, suburbs, and parks. In the early 1880s Nashville was still a compact mix of small shops and fashionable townhouses ringed by mean, disease-ridden slums, all hovering close to the river. That city was transformed by the advent of the streetcar, steam dummy train, and the electric trolley, which rapidly extended lines into the suburban periphery like spokes from the downtown hub. The automobile's popularity after World War I only accelerated the centrifugal force of the transportation revolution occurring within the city.

Downtown, in place of the jumble of shops, mansions, and shacks, there emerged a coherent central business district with new skyscrapers piercing the Nashville skyline and department stores, an arcade, and palatial movie houses offering an array of pleasures to the modern consumer. A combination of social preferences and income differentials also meant that widespread rapid transportation would produce a more socially segmented city with rich and poor, white and black, foreigner and native living in their own residential enclaves.

Though many of Nashville's blacks managed to achieve education, professional training, and considerable wealth, the masses of blacks remained the most obvious losers amid the prosperity the city enjoyed in this half-century. The New South vision of interracial harmony may have been fulfilled in Nashville, but it was a fragile arrangement and one that came at the expense of black aspirations for education, job opportunities, and genuine political power. In politics, black voters had been able at times to exert some leverage. In mayors Thomas Kercheval and Hilary Howse, and in several ward-level politicians, Nashville blacks found white allies. But their loyalty to these white politicians was rewarded too often by paltry patronage appointments, some charitable donations of coal and groceries, and protection of saloons and vice in the poor neighborhoods. Efforts at genuine social reform in public education, health, and housing made some headway in the progressive era of reform, but most of Nashville's blacks—along with many poor whites—were denied the prosperity and progress the New South had promised.

The collapse of the American economy after 1929, and the fall of Caldwell and Company in Nashville, made the New South vision seem like a dream, suddenly brought to an abrupt end. For some, who understood the New South dream as a betrayal of the southern past or the excited materialism of the 1920s as a threat to community morality, the economic crisis was a kind of vindication. For everyone, it was a reminder of the fragility of prosperity and progress in the modern world.

APPENDIXES

APPENDIX A: POPULATION AND RACE, NASHVILLE AND DAVIDSON COUNTY, 1860–1980

	Total Population				Black Population			
Year	City	% Change	County	% Change	City	% of City	County	% of County
1860	16,988	—	47,055	—	3,945	23	15,999	34
1870	25,865	52	62,896	34	9,709	38	25,412	40
1880	43,350	68	79,009	26	16,337	38	31,331	40
1890	76,168	76	108,174	37	29,382	39	41,315	38
1900	80,865	6	122,790	14	30,044	37	43,902	36
1910	110,364	36	149,478	22	36,523	33	46,710	31
1920	118,342	7	167,815	12	35,633	30	44,528	27
1930	153,866	30	222,854	33	42,836	28	51,797	23
1940	167,402	9	257,267	15	47,318	28	56,797	22
1950	174,307	4	321,758	25	58,695	34	64,381	20
1960	170,874	– 2	399,743	24	72,789	43	76,832	19
1970	426,029	149	447,877	12	87,851	21	89,223	20
1980	455,651	7	477,811	7	105,942	23	106,257	22

SOURCES: U.S. census reports, 1860–1980.
NOTE: Wherever population estimates were updated the revised figure has been used.

APPENDIX B: NASHVILLE BANK CLEARINGS, 1894–1935

Year	Clearings	Year	Clearings
1894	$47,376,346	1915	322,901,654
1895	48,747,724	1916	407,729,406
1896	49,140,006	1917	532,907,290
1897	55,129,599	1918	746,156,611
1898	57,171,411	1919	863,911,696
1899	69,181,485	1920	1,179,501,244
1900	74,318,318	1921	845,509,813
1901	79,390,995	1922	898,067,590
1902	91,877,988	1923	1,003,657,993
1903	124,589,656	1924	1,012,243,160
1904	132,854,933	1925	1,122,203,951
1905	160,153,955	1926	1,126,611,576
1906	200,682,075	1927	1,198,811,102
1907	167,780,558	1928	1,179,685,805
1908	131,477,000	1929	1,243,935,793
1909	156,414,182	1930	1,078,478,051
1910	176,616,832	1931	628,043,516
1911	231,872,569	1932	460,439,179
1912	307,042,702	1933	468,491,660
1913	366,657,389	1934	584,513,170
1914	333,647,920	1935	696,558,318

SOURCES: *Eighteenth Annual Report of Nashville Board of Trade* (Nashville, 1912), 19; Claude A. Campbell, "The Development of Banking in Tennessee" (Ph.D. diss., Vanderbilt Univ., 1932), 187n; *Polk's Nashville . . . City Directory . . . 1972* (Taylor, Mich., [1972]).

APPENDIX C: MAYORS OF NASHVILLE, 1872–1917

Mayor (Birth—Death)	Term	Party
Thomas A. Kercheval (1837–1915)	1872–73	Repub.
Kercheval	1873–74	
Morton B. Howell (1834–1909)	1874–75	Dem.
Kercheval	1875–76	
Kercheval	1876–77	
Kercheval	1877–78	
Kercheval	1878–79	
Kercheval	1879–80	
Kercheval	1880–81	
Kercheval	1881–82	
Kercheval	1882–83	
C. Hooper Phillips (1847–86)	1883–85[1]	Dem.
Kercheval	1885–87	
Kercheval	1887[2]	
Charles P. McCarver (1854–1892)	1887–89	Dem.
McCarver	1889–90[3]	
William Litterer (1832–1917)	1890–91	Dem.
George B. Guild (1834–1917)	1891–93	Dem.
Guild	1893–95	
William M McCarthy (1840–1899)	1895–97	APA[4]
Richard H. Dudley 1836–1914)	1897–99	Dem.
James M. Head (1855–1930)	1899–1901	Dem.
Head	1901–1903	
Albert S. Williams (1849–1924)	1903–1905	Dem.
Thomas O. Morris (1845–1924)	1905–1907	Dem.
James S. Brown (1858–1946)	1907–1909	Dem.
Hilary E. Howse (1866–1938)	1909–11	Dem.
Howse	1911–13	

1. Terms changed from one to two years.
2. Kercheval resigned to join Board of Public Works; term filled by McCarver.
3. McCarver resigned; term filled by Litterer.
4. American Protective Association.

Mayor (Birth—Death)	Term	Party
Howse	1913–15[5]	
Robert Ewing (1849–1932)	1915–17	Dem.

5. Ousted from office; term filled by Ewing.

NOTES

Abbreviations used frequently in the notes are as follows:

"Minutes, BOG" Minutes, Board of Governors, Commercial Club (Chamber of Commerce)

THQ *Tennessee Historical Quarterly*

TSLA Tennessee State Library and Archives

VUL Vanderbilt University Library

CHAPTER ONE

1. See Anson Nelson, "Our First Century," *American*, Apr. 25, 1880; W.W. Clayton, *History of Davidson County, Tennessee* (Philadelphia, 1880), 348–64, includes a good account of the Centennial as well.

2. *American*, June 16, 1880.

3. Ibid., Dec. 17, 1879.

4. C. Vann Woodward, *Origins of the New South, 1877–1913*, A History of the South 9 (Baton Rouge, 1951), ch. 6; and Paul M. Gaston, *The New South Creed: A Study in Southern Mythmaking* (Baton Rouge, 1970), have informed the general interpretation of the Nashville Centennial presented here.

5. *American*, Feb. 3, 1880; Mar. 26, 1880.

6. Ibid., Apr. 25.

7. Ibid., Mar. 3, 27, 1880.

8. Ibid., Apr. 25, 1880.

9. Ibid., Feb. 19, June 1, 1880.

10. Ibid., Apr. 25, 1880.

11. Ibid., Apr. 30, May 4, 1880.

12. Ibid., May 1, 1880.

13. Ibid., May 7, 1880.

14. Woodward, *Origins*, 24–25.

15. *American,* May 1, 9, 25, 28, 1880.

16. Ibid., May 11, 1880.

17. Ibid., Mar. 13, 30, Apr. 13, May 2, 1880. See also the gag letter in ibid., Apr. 15, 1880.

18. Ibid., Apr. 2, 1880.

19. Cf. Gaston, *New South Creed,* ch. 5.

20. Clayton, *History of Davidson County; Nashville Centennial Travel Guide and Business Directory* (Milwaukee, 1880).

21. Bright, *Donelson and the Pioneers of Middle Tennessee* (Washington, D.C., 1880); Charles May, *The Pioneers of Nashville and Middle Tennessee* (Nashville, 1880).

22. Albert T. McNeal, "Pioneer Days" in *American,* Apr. 30, 1880.

23. Ibid., Feb. 15, Apr. 16, 25, 1880. See also Nelson, "Our First Century"; and Charles Edwin Robert, ed., *Nashville City Guide Book* (Nashville, 1880), 3–4.

24. John Woolridge, ed., *History of Nashville, Tennessee* (Nashville, 1890; rpt. 1970), 181–92.

25. John Miller McKee, *The Panic,* rpt. in Stanley F. Horn, ed., *Tennessee's War, 1861–1865, Described by Participants* (Nashville, 1965), 64–65.

26. See, for example, Robert, ed., *Guide,* 18.

27. Jesse C. Burt, *Nashville: Its Life and Times* (Nashville, 1959), 60–61.

28. Robert, ed., *Guide,* 18.

29. Clayton, *History of Davidson County,* 168–92.

30. *American,* Feb. 17, May 18, 1880. Wheless was a Centennial official and a local industrialist.

31. Ibid., Feb. 17, May 19, 20. 1880.

32. Ibid., May 21, 1880.

33. Ibid., May 9, June 16, 1880. Mills offered to sell the statue for $12,000, less than half the original price. When the Tennessee state legislature refused to contribute funds, Mills reduced his price to $5,000. Even this amount was slow in coming, and the Centennial Commission had to make up the difference out of public subscriptions.

34. Ibid., May 21, 1880.

CHAPTER TWO

1. *Thirteenth Census of the U.S., 1910, Population* (Washington, D.C., 1913), 81–83. Population figures were much affected by suburban annexations, which are explained in subsequent chapters. The best overview of southern urban development in this period is found in Howard N. Rabinowitz,"Continuity and Change: Southern Urban Development, 1860–1900," and Blaine A. Brownell, "The Urban South Comes of Age, 1900–1940," in *The City in Southern History,* ed. Brownell and David R. Goldfield (Port Washington, N.Y., 1977), 92–122, 123–58. See also David R. Goldfield, *Cotton Fields and Skyscrapers: Southern City and Region, 1607–1980* (Baton Rouge, 1982), 80–132.

2. John Woolridge, ed., *History of Nashville, Tennessee* (Nashville, 1890; rpt. 1970), 596–601; Jesse C. Burt, Jr., "A History of the Nashville, Chattanooga

and St. Louis Railway, 1872–1916" (Ph.D. diss., Vanderbilt Univ., 1950); Jesse C. Burt, Jr., "Four Decades of the Nashville, Chattanooga & St. Louis Railway, 1873–1916," *THQ* 9(1950):99–130; Jesse C. Burt, Jr., "Edmund W. Cole and the Struggle between Nashville and Louisville and Their Railroads, 1879–1880," *Filson Club Quarterly* 26(1952):112–32. The N&C became the Nashville, Chattanooga and St. Louis (NC&StL) in 1873.

3. *Banner*, Jan. 19, 1880, clipping in "Colonel Cole's Scrapbook," MS in TSLA.

4. Ibid.

5. Maury Klein, *History of the Louisville & Nashville Railroad* (New York, 1972), 158–64; hereafter Klein, *L&N*. John F. Stover, *The Railroads of the South, 1865–1900: A Study in Finance and Control* (Chapel Hill, 1955), 210–32, also covers the expansion of the L&N in this period.

6. Klein, *L&N*, 172–73.

7. Ibid., 533–34, 315–20.

8. Rpt. in U.S. Senate, *Louisville and Nashville Railroad Co. Hearings Before the Interstate Commerce Commission*, 64th Cong., 1st sess. 1916, Sen. Doc. 461, vol. 30:369.

9. William H. Joubert, *Southern Freight Rates in Transition* (Gainesville, Fla., 1949), 179, 185.

10. Woolridge, ed., *Nashville*, 578–80; John Allison, *Notable Men of Tennessee: Personal and Genealogical*, vol. 1 (Atlanta, 1905), 43–45. William S. Speer, ed., *Sketches of Prominent Tennesseans* (Nashville, 1888), 570–72; see obituary on Baxter in *American*, Mar. 1, 1904.

11. Klein, *L&N*, 304.

12. Tennessee Central Railway Co., *The Highballer* 1, 2, 3 (Jan./Feb. 1956–Winter 1958), include a historical sketch of the road. See also Elmer G. Sulzer, "The Three Tennessee Centrals of Tennessee," *THQ* 30(1971):210–14; Margaret Campbell, "A History of Tennessee Central Railway" (M.A. thesis, George Peabody College for Teachers, 1927).

13. Klein, *L&N*, 305.

14. Ibid., 304–5. See Baxter's account of L&N efforts to frustrate the TCRR in his pamphlet *Louisville and Nashville Monopoly, Its Methods and Purposes Exposed: The Reply of Jere Baxter to Milton H. Smith* (Nashville, 1902), 12.

15. Jere Baxter, *The Facts Bearing Upon the Railroad Situation in Middle Tennessee and Especially on the Necessity for the Amendment of Terminal Company Charter* (Nashville, 1901); Citizens' Transportation Committee, *The Louisville and Nashville Railroad Monopoly: Its Bold Defiance of the Law and the People at Nashville and in Middle Tennessee, the Wrong and the Remedy* (Nashville, 1902).

16. *American*, June 10, 1898.

17. Ibid., Oct. 9, 10, 1900. Thomas B. Brumbaugh, "The Architecture of Nashville's Union Station," *THQ* 27(1968):3–12. Keith L. Bryant, Jr., "Cathedrals, Castles, and Roman Baths: Railway Station Architecture in the Urban South," *Journal of Urban History* 2(Feb. 1976):200–203.

18. *American*, Oct. 9, 10, 1900.

19. William Waller, ed., *Nashville from 1900 to 1910* (Nashville, 1972), 32–35 (hereafter *Nashville, 1900*). *Banner*, Oct. 3; Dec. 15, 16, 1900.

20. Waller, ed., *Nashville, 1900,* 35; Jesse C. Burt, *Nashville: Its Life and Times* (Nashville, 1959), 90.

21. *American,* Jan. 20, 1903; *Banner* Jan. 20, 1903. Tennessee Central Railway Co., "A History of Tennessee Central Railway Co." (Nashville, 1966), typescript in TSLA, 8.

22. Jere Baxter, *In the Grip of Monopoly: How the Louisville and Nashville Railroad Has Oppressed the Citizens of Nashville* . . . (Nashville [1901]), 16.

23. *American,* May 28, 1902; *Banner,* May 27, 28, 1902.

24. *American,* Apr. 26, 1903; *Daily News,* Apr. 27, 28, 29, 1903.

25. *American,* Mar. 1, 2, 1904.

26. Wirt Armistead, interview, Waller Collection, Special Collections, VUL; Waller, ed., *Nashville, 1900,* 39–41.

27. *Highballer,* vols. 1–3.

28. Ibid; Waller, ed., *Nashville, 1900,* 38. See James Lal Penick, Jr., *The Great Western Land Pirate: John A. Murrell in Legend and History* (Columbia, Mo., 1981).

29. Byrd Douglas, *Steamboatin' on the Cumberland* (Nashville, 1961), 195–99. See also the Byrd Douglas Papers in TSLA.

30. Ibid., 199–203. The privileged rates allowed grain to be hauled, for example, from St. Louis to Nashville, where it was milled and stored up to six months, then reshipped to Atlanta, with the freight charge set at the much lower long-haul through rate from St. Louis to Atlanta.

31. Joubert, *Southern Freight,* 179, 185. On the other hand, as Joubert explains, rates on northbound freight favored cities like Louisville and Cincinnati over Nashville. This affected Nashville's shipping rates for goods like sugar from Louisiana and coal from Alabama.

32. Douglas, *Steamboatin',* 207–26; Joubert, *Southern Freight,* 181–83.

33. Douglas, *Steamboatin'* 190–94, 213–20; obituary in *American,* Dec. 24, 1904.

34. Douglas, *Steamboatin',* 214.

35. Ibid., 215–19.

36. Ibid., 220.

37. Ibid., 235–39; Wilbur Foster Creighton, *Building of Nashville* (Nashville, 1969), 27–28; "William T. Hunter Recollections," typescript in Douglas Papers, Box 13, file 9; Douglas Anderson, "Old Times on the Upper Cumberland," *Banner,* Mar. 21–Dec. 19, 1926, clipping in Cumberland River Development Project Papers, box 2, p. 11, TSLA.

38. Creighton, *Building,* 28; Douglas, *Steamboatin',* 234–35; Nashville Chamber of Commerce, *Nashville: Progressive City of the South* (Nashville, 1903), 11, 12.

39. Douglas, *Steamboatin',* 278–80, 194; "Hunter Recollections," Douglas Papers; Anderson, "Upper Cumberland," 13–15.

40. Woolridge, ed., *Nashville,* 313–15.

41. Douglas, *Steamboatin',* 221–22, 247–82. Chart, "Average Yearly Tonnage, 1819–1950," with Douglas Papers, map drawer 1. On the Cumberland River Improvement Association, see Woolridge, ed., *Nashville,* 316–20. See *American,* Jan. 23, July 12, 16, 17, Aug. 23, Oct. 22, 1889, for accounts of the founding convention of the association. See Cumberland River Development Project

Papers; and Board of Engineers, "Transcript of Proceedings Before the Board of Engineers of River and Harbors Committee at Nashville Board of Trade, February 2nd, 1906," typescript TSLA, for a full account of Nashville's efforts to improve the river using federal aid.

42. *American,* Dec. 24, 25, 26, 1904. Fletch Coke, *Captain Ryman at Home: His Family and Neighbors on Rutledge Hill* (Nashville, 1982), 19.

43. At Ryman's death, grain dealers organized the Nashville Grain Exchange, led by Byrd Douglas, Sr., which set up its own steamboat line (with financial help from the L&N) to maintain the grain privileges. Douglas, *Steamboatin',* 251, 257–58.

44. Joubert, *Southern Freight,* 186–90.

45. John Trotwood Moore, *Tennessee: The Volunteer State, 1769–1923,* vol. 4 (Chicago, 1923), 561–62; Waller, ed., *Nashville, 1900,* 252. See also Luke Lea's obituary and biographical sketch in *Tennessean,* Nov. 19, 1945.

46. *Louisville and Nashville Hearings,* 407; Burt, *Nashville,* 91; Klein, L&N, 345–67, 368–80.

47. See 31st Annual Report of the Interstate Commerce Commission (Washington, D.C., 1917), 23–24, which reports on the outcome of L&N et al. vs. the United States et al, 242 U.S. 60. The Supreme Court ruled against the ICC injunction in behalf of the Tennessee Central, arguing that the L&N and the NC&StL were effectively one railroad and therefore the L&N was not according treatment to another road which it denied the Tennessee Central.

48. See Klein, *L&N,* 345–67, for a balanced overview of rate discrimination and other railroad "abuses."

CHAPTER THREE

1. *Manufacturing and Mercantile Resources of Nashville, Tennessee . . .* ([Nashville], 1882).

2. Arch Trawick, "An Old Time Drummer Talks About the Grocery Business, 1846–1946," typescript in Trawick Papers, TSLA.

3. Ibid; and Trawick, "Things Remembered, 1890–1910," typescript in Trawick Papers, TSLA.

4. Trawick, "Things Remembered"; William Waller, ed., *Nashville from 1900 to 1910* (Nashville, 1972), 113; Louise Davis, "Good Since the First Drop," *Tennessean,* Jan. 4, 1976; William W. Force, "The Cheek Family," in Nashville Public Library, *Nashville: A Family Town* (Nashville, 1978).

5. Trawick, "Old Time Drummer," 11, 12, 16; Trawick, "Things Remembered," 13, 15–16; William Waller, ed., *Nashville in the 1890's* (Nashville, 1970), 47–48. For an overview of the grocery industry in historical perspective, see Edward C. Hampe, Jr., and Merle Wittenberg, *The Lifeline of America: Development of the Food Industry* (New York, 1964).

6. Laura Kate Miller, "Geographical Influences in the Growth of Nashville" (M.A. thesis, George Peabody College for Teachers, 1923), 90; Clarence Colton Dawson, "History of the Flour Milling Industry of Nashville, Tennessee" (M.A. thesis, George Peabody College for Teachers, 1931).

7. James Harvey Dodd, "The Development of Manufacturing in Tennes-

see Since the Civil War," (M.A. thesis, George Peabody College for Teachers, 1955), 60; *Agricultural Trends in Tennessee: A Record of Tennessee Crop and Livestock Statistics, 1866–1947* (Nashville, 1948), 31–33.

8. [Andrew Morrison], *The City of Nashville,* The Engelhardt Series: American Cities 24 (St. Louis and Nashville, [1891]), 137–38.

9. Dawson, "Flour Milling," 28–30, 62–65. Trawick, "Things Remembered," 15–16, recalls H.G. Hill's involvement in the flour milling industry.

10. M.J. Danner, B.H. Leubke, and B.D. Raskopf, *Development and Present Importance of Nashville Livestock Market,* Rural Research Series 205, Department of Agricultural Economics and Rural Sociology, Agricultural Experiment Station, Univ. of Tennessee (Knoxville, July 30, 1946), 2–6.

11. Robert C.H. Mathews III, "North Nashville: A History of Urban Development" (M.A. thesis, Univ. of North Carolina, 1976), 48–51.

12. Ed Huddleston, *Big Wheels and Little Wagons* (Nashville, 1959), 42, 47, 58, et passim; Danner, et al., "Nashville Livestock Market," iv, 2–6.

13. Louis Garfield Kennamer, "The Woodworking Industries of Nashville" (M.A. thesis, George Peabody College for Teachers, 1922), 41–52.

14. [Morrison], *City of Nashville,* 119.

15. John Woolridge, ed., *History of Nashville, Tennessee* (Nashville, 1890, rpt. 1970), 636–39; Ethel Armes, *The Story of Coal and Iron in Alabama* (Birmingham, 1910); Anne Kendrick Walker, *Life and Achievements of Alfred Montgomery Shook* (Birmingham, 1952); J.B. Killebrew, *Life and Character of James Cartwright Warner* (Nashville, 1897); Justin Fuller, "History of the Tennessee Coal, Iron and Railroad Company, 1852–1907" (Ph.D. diss., Univ. of North Carolina, 1966).

16. Broadus Mitchell and George Sinclair Mitchell, *The Industrial Revolution in the South* (Baltimore, 1930), 2–4, 9–16, 37–38, 130–38; C. Vann Woodward, *The Origins of the New South, 1877–1913,* A History of the South 9(Baton Rouge, 1951), 131–35, 306–8.

17. Woolridge, ed., *Nashville,* 225–26.

18. Ibid., 226–27.

19. Ibid., 227; [Morrison], *City of Nashville,* 138–40.

20. Woolridge, ed., *Nashville,* 235–37, 360–61; Lester C. Lamon, *Black Tennesseans, 1900–1930* (Knoxville, 1977), 18n; Nashville Board of Trade, *Yearbook, 1908* (Nashville, 1908), 23–25.

21. Emory C. Hawk, *Economic History of the South* (New York, 1934), 108–11; Lance E. Davis. "The Investment Market, 1870–1914: The Evolution of a National Market," *Journal of Economic History* 25(1965):355–99.

22. [Morrison], *City of Nashville,* 46, lists the Fourth National's officers and directors and their occupations. Fourth National Bank, *The Fourth National Bank of Nashville, Tennessee* (Nashville, [1907]). Nashville's city directory for 1880 was used to identify bank directors and their occupations.

23. [Morrison], *City of Nashville,* 45. Woolridge, ed., *Nashville,* 292–98. Waller, ed., *Nashville, 1900,* 105–9.

24. *American,* Aug. 8, 1893; William Waller, ed., *Nashville in the 1890s* (Nashville, 1970), 97–103.

25. Waller, ed., *Nashville, 1900,* 106; *The Bankers Encyclopedia* (New York, 1915), 1729–30.

26. James E. Caldwell, *Recollections of a Life Time* (Nashville, 1923), 221–22; *Fourth National Bank.*

27. Wilbur Foster Creighton, *Building of Nashville* (Nashville, 1969), 165–66. Caldwell, *Recollections.*

28. See Thomas C. Cochran, *American Business in the Twentieth Century* (Cambridge, Mass., 1972); Edward C. Kirkland, *Industry Comes of Age: Business, Labor, and Public Policy, 1860–1897* (New York, 1961).

29. Nashville Trust Co., "Seventy Nine Years Ago," typescript in Nashville City Bank & Trust Co.; Margaret Dick, "Survival of the Fittest: Nashville City Bank at the Crossroads," *Nashville! Magazine,* July 1978; Waller, ed., *Nashville, 1890s,* 14.

30. Waller, ed., *Nashville 1900,* 105–10; James R. Kellam, Jr., *Bootstraps: A History of Commerce Union Bank, 1916–1966* ([Nashville, 1966]), 12; Lamon, *Black Tennesseans,* 184–87.

31. For a detailed example of how bank capital was invested in local enterprise, see Nashville Trust Co., "Sundry Security Register, 1889–1931," MS in Nashville City Bank & Trust Co.

32. Jack Blicksilver, "Insurance Industry," in *The Encyclopedia of Southern History,* ed. David C. Roller and Robert W. Twyman (Baton Rouge, 1979), 632–33; Blicksilver, *Industrial Insurance in the United States* (New York, 1968).

33. J. Owen Stalson, *Marketing Life Insurance: Its History in America* (1942; rpt. Homewood, Ill., 1969), 445–81.

34. Ibid., 462–81.

35. Morton Keller, *The Life Insurance Enterprise, 1885–1910: A Study in the Limits of Corporate Power* (Cambridge, Mass., 1963); Douglas North, "Capital Accumulation in Life Insurance Between the Civil War and the Investigation of 1905," in William Miller, ed., *Men in Business: Essays in the History of Entrepreneurship* (Cambridge, Mass., 1952), 238–53; B. Michael Pritchett, "Northern Institutions in Southern Financial History: A Note on Insurance Investments," *Journal of Southern History* 41(1975):391–96.

36. William Ridley Wills, "The Story of the National," transcript of speech May 1932, in Stamper Papers, box 4, in Sales Promotion Office, National Life Center. Thanks to R.A. Sobel for making these records in his office available. Mrs. James Fraser, interview, July 6, 1950, Waller Collection, Special Collections, VUL, confirms the early dependence on "Negro insurance."

37. Powell Stamper, *The National Life Story: A History of the National Life and Accident Insurance Company of Nashville, Tennessee* (New York, 1968), 1–72.

38. *Life and Casualty Mirror,* Aug. 1966, 3–5 (hereafter *Mirror*); Era Irene Emmons, *The Thrift Family: The Story of the Life and Casualty Insurance Company, 1903–1943* (Nashville, 1943); Stamper, *National Life,* 50.

39. Powell Stamper, telephone interview with author, Jan. 1980.

40. Stamper, *National Life,* 55, 82.

41. Emmons, *Thrift Family,* 23–24.

42. [A.M. Burton], *John Smith and His Success* (Nashville, 1911), copy in L&C Public Relations office. Thanks to Marilyn Watkins for her aid in making company records accessible. See also Burton, *Key to Success: Conservation Our Keynote for 1912* (Nashville, 1912).

43. Lamon, *Black Tennesseans*, 201.

44. National Life and Accident Insurance Co., *The National*, 7(Feb. 1913), includes a financial statement of the company which shows heavy investment in real estate loans. This was an investment area nationally chartered banks were forbidden to enter in this period.

45. *Annual Report of the Merchants Exchange of Nashville, Tennessee, 1881* (Nashville, 1881), 10, 36–37; Woolridge, ed., *Nashville*, 252–59. Chamber of Commerce, *Nashville in the Twentieth Century*, (Nashville, [1900]), 44.

46. Woolridge, ed., *Nashville*, 259; Board of Trade, *Yearbook, 1908*, p. 3.

47. Chamber of Commerce, *Manual, 1895* (Nashville, 1895), 11, 27, 16. See also *Nashville, . . . the Progressive City of the South . . .* (Nashville, [1903]); and the Chamber's *Manual* for 1903, 1905.

48. *Manual, 1895*, 15, 16.

49. See Carl V. Harris, *Politics and Power in Birmingham, 1871–1920* (Knoxville, 1977); William D. Miller, *Memphis During the Progressive Era, 1900–1917* (Memphis, 1957); Walter G. Cooper, *Official History of Fulton County* (Atlanta, 1934); James Michael Russell, "Atlanta, Gate City of the South, 1847 to 1885" (Ph.D. diss., Princeton Univ., 1972).

50. Chamber of Commerce, *Manual, 1903*, 28, 13.

51. Nashville Board of Trade, *Yearbook, 1906* (Nashville 1906), 4. Ida Clyde Clark, comp., *All About Nashville: A Complete Historical Guide to the City . . .* (Nashville, 1912), 136–40.

52. Miller Manier, telephone interview with author, June 1979.

53. *Commercial Club Tattler* 1(Sept. 1912):19.

54. Ibid. (June 1912):7–8.

55. *Proposed Consolidation of the Civic and Commercial Organization of Nashville: Plan and By-laws* ([Nashville, 1913]), 7; *Tattler* 6(Apr. 1917):28. Details of the consolidation can be found in "Minutes, Directors' meetings, Nashville Board of Trade, 1912–1913, 1914–1915," MS in Nashville Chamber of Commerce.

CHAPTER FOUR

1. On Methodists in the New South, see Hunter Dickinson Farish, *The Circuit Rider Dismounts: A Social History of Southern Methodism, 1865–1900* (Richmond, 1938), and Myron J. Fogde, "Methodist Church," in *The Encyclopedia of Southern History*, ed. David C. Roller and Robert W. Twyman (Baton Rouge, 1979), 814–15, which describes Methodism as the religion of the rising middle class in the New South.

2. *Chat* 3 (Apr. 6 through Nov., 1895), includes the "Leading Citizens Series." *Evening Herald*, Apr. 14 through June 23, 1889, contains several biographies of business and professional leaders in the city.

3. E.W. Crozier, comp. *The Nashville Blue Book of Select Names of Nashville and Immediate Suburbs for the Year 1896* (Nashville, 1896). Dau Publishing Co., *The Nashville Society Blue Book* (New York, 1900); see also Dau's *Blue Book* for 1907–8. *Social Directory, Nashville, Tennessee* (Nashville, 1911). At least one more directory appeared in the 1930s, Southern Social Directory Pub-

lishers, *Nashville 1937—Social Directory; The "700" of Nashville* ([Nashville?],
1937). Susan E. Cox, "The Nashville Elite, 1896–1907" (Unpublished undergraduate paper, Vanderbilt Univ., Spring 1977), analyzes the social directories
as an index of elite status.

    4. John Woolridge, ed., *History of Nashville, Tennessee* (Nashville, 1890;
rpt. 1970), 596–601.

    5. *American*, Aug. 2, 1904.

    6. William Waller, ed., *Nashville in the 1890s* (Nashville, 1970), 143–44.
See also, William Waller, ed., *Nashville from 1900 to 1910* (Nashville, 1972),
135–159. Waller's books on the 1890s and 1900s are both excellent on the social life of the city's upper classes.

    7. There were several other downtown men's clubs, some of which would
be merged into older and larger clubs. The Capital Club was absorbed into the
Hermitage Club in 1895; later, the Hermitage and University clubs merged in
1907 forming the Watauga Club, which later resumed the name of the Hermitage Club. Waller, ed., *Nashville, 1890s,* 144; Waller, ed., *Nashville, 1900,* 145.

    8. *American,* Jan. 1, 31, Feb. 5, 1892. See also notes on "Society," in Waller
Collection, box 1, Special Collections, VUL.

    9. Anne Firor Scott, *The Southern Lady: From Pedestal to Politics, 1830–
1930,* (Chicago, 1970), provides a good overview of women's changing roles in
the South. Charlotte A. Williams, comp., *The Centennial Club of Nashville:
A History from 1905–77* (Nashville, 1978), 9–145, passim.

    10. Old Oak Club Handbook, in Waller Collection, box 3, file 21.

    11. John M. Marshall, "Residential Expansion and Central City Change,"
in *Growing Metropolis: Aspects of Development in Nashville,* ed. James F.
Blumstein and Benjamin Walter (Nashville, 1975), 48–49, 52–63; Don H. Doyle,
"Saving Yesterday's City: Nashville's Waterfront," THQ 35 (1976):354–57.

    12. Marshall, "Residential Expansion," 52–63.

    13. Carole Elam, "On the Avenue, Fifth Avenue," unpublished paper, spring
1982 (early report, M.A. thesis, program in historic preservation, Middle Tennessee State Univ.).

    14. "History of Castner-Knott," typescript, Oct. 1965, courtesy of Castner-
Knott's public relations office. *Souvenir, 1903: Nashville of Today* [Nashville,
1903]); *Nashville This Week,* Apr. 7, 1930, pp. 3–7.

    15. Waller, ed., *Nashville, 1900,* 114.

    16. *Daily News,* May 2, 1903. See also *American,* May 21, 1903, and Ralph
Morrissey, "That Arcade," *Tennessean Magazine,* Sept. 2, 1956.

    17. *Reports of Departments of the City of Nashville for the Fiscal Year
Ending January 1, 1893* (Nashville, 1893), 21–22 (title varies, hereafter *Reports
of Departments, year*).

    18. *American,* Jan. 26, 1902; Waller, ed., *Nashville, 1900,* 7–8; Blanche
Henry Clark Weaver, "Shifting Residential Patterns of Nashville," THQ 8(1959):
23–24, 28–29.

    19. *American,* July 20, 1888.

    20. *Reports of Departments, 1893,* 22–23.

    21. *American,* June 30, 1905; James Summerville, "The City and the Slum:
'Black Bottom' in the Development of South Nashville," THQ 40(1981):182–83.

    22. See *American,* Dec. 18, 1906; Jan. 18, 29, Feb. 5, 6, 9, 1907.

    23. See ibid., Dec. 12, 1907, Jan. 13, Feb. 29, 1908.

24. See *Banner*, Nov. 5, 7, 1910.

25. Benjamin Walter, "Ethnicity and Residential Succession: Nashville, 1850–1920," in Blumstein and Walter, eds., *Growing Metropolis*, 23, 26–28.

26. Lindsley, *Second Report of the Nashville Board of Health for the Year Ending July 4, 1877* (Nashville, 1877).

27. *Reports of Departments, 1898*, 138.

28. *Reports of Departments, 1894*, 138.

29. Lester C. Lamon, *Blacks in Tennessee, 1791–1970* (Knoxville, 1982), 62–64.

30. *Reports of Departments, 1911*, 182.

31. Ibid.; *Reports of Departments, 1891*, 106–7, 114–15.

32. *Reports of Departments, 1888*, 94; *Reports of Departments, 1899*, 172.

33. James E. Caldwell, *Recollections of a Life Time* (Nashville, 1932), 111–13. Caldwell purchased Longview on Franklin Pike in the summer of 1878 and moved there in January 1879, years before the suburban trend described here, but his motives were widely shared in the ensuing years.

34. *American*, May 14, 1903.

CHAPTER FIVE

1. Blanche Henry Clark Weaver, "Shifting Residential Patterns of Nashville" THQ8(1959):25; John Woolridge, ed. *History of Nashville, Tennessee* (Nashville, 1890; rpt. 1970), 336; Eleanor Graham, ed., *Nashville: A Short History and Selected Buildings* (Nashville, 1974), 125–35; Fletch Coke, *Captain Ryman at Home: His Family and Neighbors on Rutledge Hill* (Nashville, 1982).

2. John Lawrence Connelly, "Old North Nashville and Germantown," THQ 39(1980):130–31; Ed Huddleston, *Big Wheels and Little Wagons* (Nashville, 1959), 31–33 and passim—reprinted from the *Nashville Banner*, published in installments from Oct. 5 to Dec. 7, 1959; Woolridge, ed., *Nashville*, 336–37; Robert C.H. Mathews III, "North Nashville: A History of Urban Development" (M.A. thesis, Univ. of North Carolina, 1976), 40–43; Benjamin Walter, "Ethnicity and Residential Succession: Nashville, 1850–1920," in *Growing Metropolis: Aspects of Development in Nashville*, James F. Blumstein and Benjamin Walter (Nashville, 1975), 15–16. See also Phyllis Hahn, "German Settlers in Nashville, Tennessee" (M.A. thesis, Vanderbilt Univ., 1935).

3. Mark B. Riley, "Edgefield: A Study of an Early Nashville Suburb," THQ 37(1978):138–44.

4. Jean Martin, "Mule to MARTA," *Atlanta Historical Bulletin* 19 (1975):23.

5. Woolridge, ed., *Nashville*, 339; George E. Frazer, comp., *Charters, Amendments, County Grants, City Franchises, and Private Property Rights-of-Way of the Nashville Railway and Light Company and the Preceding Street Railway Companies Heretofore Operating in the City of Nashville and Davidson County Tennessee, from February 29, 1860 to May 1, 1911* (n.p., [1911?]), 3–8, 28–31, 121–28, 168.

6. Woolridge, ed., *Nashville*, 339–40; Chamber of Commerce, *Nashville in the 20th Century* (Nashville, [1900?]), 15–16; William Waller, ed., *Nashville in the 1890s* (Nashville, 1970), 4–6.

7. Chamber of Commerce, *Nashville in the 20th Century;* Frazer, comp., *Charters,* 209–233; William Waller, ed., *Nashville from 1900 to 1910* (Nashville, 1972), 41–43.

8. Weaver, "Shifting Residential Patterns," 29–30.

9. W.W. Clayton, *History of Davidson County, Tennessee* (Philadelphia, 1880), 222; Woolridge, ed., *Nashville,* 226.

10. Mathews, "North Nashville," 48–56; Connelly, "Old North Nashville," 140; *Tennessean,* Jan. 16, 1977. On Germantown's past see John Lawrence Connelly, *North Nashville and Germantown: Yesterday and Today* (Nashville, 1982).

11. *Second Annual Report of the Department of Fire Prevention, State of Tennessee, from January 1, 1916 to December 31, 1916* (Jackson, Tenn., 1917), 16, 24–26.

12. *American,* May 22, 1890.

13. Ibid., May 19, 20, 22, 23, 24, 25, 1890.

14. *Evening Herald,* May 10, 1891.

15. Waller, ed., *Nashville, 1890s,* 185–86n. See Murphy's obituary in *Banner,* Dec. 24, 1900.

16. *Banner,* Dec. 24, 1900; *Nashville Daily News,* Feb. 6, 1902.

17. *Daily News,* Jan. 19, 1902; *American,* Jan. 19, 1902; Frazer, comp., *Charters,* 280–82.

18. *Daily News,* Feb. 4, 1902.

19. As part of the settlement of Nashville Railway's prolonged court battle to consolidate, the company not only bought the park land and deeded it to the city, it also promised to pay 2 percent of the first $1 million in fares annually to fund the maintenance of all city parks. *American,* Oct. 4, 1902. The consent decree filed by the city and the street railway company may be found in "Ordinances Enacted, City Council, City of Nashville, January 4, 1896 to January 30, 1906," Oct. 3, 1902, pp. 415–17, Metropolitan Clerk's vault, Metropolitan Nashville and Davidson County Courthouse.

20. *American,* May 21, 1905.

21. Ibid., July 1, 1905.

22. Ibid., Feb. 26, Mar. 4, 5, 26, May 7, July 1, 1905; *Banner,* Mar. 4, 1905. See also Cindy Young, "The Growth and Development of the Richland-West End Neighborhood" (unpublished undergraduate paper, Vanderbilt Univ., spring 1979).

23. Waller, ed., *Nashville, 1900,* 147–49; Morgan B. Reynolds, *Seventy Years of Belle Meade Country Club, 1901–1971* (Nashville, 1971), 3–4.

24. *Tennessean,* Dec. 8, 1912, Feb. 1, 8, Mar. 2, 23, 30, Apr. 2, 1913. Sales figures are given in "Direct Index to Warranty Deeds," vol. R, Apr. 15, 1817, to Feb. 10, 1924, Davidson County, Tenn. These documents are located in the office of the Register of Deeds, Metropolitan Nashville and Davidson County Courthouse.

25. *American,* June 15, 1902; Herschel Gower, "Belle Meade: Queen of Tennessee Plantations," THQ 22(1963):203–22.

26. Waller, ed., *Nashville, 1900,* 17–19; Margaret Lindsley Warden, "Fabulous Belle Meade" *Tennessean Magazine,* May 7, 1950; idem, "The Breaking," *Tennessean Magazine,* May 14, 1950; Gower, "Belle Meade," 219–20.

27. Waller, ed., *Nashville, 1900,* 19–21; *American,* Apr. 10, 1906.

28. Waller, ed., *Nashville, 1900*, 21–22, 284, 302; *American*, Oct. 32, 1909; Reynolds, *Belle Meade Country Club*, 8, 10–11.

29. Henry Francis Beaumont, *West Nashville: Manufacturing Metropolis of the South* (Nashville, 1908), 1–5; Nashville Land Improvement Co., *West Nashville* (Nashville, [1900?]), 3–6.

30. Beaumont, *West Nashville*, 1–2.

31. Ibid., 8–10.

32. Second Biennial Report of the Board of Prison Commissioners, *House and Senate Journal*, 51st Assembly, 1899, app. 735–37, cited in Jesse Crawford Crowe, "Agitation for Penal Reform in Tennessee, 1870–1900" (Ph.D. diss., Vanderbilt Univ., 1954), 319. The statute allowing convict labor for private firms within the penitentiary is found in *Acts of the State of Tennessee, 48th General Assembly, 1893*, ch. 78, pp. 96–105.

33. Beaumont, *West Nashville*, 4–5; Nashville Land Improvement Co., *West Nashville*, 3–4; Second Biennial Report of the Board of Prison Commissioners, 22–25.

34. *Nashville Daily News*, May 20, 1903; Beaumont, *West Nashville*, 14–15.

35. Waller, ed., *Nashville, 1900*, 289; *Nashville Daily News*, May 20, 1903.

36. Nashville Land Improvement Co., *West Nashville*, 6.

37. Nashville Land Improvement Co., *Fourteenth Regular Annual Meeting of Stockholders; Synopsis of Reports* (Nashville, 1901), 9; Beaumont, *West Nashville*, 3.

38. Beaumont, *West Nashville*, 3; Nashville Land Improvement Co., *West Nashville*, 6; idem, *Fourteenth Regular Annual Meeting*, 4.

39. Walter, "Ethnicity and Residential Succession," 6–7.

40. Ibid., 10–12.

41. Ibid., 11–12.

42. Ibid.

43. *Saint Patrick's Church* [Nashville, 1891?], pamphlet with membership list; and "Saint Patrick's Church" [Nashville, n.d.], both located in the Diocese Archives, Nashville, and loaned to the author courtesy of Sam Shannon.

44. Federal Writers' Project, Work Projects Administration, *Tennessee: A Guide to the State* (New York, 1939), 397–98. For more on the Irish gypsies and their persistence in the twentieth century, see *The Tennessee Register*, June 6, 1977. My thanks to Sam Shannon for bringing this article to my attention.

45. Pat Willard, "The Irish in Nashville, 1880–1910" (unpublished undergraduate paper, spring 1980).

46. *Catholic Herald*, Apr. 29, 1899.

47. Willard, "Irish."

48. Walter, "Ethnicity and Residential Succession," 12.

49. Hahn, "German Settlers in Nashville," 11–12.

50. Walter, "Ethnicity and Residential Succession," 13–14; Huddleston, *Big Wheels*, 31; Joseph Tant McPherson, "Nashville's German Element, 1850–1870" (M.A. thesis, Vanderbilt Univ., 1957), 32, 34–36, 42–58.

51. Walter, "Ethnicity and Residential Succession," 14–16; Charles E. Robert, *Nashville and Her Trade for 1870* (Nashville, 1870), 46.

52. Huddleston, *Big Wheels*, 7–8, 20, 32–33; Walter, "Ethnicity and Residential Succession," 16; Mathews, "North Nashville," 40–43; Hahn, "German

Settlers in Nashville," 25–58; McPherson, "Nashville's German Element," 89–114.

53. The lives and careers of these German-Americans of late nineteenth and early twentieth century Nashville are recounted in passing in Huddleston, *Big Wheels*, chs. 17–44. On the origins of the German-American bank, see Connelly, "Old North Nashville," 143. See also McPherson, "Nashville's German Element," ch. 3: "Occupational Structure," passim; and Cindy Albrecht, "The German Contingent in Nashville, Tennessee, 1880–1930" (unpublished undergraduate paper, spring 1981).

54. Connelly, "Old North Nashville," 143.

55. Mathews, "North Nashville," 44–56.

56. Fedora S. Frank, *Five Families and Eight Young Men* (Nashville, 1962), 23–26, 38–52, passim.

57. Department of the Interior, U.S. Census Office, *Report on Statistics of Churches in the United States at the 11th Census, 1890* (Washington, D.C., 1894), 112–13. Department of Commerce, U.S. Bureau of the Census, *Religious Bodies, 1916* (Washington, D.C., 1919), Prt. I, 442–44. See also Department of Commerce and Labor, U.S. Bureau of the Census, *Religious Bodies: 1906* (Washington, D.C., 1910), Prt. I, 448, which indicates there were 275 "heads of families" who were members of Jewish congregations. There may have been many more people of Jewish background in Nashville who were not members of a Jewish congregation. The census of 1910 showed Nashville had almost 600 Russian-born residents and 335 children of Russian-born parents, plus another 353 persons born in Hungary or of Hungarian parents; many of the Russians and Hungarians were probably Jewish by identity if not religious affiliation. *Thirteenth Census of the United States, 1910*, vol. 3, *Population* (Washington, D.C., 1913), 762. A religious survey of Nashville in 1899 showed that 583 identified themselves as Jews, about 3 percent of all those who gave a religious preference. The results of the survey were published in *Banner*, Jan. 20, 1899.

58. Frank, *Five Families*, 54–75; Walter, "Ethnicity and Residential Succession," 17–18.

59. Fedora S. Frank, *Beginnings on Market Street: Nashville and Her Jewry, 1861–1901* (Nashville, 1976), 1–23; Walter, "Ethnicity and Residential Succession," 18–19.

60. C. Vann Woodward, *The Strange Career of Jim Crow* (New York, 1955, 3rd rev. ed. 1974), interprets the historical circumstances leading to segregation.

61. Howard N. Rabinowitz, *Race Relations in the Urban South, 1865–1890* (New York, 1978), 64, citing Bureau of the Census, *Eleventh Census of the United States, 1890, Population*, vol. 1, pt. 2 (Washington, D.C., 1893), 634, 696, 718. Faye Wellborn Robbins, "A World within a World: Black Nashville, 1880–1915" (Ph.D. diss., Univ. of Arkansas, 1980), 319–22, summarizes some of the occupational data for Nashville blacks from the federal censuses of 1890, 1900, and 1910.

62. Rabinowitz, *Race*, 248–49, 330. Rabinowitz mentions a "Blue Vein Society" organized by Nashville mulattoes in 1889; see 402n, citing *Banner*, Aug. 20, 1889. See also Louis Clausiel Perry, "Studies in the Religious Life of the Negro in the City of Nashville, Tenn." *Vanderbilt University Quarterly* 1(1901):90–91, for a discussion of the "blue-vein" elite.

63. Rabinowitz, *Race*, 239–43; Joseph H. Cartwright, *The Triumph of Jim Crow: Tennessee Race Relations in the 1880s* (Knoxville, 1976), 119–37; Lester C. Lamon, *Black Tennesseans, 1900–1930* (Knoxville, 1977), 89.

64. Rabinowitz, *Race*, 91; W.N. Hartshorn, *An Era of Progress and Promise, 1863–1910* (Boston, 1910), 415; Herbert Leon Clark, "The Public Career of James Carroll Napier: Businessman, Politician, and Crusader for Racial Justice, 1845–1940" (D.A. thesis, Middle Tennessee State Univ., 1980). Cordell Hull Williams, "The Life of James Carroll Napier From 1845 to 1940" (M.A. thesis, Tennessee A&I, 1955).

65. Rabinowitz, *Race*, 218; Hartshorn, *Era*, 445; William J. Simmons, *Men of Mark: Eminent Progressive and Rising* (Cleveland, 1887), 296–301; James T. Haley, comp., *Afro-American Encyclopedia or, The Thoughts, Doings and Sayings of the Race* (Nashville, 1896), 220.

66. Rabinowitz, *Race*, 92–93; Haley, comp., *Afro-American*, 59–62.

67. Lamon, *Black Tennesseans*, 18n.

68. Robbins, "World," 1–96, covers in detail the founding of Nashville's several black colleges; see 239–52 on the black and mulatto elites and their relationship to Fisk and Meharry in particular. See also the sources cited in ch. 8 of the present volume for more on the history of these black colleges.

69. The segregation indices were derived from ward-level population figures in the published federal censuses for 1890, 1900, and 1910. In all instances, the percentage distribution of all blacks in each ward was compared with that of all whites. Had native-born whites been isolated, the indices would probably have been higher. See Karl E. Taeuber and Alma F. Taeuber, *Negroes in Cities: Residential Segregation and Neighborhood Change* (1965; rpt. New York, 1969), 28–31, and app. A, for a thorough explanation of the measurement of segregation.

70. Joe M. Richardson, *A History of Fisk University, 1865–1946* (University, Ala., 1980), 25–39.

71. Weaver, "Shifting Residential Patterns" 29–30; Robbins, "World," 110–17.

72. Rabinowitz, *Race*, 175, 401, citing *American*, Aug. 29, 1879; *Banner*, May 26, 1882; June 9, 1883. See Howard N. Rabinowitz, "Half a Loaf: The Shift From White to Black Teachers in the Negro Schools of the Urban South, 1865–1890," *Journal of Southern History* 40(Nov. 1974): 565–94, for a more detailed account of this issue.

73. Rabinowitz, *Race*, 177; D.N. Crosthwait, "The First Black High School in Nashville," *Negro History Bulletin* 37(June/July 1974): 266–68.

74. Rabinowitz, *Race*, ch. 6, esp. 138, 142, 147.

75. Ibid., ch. 8, esp. 185, 188, 189, 190.

76. Lamon, *Black Tennesseans*, 4–5, 176–79.

77. Ibid., 184–87.

78. Ibid., 179–80.

79. Ibid., 14–16. The *Globe* did not actually begin publication until Jan. 1906.

80. W.E.B. DuBois, *Autobiography* ([New York], 1968), 121. August Meier, *Negro Thought in America, 1880–1915: Racial Ideologies in the Age of Booker T. Washington* (Ann Arbor, 1963), is the best treatment of the Washington-DuBois debate.

81. Lamon, *Black Tennesseans*, 20–22.

82. *American*, Mar. 5, 1904, quoted in ibid., 23–24.

83. Ibid., 24.

84. *Banner*, Sept. 29, 1905, quoted in ibid., 27–28.

85. Ibid., 33–34.

86. Quoted in ibid., 35.

87. See August Meier and Elliott Rudwick, "The Boycott Movement Against Jim Crow Streetcars in the South, 1900–1906," *Journal of American History* 55(Mar. 1969): 756–75; idem., "Negro Boycotts of Jim Crow Streetcars in Tennessee" *American Quarterly* 21 (1969): 755–63; and "Fighting 'Jim-Crowism' in Nashville" *Literary Digest* 31(Oct. 7, 1905): 474–75.

CHAPTER SIX

1. James E. Caldwell, *Recollections of a Life Time* (Nashville, 1923), 72.

2. John Patrick McDowell, *The Social Gospel in the South: The Woman's Home Mission Movement in the Methodist Episcopal Church, South, 1886–1939* (Baton Rouge, 1982); Sydney E. Ahlstrom, *A Religious History of the American People* (New Haven, 1972); James Douglas Flamming, "The Sam Jones Revivals and Social Reform in Nashville, Tennessee, 1885–1900" (M.A. thesis, Vanderbilt Univ., 1983), 1–7, 130–36.

3. Flamming, "Jones Revivals," 15–16, 152, 153, citing U.S. Department of Interior, Census Office, *Report on Statistics of Churches in the United States at the Eleventh Census, 1890* (Washington, D.C., 1894), 112–13. See also *Banner*, Jan. 20, 1899, for the summary of a church survey done by Nashville churches, which shows a similar pattern. All data in the discussion that follows are drawn from these sources and those cited in Table 3.

4. Hunter Dickinson Farish, *The Circuit Rider Dismounts: A Social History of Southern Methodism, 1865–1900* (Richmond, 1938), 349, quoted in Flamming, "Jones Revivals," 16.

5. John Woolridge, ed., *History of Nashville, Tennessee* (Nashville, 1890; rpt. 1970), 453–65; Alfred Leland Crabb, *Nashville: Personality of a City* (Indianapolis, 1960), 141–48, provide brief overviews of the history of Methodism in Nashville.

6. Woolridge, ed., *Nashville*, 468; Crabb, *Nashville*, 134–35.

7. Flamming, "Jones Revivals," 20–21. On the Presbyterians, see Woolridge, ed., *Nashville*, 465–72; Crabb, *Nashville*, 127–39.

8. Milton L. Baughn, "Social Views Reflected in Official Publications of the Cumberland Presbyterian Church, 1875–1900" (Ph.D. diss., Vanderbilt Univ., 1954), cited in Paul E. Isaac, *Prohibition and Politics: Turbulent Decades in Tennessee, 1885–1920* (Knoxville, 1965), 23n, 75, 75n; Woolridge, ed., *Nashville*, 472–75, 494–98; Crabb, *Nashville*, 139–41, 159–60.

9. Flamming, "Jones Revivals," 21–22. Rufus Buin Spain, *At Ease in Zion: A Social History of Southern Baptists, 1865–1900* (Nashville, 1967), provides a good overview of this denomination.

10. Woolridge, ed., *Nashville*, 475–88, 502, 505; Crabb, *Nashville*, 148–57; Spain, *At Ease in Zion*.

11. Isaac, *Prohibition*, 23.

12. Woolridge, ed., *Nashville*, 499–501; Crabb, *Nashville*, 160–67; George Flanigan, ed., *Catholicity in Tennessee* (Nashville, 1937).

13. *Banner*, Mar. 25–May 10, 1885, describes the planning preliminary to Jones's 1885 visit, as referred to in Flamming, "Jones Revivals," 24–25. On Jones see Harold Ivan Smith, "An Analysis and Evaluation of the Evangelistic Work of Samuel Porter Jones in Nashville, 1885–1906" (M.A. thesis, Scarritt College for Christian Workers, 1974); Richard L. Wilson, "Sam Jones: An Apostle of the New South," *Georgia Historical Quarterly* 57(1973): 459–74; Walt Holcomb, *Sam Jones* (Nashville: Methodist Publishing House, 1947).

14. *Banner*, May 14, 1885, quoted in Flamming, "Jones Revivals," 39.

15. *Banner*, May 19, 1885; *Daily American*, May 27, 1890, both quoted in Flamming, "Jones Revivals," 36–37.

16. Flamming, "Jones Revivals," 110, citing *American*, Apr. 4, 1886, describes the reformed hall, also known as Ryman Temperance Hall, as "an intimidating sight for any sot who inadvertently stumbled through the door." It had a life-sized portrait of Sam Jones, murals depicting the ruin of a drunken man with his weeping family exposed to the winter chill, another showing a barroom murder, and a more comforting scene showing the WCTU ladies reforming a drunken man. See also Herman A. Norton, *Religion in Tennessee, 1777–1945* (Knoxville, 1981), 83, et passim, for a summary of the Ryman conversion story and a good overview of social reform and its relationship to southern religion.

17. Norton, *Religion*, 84. See also, Smith, "Jones in Nashville," 60, 63–64; and Jerry Eugene Henderson, "A History of the Ryman Auditorium in Nashville, Tennessee: 1892–1920" (Ph.D. diss., Louisiana State Univ., 1962; copy in Ben West Public Library, Nashville Room).

18. Flamming, "Jones Revivals," 51–56; Howard N. Rabinowitz, *Race Relations in the Urban South, 1865–1890* (New York, 1978), 142–43, 371.

19. Flamming, "Jones Revivals," 57–58, cites the *Twenty Third Annual Report of the United Charities, Nashville, Tennessee, 1904* (Nashville, 1904), 7–9, which states that this Thanksgiving drive was the actual origin of the Nashville Relief Society. Cf. Sarah S. Morrow, *The Legacy of Fannie Battle* (Nashville, 1980), 12.

20. Morrow, *Legacy*, 12–13.

21. *American*, Jan. 23, 1882, quoted in ibid., 13.

22. Ibid., 15–17.

23. Roy Lubove, *The Professional Altruist: The Emergence of Social Work as a Career, 1880–1930* (Cambridge, Mass., 1965), provides a thorough history of professional social work.

24. Louise L. Davis, "She Didn't Look the Other Way," *Tennessean Magazine*, Dec. 14, 1958, p. 15, cited in Flamming, "Jones Revivals," 66–67; *Banner*, Apr. 8, 1901.

25. Morrow, *Legacy*, 17–21; Flamming, "Jones Revivals," 84–85.

26. *Banner*, May 28, 1885; *Union*, June 7, 8, 1885, cited in Flamming, "Jones Revivals," 68–69.

27. *History of the Woman's Mission Home and the Annual Reports for the Year 1893* (Nashville, 1894), 2; Otto Wilson, *Fifty Years Work With Girls, 1883–1933: A Story of the Florence Crittenton Homes* (Alexandria, Va., 1933), 352–53, both cited in Flamming, "Jones Revivals," 81–82.

28. John C. Ferris, *Homes For the Homeless; or Fourteen Years Among the Orphans* (Nashville, 1895), 11–12, 217–19; *First Biennial Report of the Tennessee Industrial School, 1887–1888*, 18; *Sixth Biennial Report of the Tennessee Industrial School, 1897–98*, 65, both cited in Flamming, "Jones Revivals," 75–78.

29. Rabinowitz, *Race*, 142–43, 210–11, 248; Flamming, "Jones Revivals," 74.

30. Flamming, "Jones Revivals," 72–74; Woolridge, ed., *Nashville*, 567–68. See also *Union*, May 2, 1887, which provides a useful retrospective at the twelfth anniversary of the YMCA.

31. Charles T. Wyatt, *History of the Development of Watkins Institute, Nashville, Tennessee* (Nashville, 1935); Louise Davis, "A Hungry Orphan's Will," *Tennessean Magazine*, July 16, 1972, pp. 18–21; Wilson E. Wood, "The Development of Watkins Institute as an Educational Service to the Community" (unpublished paper, winter 1951, in Watkins Institute Library). A typescript of Samuel Watkins's will is also located in the institute's library.

32. Isaac, *Prohibition*, 11.

33. Ibid., 13–15, 18, 33.

34. *Nashville Union*, July 19, 1886, quoted in ibid., 21–22.

35. Ibid., 28–29.

36. Ibid., 30–31.

37. *Union*, Nov. 2, 1886, quoted in ibid., 30–31.

38. *Union*, Feb. 19, 1887.

39. *Banner*, June 7, 13, 18, July 4, 21, Aug. 2, 1887.

40. Isaac, *Prohibition*, 45; *Banner*, June 6, 7, July 9, Sept. 17, 1887.

41. The *American* remained opposed to constitutional prohibition over the next twenty years, until it was bought by Luke Lea and merged into his strong prohibitionist newspaper, the *Tennessean*.

42. *Banner*, June 13, 1887; Isaac, *Prohibition*, 36.

43. *Banner*, Sept. 22, 1887. For examples of integrated rallies see *Banner*, Aug. 12, 13, 15, 1887, and the "Prohibition Column" of *Banner*, Sept. 15, 1887, addressed "To Laboring Men of Davidson County—White and Colored."

44. *American*, Aug. 13, 1887, quoted in Isaac, *Prohibition*, 46.

45. Quoted in ibid., 52–53.

46. *Banner*, Sept. 29, 1887.

47. *Banner*, Sept. 29, 1887; Isaac, *Prohibition*, 54–55.

48. *Banner*, Oct. 1, 1887.

49. *American*, Oct. 17, 1887, quoted in Isaac, *Prohibition*, 57. This was only a rough estimate, but one made by a newspaper that favored defeat of prohibition and had no reason to discredit black voters opposing the amendment.

50. *Banner*, Oct. 1, 1887.

51. Isaac, *Prohibition*, 57; Rabinowitz, *Race*, 314–15, 318–19.

52. J. Morgan Kousser, *The Shaping of Southern Politics: Suffrage Restriction and the Establishment of the One-Party South, 1880–1910*, Yale Historical Publications, Miscellany, 102 (New Haven, 1974), 104.

53. See Kercheval's obituary in *Banner*, Mar. 23, 1915.

54. Rabinowitz, *Race*, 283.

55. Joseph H. Cartwright, *The Triumph of Jim Crow: Tennessee Race Relations in the 1880s* (Knoxville, 1976), 124.

56. *American*, May 21, 22, June 5, 1881.

57. Ibid., Sept. 4–20, 1881; *Banner*, Sept. 26, 1881.

58. *American*, Dec. 9, 1882.

59. Ibid., Sept. 23, 1883, quoted in Cartwright, *Triumph*, 121. Colyar's biographer argues that this reform was motivated by broader partisan goals of Colyar and his business allies, who wanted to regain power in Nashville and expand their base in state Democratic politics. See Thomas Woodrow Davis, "Arthur S. Colyar and the New South, 1860–1905" (Ph.D. diss., Univ. of Missouri, 1965), 327, cited in Cartwright, *Triumph*, 121–22.

60. *American*, Mar. 7, 1883.

61. Ibid., Mar. 22, 1883.

62. See ibid., Mar. 1, 1883, for a long petition of citizens favoring the reform charter. For the Republican opposition view see *Daily World*, Mar. 2, 3, 6, 1883.

63. *American*, Oct. 10, 1883, quoted in Cartwright, *Triumph*, 123.

64. Ibid., 126.

65. *American*, Oct. 19, 1983.

66. *Banner*, Oct. 12, 1883. Cartwright, *Triumph*, 129, argues that black defection was more limited than Colyar claimed.

67. Cartwright, *Triumph*, 130, 135, 136. Convict labor, predominantly black, was no longer allowed to work for the city, as it apparently had been under Kercheval. Also, the practice of paying black city workers in scrip, redeemable only at stores operated by Kercheval cronies who charged exorbitant prices, was abandoned for cash payments. Ibid., 133–34.

68. Minutes of the City Council," Feb. 14, 1884, p. 74; Feb. 28, 1884, p. 83, MS in City Clerk's Vault, Metropolitan Nashville and Davidson County Courthouse.

69. Ibid., Feb. 28, 1884, p. 83.

70. Ibid., Sept. 11, 25, 1884, pp. 217–18, 222. There was also considerable opposition among whites to the establishment of a Negro fire company in East Nashville; see *American*, Jan. 8, 14, 1884. See also *Banner*, Oct. 18, 1893, for an account of whites' trying to end this black fire company. See also, Rabinowitz, *Race*, 295–96, 411–12, n.42, for more references to the fire company issue.

71. See, for example, William H. Young's denunciation of Kercheval's treatment of his fellow blacks in *Banner*, Oct. 6, 1885.

72. Rabinowitz, *Race*, 296, 411–12, n.42.

73. Cartwright, *Triumph*, 135–36; Rabinowitz, *Race*, 296–97. Kercheval polled 3,750 votes against Phillips's 5,023 in 1883. In 1885 he won only 345 additional votes (4,095), but the Reform mayoral candidate, Maj. Andrew W. Wills, a Republican, won only 3,595, down 1,428 from the 1883 reform vote. *Banner*, Oct. 9, 12, 1885.

74. *Banner*, Oct. 9, 1885. This account reports incorrectly that the 1885 election was Kercheval's tenth, instead of eleventh, mayoral election victory (see app. C).

75. Ibid., Oct. 13, 14, 1887.

76. See Rabinowitz, *Race*, 305.

77. Kousser, *Southern Politics*, 108–9, reports the methods of fraud and intimidation used by black-belt Democrats to gain office in 1888. The voting

laws that followed guaranteed that strong-arm tactics would no longer be necessary, except in emergencies.

78. Ibid., 110–11. To further skew the Dortch Law against Republicans, one provision, later deleted, allowed those who could have voted before 1857 to receive assistance in marking their ballot, a loophole to allow illiterate whites to exercise their franchise.

79. Ibid., 113.

80. Ibid., 114–16; Rabinowitz, *Race,* 325–26. The effect of the poll tax on poor whites created much discontent over this provision of disfranchisement, but Kousser demonstrates that black-belt, or West Tennessee, Democrats cracked the party whip to push this measure through.

81. *American,* Nov. 11, Dec., 24, 1890, quoted in Cartwright, *Triumph,* 214–15.

82. *Banner,* Oct. 11, 1889. The Democratic vote was also down, to 2,682, about 65 percent of the average in the 1881, 1883, and 1885 mayoral elections (the Democrats did not run a candidate in 1887). A prohibition candidate took some of these votes, 789, but the total turnout, 4,613, was only 63 percent of the average in the four previous mayoral elections. Returns give an idea of how the restrictive voting laws affected blacks: the heavily black Fourth Ward polled only 229 mayoral votes, including only 85 for the Republican mayor, in 1889, about one-third the total average turnout since 1881, and about one-fifth the average Republican vote since 1881. See also Rabinowitz, *Race,* 326.

83. Cartwright, *Triumph,* 238; Rabinowitz, *Race,* 327.

84. Cartwright, *Triumph,* 238.

85. *Banner,* Nov. 11, 1890.

86. *American,* July 21, 1890.

87. *Banner,* Sept. 23, 28, 1893. Waller, *Nashville, 1890s,* 85. See also *Banner,* Nov. 6, 1892; Oct. 31, Nov. 3, 1894, for coverage of continued conflict between white and black Republicans in the 1890s.

88. William Waller, ed., *Nashville in the 1890s* (Nashville, 1970), 85; *Banner,* Sept. 8, 1897. Kousser, *Southern Politics,* 72–82, deals with white primaries throughout the South.

89. Black voters and politicians did maintain some leverage in the system even in the darkest days of the 1890s. See the controversy over white efforts to displace the black fire company in *Banner,* Oct. 18, 1893, and subsequent issues, for an example of black and Republican resistance to racial repression.

90. C. Vann Woodward, *The Strange Career of Jim Crow* (New York, 1955, rev. ed. 1957), 64, 49–95, passim.

91. *Banner,* Apr. 30, 1892. See also *Banner,* May 21, 1892, for an account of another attempted lynching in Nashville, and Rabinowitz, *Race,* 40, 52–54, for accounts of earlier lynchings.

CHAPTER SEVEN

1. On the Crump regime, see William D. Miller, *Mr. Crump of Memphis* (Baton Rouge, 1964); idem, *Memphis During the Progressive Era* (Memphis, 1957).

2. Howse-Wilson Hall, a home for nurses, erected in 1931–32 at the City Hospital (now General Hospital) was named to honor the mayor's beloved wife, Jennie Wheeler Howse. She shared the honor with Felix Z. Wilson, one of her husband's arch political foes.

3. Herman Justi, ed., *Official History of the Tennessee Centennial Exposition: Opened May 1, and Closed October 30, 1897* (Nashville, 1898), 439.

4. C. Vann Woodward, *Origins of the New South, 1877–1913,* A History of the South 9(Baton Rouge, 1951), 124–25.

5. Justi, ed., *Official History,* 27–29.

6. Ibid., 29–31, 37. See ch. 2, above, on the L&N battle with Jere Baxter, which coincided with the Centennial Exposition.

7. Justi, ed., *Official History,* 96.

8. Ibid., 481–83, 489–91.

9. Ibid., 146; Anne Firor Scott, *The Southern Lady: From Pedestal to Politics, 1830–1930* (Chicago, 1970), 105–231, provides a good overview of the "new woman" in the South. Women, the *Official History of the Exposition* remarked, are "the poetry of life. . . . But they demonstrated the fact that a woman can execute as well as inspire, reason as well as see, add strength as well as grace, fight as well as crown." It added, "she is strong without becoming masculine, and gracious without becoming weak. She has her rights and retains her privileges. . . . Such is the woman who has been mother, wife, daughter, sister, in the homes of Tennessee, and whose sweet, noble, inspiring preserver has suffered the struggles of a hundred years and crowned the summit of the century with a halo of ineffable light."

10. Justi, ed., *Official History,* 145–50.

11. Ibid., 151–53.

12. Ibid., 264–76.

13. Ibid., 327–30.

14. Ibid., 193–94.

15. Ibid., 198, 202–3.

16. Ibid., 196–98, 202.

17. Ibid., 208–9.

18. Ibid., 204.

19. Ibid., 336–51, 360–89, 413–32.

20. Ibid., 366–89, 413–23.

21. Ibid., 474.

22. The quoted phrase is from Woodward, *Origins,* 154–58.

23. Ibid., 129–40, quote on 138.

24. Robert Love Taylor, *Echoes: Centennial and Other Notable Speeches, Lectures and Stories* (Nashville, 1899), 24–28.

25. For biographical data on the mayors of the 1890s, see William Waller, ed., *Nashville in the 1890s* (Nashville, 1970), 78–96.

26. On Vertrees's importance to local politics see the interviews with Wirt Armistead and George Armistead in Waller Collection, Special Collections, VUL.

27. Biographical information on Head is found in *Daily News,* Apr. 25, 1902; William Waller, ed., *Nashville from 1900 to 1910* (Nashville, 1972), 3–5. See also James M. Head, "One Mayor's Experience" National Municipal League, Conference for Good City Government, *Proceedings* (1906):269–79. Head's nu-

merous contributions to Nashville's development in the early twentieth century deserve more thorough scholarly attention.

28. The details behind what was known as the "Simmons Hall Bill" charter can be followed in detail in the *Banner*, Mar. 28, Apr. 1, 3, 6, 7, 1899. See also Waller, ed., *Nashville, 1900*, 5, and Hill McAlister interview, Waller Collection, box 2, 7–8, Special Collections, VUL. For the complete text of the new charter see Senate Bill Number 464, Chapter 204, *Acts of Tennessee, 1899*, 405–22.

29. *Banner*, Apr. 7, 1899.

30. Head was also an avowed "wet" but was the clear choice of the temperance movement over Kinney. See *Banner*, Sept. 29, 1899, for primary election results, and *Banner*, Oct. 13, 1899, for general election results and commentary.

31. *Banner*, Oct. 14, 1903.

32. James M. Head, "Message of the Mayor," Jan. 11, 1900, in *Reports of Departments, 1900*, 8.

33. *Daily News*, June 16, 1903, 10; *Banner*, Oct. 14, 1903. Waller, ed., *Nashville, 1900*, 41–42. Partly as a result of the battle with Mayor Head, the company was reorganized in 1903 as Nashville Railway and Light Company, with Percy Warner as president and the stock owned mostly by local capitalists. It had been controlled by a Baltimore-based syndicate before this time. See ch. 3, and Waller, ed., *Nashville, 1900*, 42.

34. *Banner*, Oct. 14, 1903; *Daily News*, June 16, 1903; Head, "Message of the Mayor," Jan. 9, 1902, in *Reports of Departments, 1902*, 6; Head, "Message of the Mayor," Jan. 29, 1903 in *City Reports of Departments, 1903*, 19.

35. Waller, ed., *Nashville, 1900*, 84–86; *Banner*, Oct. 14, 1903; Head, "Message," Jan. 29, 1903, 14–15.

36. Head, "Message," Jan. 29, 1903, 15–16; *Banner*, Oct. 14, 1903; Waller, ed., *Nashville, 1900*, 32–36.

37. On municipal ownership and socialism in the progressive era, see Howard P. Chudacoff, *The Evolution of American Urban Society*, 2nd ed. (Englewood Cliffs, N.J., 1981), 170–73; and Bruce Stave, ed., *Socialism and the Cities* (Port Washington, N.Y., 1975).

38. See James M. Head, "Municipal Construction *Versus* the Contract System," *Arena* 31(Apr. 1904): 337–52, for the mayor's own statement on municipal ownership, which portrays Nashville as a national model for progressive reform. See also Head, "Nashville, Tennessee, Municipal Government," *Arena* 30(Apr. 1903):345–51.

39. Paul E. Isaac, *Prohibition and Politics: Turbulent Decades in Tennessee, 1885–1920* (Knoxville, 1965), 78–79, 90. An 1899 law extended the Four-Mile Law to towns under, 2,000 by reincorporation; the Adams Act allowed towns up to 5,000 population to go dry.

40. Waller, ed., *Nashville, 1900*, 76–77.

41. Ibid., 78–79; *Banner*, May 15, 1903. Howard Brooks, "Nashville's Reform Constituency During the Progressive Era" (unpublished undergraduate paper, Feb. 1981), 10–12; Brooks follows the reform movement from the mid-1890s through 1913 with careful analysis of electoral behavior.

42. Brooks, "Reform," 21–22, app. 8, 9, 41, includes election results by wards and analysis of the voting population of each ward from census materials.

43. *American*, May 15, 1903, quoted in Waller, ed., *Nashville, 1900*, 80–81.

44. *American*, May 19, 1905; *Banner*, May 18, 1905.

45. Waller, ed., *Nashville, 1900*, 87; Isaac, *Prohibition*, 126.

46. Davidson County representative and, later, county judge Litton Hickman was a major force behind this annexation. *Banner*, Jan. 21, 23, 24, 25, 27, 31, Feb. 1, 1905.

47. *American*, Mar. 17, 1907, quoted in Isaac, *Prohibition*, 127 (St. Patrick's Day may not have been the most opportune time to declare a crusade for prohibition in Nashville).

48. Isaac, *Prohibition*, 127.

49. Ibid., 107.

50. Ibid., 108–9.

51. Ibid., 14932–44.

52. *Tennessean*, June 14, 1908, quoted in ibid., 147–48.

53. *Tennessean*, June 16, 17, 1908, quoted in ibid., 148.

54. Waller, ed., *Nashville, 1900*, 93–100, includes a detailed account by J.C. Bradford, who was a friend of Robin Cooper. See also Hugh Walker's careful review of the evidence in *Tennessean*, Apr. 19, 26, May 3, 24, 1981.

55. *Tennessean*, Nov. 10, 1908. Waller, ed., *Nashville, 1900*, 97–98; Isaac, *Prohibition*, 157–59.

56. Isaac, *Prohibition*, 165–67. The Carmack statue was finally erected in 1925. Later, a tunnel to ease the passage of legislators into the statehouse was constructed directly under Carmack's memorial. It was named after Lem and Reagor Motlow, legislators and distillers of Jack Daniel whiskey. Ibid., 167–68n.

57. *Banner*, July 1, 1909. The saloons along Fourth Street continued as speakeasies, and patrons entered at the rear alley. Known as Printers Alley, this area became a famous resort during prohibition and remains the heart of Nashville's nighttime entertainment.

58. Biographical information on Hilary Howse is available in his obituaries, *Tennessean*, Jan. 3, 1938, *Banner*, Jan. 3, 1938, and in *Banner*, Dec. 21, 1934. Howard S. Brooks, "Nashville's Municipal Politics, 1909–1938: Hilary Howse and the Decline of the 'Moral Wave'" (unpublished undergraduate paper, Apr. 1980), 3–4, includes a good summary of Howse's political career. George Barker's colorful account of Howse and the prohibition era "The Era of Nickel Beer, Free Lunch" and "Behind the Western Front" in *Tennessean Magazine*, June 6, 13, 1965, from which the quote is taken. See also John Trotwood Moore, *Tennessee: The Volunteer State* 3 (Chicago, 1923), 866–69; Will T. Hale and Dixon L. Merritt, *A History of Tennessee and Tennesseans . . .* 4(Chicago, 1913), 992.

59. *American*, Oct. 13, 1909.

60. *Banner*, Aug. 23–25, Sept. 1, 1909. See also, *Banner*, Sept. 14, 16, 1909, for colorful account of the heated primary campaign; Isaac, *Prohibition*, 172–73; Waller, ed., *Nashville, 1900*, 103.

61. *Banner*, Sept. 25, 1909.

62. Ibid., Oct. 15, 1909.

63. *Tennessean*, May 11, 1911.

64. Steve R. Dozier, "Prohibition and the Enforcement of the Nashville Police Department, 1905–1933" (unpublished undergraduate seminar paper, Dec. 1978), 9, app. B. App. B. shows arrests records.

65. Litton Hickman interview, in Waller Collection, box 2, 9–10, Special Collections, VUL.

66. John D. Buenker, *Urban Liberalism and Progressive Reform* (New York, 1973); J. Joseph Huthmacher, "Urban Liberalism and the Age of Reform," *Mississippi Valley Historical Review* 49(Sept. 1962): 231–41.

67. For the distinctions between structural and social reform, see Melvin G. Holli, *Reform in Detroit: Hazen S. Pingree and Urban Politics* (New York, 1969), 161–81.

68. *Banner*, Sept. 9, 1909; Feb. 8, Apr. 11, 12, 29, July 8, 1910; May 6, 22, 1911.

69. Ibid., Nov. 30, 1910; "Annual Message of Honorable Hilary E. Howse, Mayor of Nashville, Tennessee," Nov. 6, 1911, in *Reports of Departments, 1911*, 9, 13, 14, 17.

70. Lester C. Lamon, *Black Tennesseans, 1900–1930* (Knoxville, 1977), 17, 42, 53, 101.

71. *Banner*, July 5, 1912.

72. *Globe*, Dec. 16, 1910. See also, "Annual Message," 1911, p. 19, on the Carnegie Library. This library was recently reopened as a depository for an Afro-American history collection.

73. *Banner*, Oct. 13, 1911; Brooks, "Reform," 54.

74. *Banner*, Oct. 13, 1911.

75. *Thirteenth Census of the United States: 1910. Population* 3 (Washington, D.C., 1913), 766; *Banner*, Oct. 15, 1909, Oct. 13, 1911; Lamon, *Black Tennesseans*, 51–53, shows blacks remained loyal to the party of Lincoln in national elections, but they allied with friendly Democrats like Howse and Gov. Patterson in local and state elections.

76. *Banner*, Aug. 16, Sept. 20, 1907; *Banner*, Oct. 26, 1910; Jan. 26, Feb. 9, 15, 16, 17, 21, Mar. 30, 1911. Patricia S. Miletich, "The Launching of Nashville's Commission Government, 1910 to 1915" (unpublished graduate seminar paper, May 1979), 5.

77. Max York, "The Night the Reservoir Broke," *Tennessean Magazine*, Aug. 29, 1971.

78. *Banner*, Nov. 5, Dec. 28, 1912; "Minutes, Directors Meetings, Board of Trade Executive Committee," Nov. 8, 14, 1912, in Nashville Chamber of Commerce.

79. Multiple versions of this plan were introduced by different interest groups to the state legislature. The final version is in ch. 22, Senate Bill no. 236, *Acts of Tennessee, 1913*, pp. 49–119, also published as *The Charter of the City of Nashville. The Commission Form of Government Act of 1913, and Subsequent Amendments* (Nashville, 1915).

80. *Commercial Club Tattler* 1(Oct. 1912): 19.

81. "Annual Message of Hon. Hilary E. Howse, Mayor of Nashville, Tennessee" *Reports of Departments, 1912*, 7.

82. The passage of the commission charter through the legislature can be followed in the *Banner*, Jan. 18, 30, Feb. 5, 7, 11, 12, 17, 19, 1913. Gov. Ben Hooper refused to sign, or veto, the bill, and in a special message to the legislature he objected to the lack of citizen approval of the new charter and the "perpetuation of so much of the machinery and officials of the present city government." See *Banner*, Feb. 19, 1913.

83. *Banner,* Feb. 19, 20, 1913.

84. *Democrat,* Sept. 6, 1913; *Banner,* Aug. 28, Sept. 10, 1913.

85. *Banner,* Sept. 9, 1913.

86. *Banner,* Sept. 10, 1913. This cartoon as well as clippings on local politics in this period are collected in the Edwin A. Price Scrapbook, Scrapbook Collection, box 1, file 1, TSLA.

87. *Banner,* Aug. 28, Sept. 4, 1913; *Democrat,* Aug. 26, 1913.

88. Total registration was up from 13,878 to 19,143. *Banner,* Sept. 4, 1913.

89. Ibid., Sept. 3, 1913. *Globe,* Aug. 22, 1913.

90. Ibid., Sept. 12, 1913.

91. *Tennessean,* Sept. 12, 1913.

92. *Banner,* Sept. 12, 1913. The *Banner,* in one of the few objective attempts to analyze the bases of machine power in Nashville, also attributed much of Howse's strength to the Elks and Eagles and other "secret orders." Howse was an active member of several men's fraternal organizations.

93. *Banner,* Sept. 12, 1913.

94. This letter is in "Minutes, Board of Trade Directors Meetings," Oct. 16, 1913, p. 499. It apparently was sent to other businessmen's associations and printed in the newspapers.

95. George L. Sioussat, "Municipal Affairs in Nashville, 1915," *National Municipal Review* 4(Oct. 1915): 646–51, is the best summary of the events surrounding the 1915 crisis.

96. "Minutes, BOG," Mar. 20, 1915.

97. *Banner,* Mar. 15, 1915.

98. Ibid., May 25, 1915.

99. *Tennessean,* Mar. 30, 1915.

100. Ibid., Mar. 31, 1915.

101. *Banner,* June 4–24, 1915. The Price Scrapbook includes all the important clippings on the crisis of 1915.

102. *Banner,* June 24, 25, July 3, 1915. See also "Minutes of Public Safety Committee," June 24 through Dec. 26, 1915, in Nashville Chamber of Commerce.

103. *Banner,* June 15, 17, 23, 25, 1915.

104. Ibid., July 7, 1915.

105. Ibid., July 8, 9, 20, 1915.

106. Sioussat, "Municipal Affairs," 651, 647; *Banner,* July 8, 1915.

107. *Banner,* July 21, 1915; Sioussat, "Municipal Affairs," 647, 651.

108. *Banner,* July 21, 1915.

109. Ibid., July 27, 1915.

110. Ibid., June 26, July 27, 1915; "A City in the Hands of a Receiver," *Outlook,* Sept. 1, 1915, p. 11.

111. *Banner,* Aug. 10, 11, 1915.

112. Sioussat, "Municipal Affairs," 649–51; *Tennessean,* July 31, 1915.

113. Sioussat, "Municipal Affairs," 650.

114. "Minutes, Boards of Commissioners, 1915," 150–87, City Clerk's Vault, Metropolitan Nashville and Davidson County Courthouse.

115. *Banner,* Nov. 30, 1915.

CHAPTER EIGHT

1. See app. A for figures on city and county population, by race, from 1860 to 1980.

2. Blaine A. Brownell, *The Urban Ethos in the South, 1920–1930* (Baton Rouge, 1975), 15, et passim.

3. George Brown Tindall, *The Emergence of the New South, 1913–1945* A History of the South 10 (Baton Rouge, 1967), 64.

4. *Tennessean*, Apr. 3, 1917.

5. "Minutes, Board of Governors Meeting, Commercial Club" (hereafter "Minutes, BOG"), Apr. 5, 1917, MS in Chamber of Commerce.

6. See Lea's account of "The Kaiser Story," MS in TSL.

7. Jesse C. Burt, *Nashville: Its Life and Times* (Nashville, 1959), 103.

8. *Tennessean*, July 16, 1918.

9. Ibid., May 16, 1917.

10. Ibid., Mar. 30, Apr. 3, 24, 27, May 16, 17, July 26, Aug. 7, 1917.

11. Ibid., Jan. 28, 1918.

12. Ibid., Feb. 18, 28, Mar. 15, 1918.

13. In April 1917 a labor recruiter was arrested at Union Station. Ibid., Apr. 9, 1917. See also, "Minutes, BOG," May 17, 1923, for the chamber's response to black labor recruiters.

14. Samuel H. Shannon, "Agricultural and Industrial Education at Tennessee State University During the Normal School Phase, 1912–1922" (Ph.D. diss., George Peabody College for Teachers, 1974), 224–25.

15. See app. A for population data on blacks in Nashville and Davidson County, 1860–1980. On the black migration, see Florrette Henri, *Black Migration: Movement North, 1900–1920* (New York, 1975); Louise V. Kennedy, *The Negro Peasant Turns Cityward: Recent Migrations to Northern Centers* (New York, 1930).

16. See Anne Firor Scott, *The Southern Lady: From Pedestal to Politics, 1830–1930* (Chicago, 1970), 185–231.

17. See Rose L. Gilmore, *Davidson County Women in the World War, 1914–1919* (Nashville, 1923), for a full account of women's activities in this period. *Tennessean*, July 22, 1917.

18. *Tennessean*, July 22, Oct. 12, 23, 1917; Jan. 11, Apr. 4, 5, May 24, July 4, 1918.

19. See ibid., Jan. 30, 1918, for an account of women workers at the Edgefield and Nashville Furniture Manufacturing Co.

20. Lou Cretia Owen, "Diary, 1918–1919," 9, MS in TSL.

21. *Tennessean*, Apr. 8, 1923, gives the histories of the Altrusa Club and the Business and Professional Women's Club. See also ibid., Apr. 13, 1917.

22. Ibid., Oct. 18, 1917.

23. Owen, "Diary," 5.

24. Commercial Club, "Minutes, Committee Meeting," July 7, 14, 1916; "Minutes BOG," Apr. 24, Dec. 6, 1917; Apr. 5, 1918.

25. *Tennessean*, Jan. 14, 1918.

26. "Minutes, BOG," July 26, 1918; *Tennessean*, Feb. 24, 1918.

27. *Tennessean,* Feb. 16, 1918. The average daily wage for common laborers in Nashville was approximately $2.00 at this time.

28. Owen, "Diary," 57, 79, 123.

29. See David Edward Brand, "Fill the Empty Shell: The Story of the Government Munitions Project at Old Hickory, Tennessee, 1918–1919" (M.A. thesis, Vanderbilt Univ., 1971), 41–44, 59–60, 67–70; Owen, "Diary," 3, 52; *Tennessean,* July 27, 1918; "Minutes, BOG," Oct. 10, 1918.

30. Brand, "Empty Shell," 36–37, 47–51. Brand shows that pressure from local businessmen kept powder plant wages lower than the federal government wished.

31. Owen, "Diary," 65.

32. Ibid., 7.

33. Glenn Rogers, "Localization of a Few Selective Industries in Nashville" (M.A. thesis, George Peabody College for Teachers, 1932), 14–27, 29–58. One important new avenue in metal works was Harry Dyer's Nashville Bridge Co., which applied mass production techniques borrowed from the automobile industry to the construction of barges. *Nashville This Week,* Apr. 5, 1926, p. 9; Apr. 25, 1927, p. 25.

34. See Brownell, *Urban Ethos,* for an insightful analysis of the "commercial-civic elite" in Nashville and other southern cities during the 1920s.

35. Ernest Goodrich, "Report of an Industrial Survey of Nashville, Tennessee for the Commercial Club of Nashville," 1920, typescript in Chamber of Commerce.

36. Ibid., 774.

37. "Minutes, BOG," Apr. 17, 1919; May 18, 1920; "Minutes, Committee Meetings: Charter Committee," Aug. 4, 1920. See the Nashville Industrial Corporation's promotional pamphlet "Old Hickory" (Nashville, [1920?]).

38. *Nashville Review,* Sept. 15, 1921, pp. 34–35; Apr. 20, 1922, pp. 16–17. "Minutes, BOG," July 25, 1923.

39. *Tennessean,* Nov. 24, 1920. See also ibid., May 12, July 2, Aug. 9, Sept. 8, 1920; Jan. 2, 9, 16, Nov. 20, 1921; May 21, 1922.

40. Ibid., Dec. 3, 1920.

41. Ibid., July 14, 1923; Tindall, *Emergence of New South,* 87.

42. *Nashville This Week,* Aug. 1, 1927, p. 10; *Tennessean,* Oct. 8, 10, 1925; Jan. 10, 1926; July 25, 1927; Mar. 1, 28, 1929; May 5, 1930.

43. *Nashville This Week,* Nov. 30, 1925, p. 5; Chamber of Commerce, "Minutes Industrial Committee," Mar. 19, 1924; "Minutes, BOG," Nov. 12, 1925; "Minutes, Joint Meeting of Sub-Committees of BOG and Industrial Committee," Nov. 18, 1925.

44. "Minutes, BOG," Nov. 12, 1925.

45. *Nashville This Week,* Nov. 30, 1925, p. 4; May 3, 1926, p. 9; *Tennessean,* Apr. 25, 1926. See Chamber of Commerce, "Minutes, Industrial Committee," Jan. 11, 1921, for an example of how the Thomas Henry Co. move was financed.

46. *Nashville This Week,* Feb. 6, 1928, p. 8.

47. *Tennessean,* Nov. 18, 1928; Oct. 19, 1930; *Banner,* Apr. 1, 1950. "Minutes, BOG," Apr. 2, Sept. 11, 1924.

48. *Fifteenth Census of the United States: 1930, Population 5, General*

Report on Occupations (Washington, D.C., 1933), 65–67; *Fourteenth Census of the United States Taken in the Year 1920*, 4, *Population*, 1910, *Occupation Statistics* (Washington, D.C., 1914), 167.

49. *Nashville This Week*, Nov. 5, 1928, p. 22.

50. William E. Leuchtenburg, *The Perils of Prosperity, 1914–32*, Chicago History of American Civilization (Chicago, 1958), 188–89.

51. *Nashville This Week*, Apr. 7, 1930, pp. 3–5.

52. *Tennessean*, Sept. 22, 1926.

53. Ibid., July 1, 1923.

54. Ibid., June 24, 1923; Jan. 20, 1924.

55. Ibid., Mar. 11, June 26, 1924.

56. *Nashville This Week*, Mar. 7, 1927, p. 11.

57. Ibid.; *Nashville City Directory 1928* (Nashville, 1928), 34–35; see *Tennessean*, July 13, 1983, for a good review of the early movie houses in Nashville based on an interview with Kermit Stengel, Jr., grandson of Tony Sudekum.

58. Leuchtenburg, *Perils*, 158–77.

59. *Analysis of Nashville's Retail Trade* (Nashville, 1932), 40.

60. *Tennessean*, Mar. 9, 1926.

61. John A. DeWitt, Jr., "Early Radio Broadcasting in Tennessee," THQ 31 (1972): 80–94.

62. Louise Davis, "Nashville-Made Autos . . . ," *Tennessean*, May 30, 1982.

63. *Retail Trade*, 40.

64. Charles E. Allred et al., *Human and Physical Resources of Tennessee: Financial Institutions [and] Insurance*, Rural Research Series, 66 (Knoxville, 1937), ii; John B. McFerrin, *Caldwell and Company: A Southern Financial Empire* (n.p., 1939; rev. Nashville, 1969).

65. *Tennessean*, Mar. 4, 1923; June 16, 1929.

66. *Nashville This Week*, Sept. 28, 1925, pp. 18–19.

67. Leuchtenburg, *Perils*, 201.

68. *Tennessean*, Jan. 18, 1925.

69. Ibid., Mar. 4, 1923.

70. See, for examples, ibid., Dec. 31, 1922; Mar. 4, 1923; Dec. 13, 1925; Apr. 9, 1926; Apr. 2, 1927; Aug. 4, 1929.

71. Brownell, *Urban Ethos*, 116–24; Howard L. Preston, *Automobile-Age Atlanta* (Athens, Ga., 1979).

72. Brownell, *Urban Ethos*, 124; see also Brownell's, "A Symbol of Modernity: Attitudes Toward the Automobile in Southern Cities in the 1920s," *American Quarterly* 24 (1972): 20–44.

73. Edwin Mims, *Chancellor Kirkland of Vanderbilt* (Nashville, 1940), 219–20.

74. Robert A. McGaw, *A Brief History of Vanderbilt University* (Nashville, 1973), 29.

75. Mims, *Kirkland*, 207.

76. Ibid.

77. *The Encyclopedia of Southern History*, ed. David C. Roller and Robert W. Twyman (Baton Rouge, 1979), 512–13.

78. Mims, *Kirkland*, 219.

79. *Tennessean,* Feb. 20, 1926.

80. Ibid., Dec. 27, 1925; Feb. 20, 1926.

81. Alfred L. Crabb, "The Historical Background of Peabody College: Covering a Period of One Hundred and Fifty-five Years," *Bulletin* George Peabody College for Teachers 30 (Oct. 1941):27–38.

82. Ibid.; *Tennessean,* Jan. 22, 1925.

83. *Tennessean,* June 29, Sept. 13, Dec. 11, 1923; Jan. 28, 1926; Aug. 18, 1929.

84. A.F. Kuhlman, ed., *The Development of University Centers in the South: Papers presented at the Dedication of the Joint University Library* (Nashville, 1941), 10–14, 82–92.

85. Joe M. Richardson, *A History of Fisk University, 1865–1946* (University, Ala, 1980), 55–70. Richardson notes that a "few vocational courses were taught . . . , but never to the injury of the college." Ibid., 59.

86. Ibid., 59–60, 66–68. In addition to being a member of the Board of Trustees, Washington was tied to Fisk through his wife, an alumna, and his son, who attended Fisk.

87. Ibid., 102–19.

88. Ibid., 123–24.

89. *Tennessean,* Mar. 1, Dec. 23, 1920; Jan. 4, 1922. James Summerville, *Educating Black Doctors: A History of Meharry Medical College* (University, Ala. 1983).

90. Charles Victor Roman, *Meharry Medical College: A History* (Nashville, 1934), 155–63.

91. Lester C. Lamon, *Black Tennesseans, 1900–1930* (Knoxville, 1977), 88–101.

92. Ibid., 102–6.

93. Shannon, "Agricultural and Industrial Education at Tennessee State University," provides an excellent overview of the early history of TSU. See also Shannon, "Land Grant College Legislation and Black Tennesseans: A Case Study in the Politics of Education," *History of Education Quarterly* 22(Summer 1982): 139–57.

94. Alfred Leland Crabb, *Nashville: Personality of a City* (Indianapolis, 1960), 204–5.

95. Ibid., 206.

96. *Tennessean,* Oct. 21, 1927. On Roger Williams University, see Eugene Teselle, "The Nashville Institute and Roger Williams University: Benevolence, Paternalism, and Black Consciousness, 1867–1928," THQ 41(1982): 360–79; Faye Wellborn Robbins, "A World within a World: Black Nashville, 1880–1915" (Ph.D. diss., Univ. of Arkansas, 1980), 4–7; Ruth Marie Powell, "The History of Negro Educational Institutions Sponsored by the Baptists of Tennessee from 1864 to 1934" (M.A. thesis, Tennessee A&I, 1953).

97. Crabb, *Nashville,* 196–98.

98. *Nashville This Week,* Aug. 25, 1930, p. 5. Vanderbilt University claimed $25 million in assets, Peabody College $8 million, leaving about $9 million among the other colleges.

99. *Banner,* July 15, 1923; *Tennessean,* May 1, 1920, both quoted in Brownell, *Urban Ethos,* 131–32.

CHAPTER NINE

1. George Barker, "The Rogers Caldwell Story," *Tennessean Magazine,* Oct. 20, 27, Nov. 3, 1963.

2. Powell Stamper, *The National Life Story: A History of the National Life and Accident Insurance Company of Nashville, Tennessee* (New York, 1968); *Our Shield,* Feb. 17, 1931; *Mirror,* Feb. 5, 1931, p. 3. Nashville's economy was never truly "depression proof," but the insurance industry continued to grow in the 1930s: National Life nearly tripled its assets to $83.5 million by 1940, while Life & Casualty more than doubled its assets to reach $28.5 million by 1940. *Our Shield,* Feb. 10, 1941, pp. 10–11; *Mirror,* Mar. 7, 1935, p. 4; Feb. 13, 1941, p. 2.

3. Stamper, *National Life,* 84, 114–14; Era Irene Emmons, *The Thrift Family: The Story of the Life & Casualty Insurance Company, 1903–1943* (Nashville, 1943).

4. Stamper, *National Life,* 85–86; Emmons, *Thrift Family,* 37–38.

5. Stamper, *National Life,* 84, 137–38; Emmons, *Thrift Family,* 37.

6. Lester C. Lamon, *Black Tennesseans, 1900–1930* (Knoxville, 1977), 201. Discussions of the shift from industrial to ordinary insurance can be found in Stamper, *National Life,* 102–10, 112–13, and Emmons, *Thrift Family,* 41.

7. See, for examples, *Mirror,* May 15, 1924, p. 1; May 22, 1924, p. 8; June 5, 1924, p. 5; July 9, 1925, p. 7; June 9, 1927, p. 4; Aug. 22, 1929, p. 3.

8. Ibid., Apr. 24, 1924, p. 1; Jan. 31, 1924, p. 1; Mar. 13, 1924, 2; Mar. 20, 1924, p. 1; Apr. 24, 1924, p. 1; Sept. 17, 1925, p. 9; Aug. 27, 1925, p. 6; Apr. 9, 1925, p. 3; May 27, 1926, p. 3; May 30, 1929, p. 2.

9. Ibid., Mar. 31, 1927, pp. 1, 4; May 30, 1929, pp. 1, 2.

10. Stamper, *National Life,* 106–7, 110.

11. *Our Shield,* Mar. 23, 1926, p. 18; Jan. 26, 1926, p. 18.

12. Charles K. Wolfe, *Tennessee Strings: The Story of Country Music in Tennessee* (Knoxville, 1977), 54–74; Stamper, *National Life,* 124–27.

13. *Our Shield,* Mar. 16, 1926, p. 23; Richard A. Peterson, "Single Industry Firm to Conglomerate Synergistics: Alternative Strategies for Selling Insurance and Country Music," in *Growing Metropolis: Aspects of Development in Nashville* ed. James Blumstein and Benjamin Walter (Nashville, 1975), 341–57; Richard A. Peterson and Paul DiMaggio, "The Early Opry: Its Hillbilly Image in Fact and Fancy," *Journal of Country Music* 4(1973): 39–50; Charles K. Wolfe, *The Grand Ole Opry: The Early Years, 1925–35* (London, 1975).

14. *Mirror,* Nov. 25, 1926, pp. 5–7; Mar. 30, 1928, p. 5.

15. Ibid., Oct. 4, 1928, p. 2; June 10, 1926, pp. 5, 8; June 24, 1926, p. 5; Sept. 2, 1926, pp. 1–2. See also Burton's 1932 publication *Gleanings* and Emmons, *Thrift Family,* 43, 53–54.

16. *Mirror,* Mar. 10, 1927, p. 5; Mar. 31, 1927, pp. 1–3.

17. *Tennessee National News,* Sept. 5, 1922; *Tennessean,* Aug. 24, 1924.

18. Claude A. Campbell, "The Development of Banking in Tennessee" (Ph.D. diss., Vanderbilt Univ., 1932), 187; *Polk's Nashville City Directory, 1941* (Nashville, 1941), 12.

19. *The Rand-McNally Bankers' Directory . . .* (Chicago, 1915), 984–85; *Moody's Manual of Investments* (New York, 1930); *Tennessean,* May 12, 1929.

20. Ernest Goodrich, "Report of an Industrial Survey of Nashville, Tennessee for the Commercial Club of Nashville," 1920, typescript in Chamber of Commerce," 159, 163, 773–75; James R. Kellam, Jr., *Bootstraps: A History of Commerce Union Bank, 1916–1966* (Nashville, 1966), 29–30; 1929 loans and resources derived from *Moody's*, 1930.

21. *Rand-McNally*, 1915, pp. 984–85.

22. Kellam, *Bootstraps*, 11–28.

23. Ibid., 23–25.

24. Ibid. For a time in 1929 Caldwell threatened to abandon Fourth and First's national charter and reorganize under the state charter granted to Nashville Trust. This would have allowed Caldwell to operate with less federal interference but at the cost of losing the public confidence a national bank normally enjoyed. This plan was rejected for a plan to set up a holding company, Fourth and First Banks, Inc., through which Caldwell could control his empire. John B. McFerrin, *Caldwell and Company: A Southern Financial Empire* (1939; rev., Nashville, 1969), 64–66; *Tennessean*, May 28, 1929.

25. Houston obituary, *Tennessean*, Sept. 16, 1956; *Tennessean*, May 21, 1969; Kellam, *Bootstraps*, 32.

26. Wilbur Foster Creighton, *Building of Nashville* (Nashville, 1969), 171–72; Margaret Dick, "Survival of the Fittest: Nashville City Bank at the Crossroads," *Nashville! Magazine*, July 1978; my conversation with John Hardcastle, July 1980, confirmed that Nelson, not Caldwell, added the parapet, which contradicts Dick's account.

27. Stamper, *National Life*, 140–41.

28. *Tennessean*, July 3, 15, 1927; *Nashville This Week*, May 14, 1927; *Nashville This Week*, May 14, 1927, p. 11; July 11, 1927, p. 7; July 25, 1927, p. 7; July 23, 1928, p. 16; *Tennessean*, Apr. 21, 1929; Third National Bank, *Nashville, 1927–52: Twenty Five Years of Progress* (Nashville, 1952); Louise Littleton Davis, "Third National Bank," in John Egerton, ed., *Nashville: The Faces of Two Centuries, 1780–1980* (Nashville, 1980), 360–61.

29. McFerrin, *Caldwell*, 2.

30. Ibid., 3–4; T.H. Alexander, "A Rich Man's Son Earns His Own Success," *The New South* 1 (Mar. 1927). Barker, "Rogers Caldwell Story."

31. *Tennessean*, July 18, 1928, quoted in McFerrin, *Caldwell*, 106; see also 9–11.

32. McFerrin, *Caldwell*, 11–14.

33. Ibid., 18–23, 252–53.

34. Ibid., 62–63.

35. Ibid., 64–80.

36. Ibid., 87–98.

37. David D. Lee, *Tennessee in Turmoil: Politics in the Volunteer State, 1920–1932* (Memphis, 1979), xiv, 81.

38. Ibid., 10–13.

39. *Banner*, Dec. 31, 1930, quoted in McFerrin, *Caldwell*, 103; Lee, *Tennessee*, 79–84.

40. McFerrin, *Caldwell*, 104–7; Stanley J. Folmsbee, Robert E. Corlew, Enoch L. Mitchell, *Tennessee: A Short History* (Knoxville, 1969), 491–93; Lee, *Tennessee*, 85–97.

41. McFerrin, *Caldwell*, 108, 144.

42. Ibid., 108–11, 113.

43. Ibid., 120–21.

44. Ibid., 122.

45. Ibid., 126–40.

46. Ibid., 177; Jesse Hill Ford, *Mr. Potter and His Bank: A Life of Edward Potter, Jr.* (Nashville, 1978), 34–36, and corrections in front.

47. Ford, *Potter*, 34–36; *Banner*, Nov. 13, 1930.

48. See Ford, *Potter*, 38–40, for an interesting account of the final hours of Caldwell and Co.

49. *Tennessean*, Nov. 28, 1930.

50. Ibid., Oct. 10, 1968.

51. Polk's *Nashville City Directory, 1941*, 12.

52. McFerrin, *Caldwell*, 189; *Time* 17 (June 8, 1931), 19, quoted in ibid., 191.

53. McFerrin, *Caldwell*, 205.

54. Ibid., 219–20. See *Banner* reporter Brainard Cheney's reminiscence of Lea in Egerton, ed., *Nashville*, 231.

55. McFerrin, *Caldwell*, 205, 210–14.

56. Ibid., 223.

57. Alexander, "Rich Man's Son," 23, quoted in McFerrin, *Caldwell*, 116.

58. Barker, "Rogers Caldwell Story."

ESSAY ON SELECTED SOURCES

The sources used for particular facts and topics are cited in the notes throughout the text. Rather than repeat all those in a long list, I have thought it more logical to identify the most useful and accessible sources to guide the interested reader who may wish to pursue certain topics further.

The most important source for a history of this kind is the local newspapers. A wealth of insights on the local community, though often buried in state and national political news, can be culled from them. Researchers must be aware of the papers' often heavy political bias and their tendency to interpret community affairs from viewpoint of the local business elite. They must also be willing to mine what is often low-density historical ore. Research for this book involved scanning and taking notes from at least one, and often two, daily newspapers published over the course of a half-century. No index exists for any of the Nashville newspapers in this period, so the tedious process of scanning the daily press was unavoidable.

There were many newspapers in the city in these years, but the most important were the *Banner*, the *American*, to 1910, and the *Tennessean*, beginning in 1907. All these newspapers operated under varying names and over the years were involved in numerous mergers. Each varied in quality and historical value as publishers and editors changed. Generally, the *American*, a "regular" Democratic newspaper, was found to be the most consistently thorough reporter of local affairs during the 1880s, but its thoroughness declined during the 1890s and it became an L&N organ in 1895. Under the ownership of Edward B. Stahlman, the *Banner* was politically "independent" but was also sympathetic to the L&N. It provided good coverage of local affairs and so was used extensively for the 1890s. The founding of the *Tennessean* by Luke Lea in 1907, which merged with the *American* in 1910, established a tradition of two strong rival newspapers that continues to this day. Stahlman of the *Banner* and Lea of the *Tennessean* divided on virtually every important issue, and their feud was often personal and vitriolic to the point of seriously distorting local news. Generally, the *Tennessean* favored whatever came under the umbrella of progressive reform and usually shared the perspective of downtown business interests, whereas the *Banner* backed the Hilary Howse political machine and opposed Lea's brand of business progressivism. Once these biases are taken into account, the city's newspaper rivalry provides the historian a certain advantage, allowing one to view nearly every issue and event from two different angles.

Three other newspapers deserve mention, though none lived long enough or was saved consistently enough to be of great use to historians of this period. The *Evening Herald*, 1889–92, is particularly good on the city's economy and business elites. So is Jere Baxter's *Daily News*, 1901–1905, which also offers the only view independent of L&N influence before Lea's *Tennessean* came on the scene in 1907. The *Globe*, a black-owned newspaper, was founded in 1905 during the streetcar boycott and until its demise in 1960 remained a durable voice for Booker T. Washington's program of black self-help and occasional militant opposition to white oppression. Unfortunately, the *Globe's* files are incomplete, with no issues preserved from the vitally important 1920s. Still, it provides an important window into black Nashville that was largely ignored by the leading newspapers.

Readers interested in the history of the South in this period could do no better than to begin with C. Vann Woodward, *Origins of the New South, 1877–1913*, A History of the South 9 (Baton Rouge, 1951). George Brown Tindall's *The Emergence of the New South, 1913–1945*, A History of the South 10 (Baton Rouge, 1967), continues the story in the same series with an equally thorough and insightful account of the region. Paul M. Gaston, *The New South Creed: A Study in Southern Mythmaking* (Baton Rouge, 1970), deals with the rhetoric and ideals of New South advocates. Dewey W. Grantham's *Southern Progressivism: The Reconciliation of Progress and Tradition* (Knoxville, 1983) appeared too late to inform this study of Nashville, but it is a thorough and perceptive overview of the subject.

Until recently little had been done by professional scholars on the cities of the South. Blaine A. Brownell and David R. Goldfield, eds., *The City in Southern History* (Port Washington, N.Y., 1977), has helped fill that void; see especially the essays by Howard N. Rabinowitz, "Continuity and Change: Southern Urban Development, 1860–1900," and Blaine A. Brownell, "The Urban South Comes of Age, 1900–1940." Blaine A. Brownell, *The Urban Ethos in the South, 1920–1930* (Baton Rouge, 1975), is a fine account of Nashville and other cities with emphasis on the civic elite. David R. Goldfield, *Cotton Fields and Sky-scrapers: Southern City and Region, 1607–1980* (Baton Rouge, 1982), interprets the urbanization of Dixie in a provocative overview. Gold-field and Brownell have incorporated their knowledge of southern cities into a broader survey of American urban history in *Urban America: From Downtown to No Town* (Boston, 1979). For another good synthe-sis of the scholarship in this field, see Howard P. Chudacoff, *The Evo-lution of American Urban Society,* 2nd ed. (Englewood Cliffs, N.J., 1981).

Nashville's history up to the Centennial is covered in a fashion by W. Woodford Clayton, *History of Davidson County, Tennessee* (Phila-delphia, 1880), but it is so poorly organized and hastily written the job had to be redone in John Woolridge, ed., *History of Nashville, Ten-nessee* (Nashville, 1890; rpt. 1970), a generally reliable compilation of factual material that aims to please. [Andrew Morrison], *The City of Nashville,* The Engelhardt Series: American Cities 24 (St. Louis and Nashville, [1891]), contains some history but is most useful as a con-temporary guide to the city, its business and institutional life. The chronicle of Nashville's history was extended in two volumes edited by William Waller: *Nashville in the 1890s* (Nashville, 1970) and *Nash-ville from 1900 to 1910* (Nashville, 1972). Both are valuable, especially on the neighborhoods and personalities of the business and social elite. The notes from interviews with Nashville's leading citizens in the Wal-ler Collection, Special Collections, Vanderbilt University Library, often provide valuable insights and details that did not find their way into the published volumes. Wilbur Foster Creighton, *Building of Nashville* (Nashville, 1969), includes useful information on the city's business history. Eleanor Graham's *Nashville: A Short History and Selected Buildings* (Nashville, 1974) is a useful guide to the city's architectural history. Alfred Leland Crabb, *Nashville: Personality of a City* (India-napolis, 1960), deals with selected topics and is usually reliable. Jesse C. Burt, *Nashville: Its Life and Times* (Nashville, 1959), is useful on rail-road history but is poorly organized and not deeply researched. Wil-liam Henry McRaven, *Nashville: Athens of the South* (Chapel Hill, 1949), is a popular account of uneven quality. John Egerton, ed., *Nash-ville: The Faces of Two Centuries, 1780–1980* (Nashville, 1980), is a finely written and beautifully illustrated volume commemorating the city's bicentennial. Louise Davis's "Gallery of Nashville Commerce" at the end of the Egerton book is very useful to a study of Nashville's busi-ness history. For Tennessee history Stanley J. Folmsbee, Robert Corlew, and Enoch L. Mitchell, *History of Tennessee,* 4 vols. (New York, 1960), is usually the most reliable. Their *Tennessee: A Short History,* 2nd ed. (Knoxville, 1981), is an updated, condensed version available in paperback.

As a commercial center Nashville's economic history is tied to the L&N, and the history of that mighty road is thoroughly covered in Maury

Klein, *History of the Louisville & Nashville Railroad* (New York, 1972). The role of the NC&StL and its absorption into the L&N system has been thoroughly explored by Jesse C. Burt, Jr., in "A History of the Nashville, Chattanooga and St. Louis Railway, 1872–1916" (Ph.D. diss., Vanderbilt Univ., 1950), and two articles: "Four Decades of the Nashville, Chattanooga & St. Louis Railway, 1873–1916," *Tennessee Historical Quarterly* 9(1950):99–130; "Edmund W. Cole and the Struggle Between Nashville and Louisville and Their Railroads, 1879–1880," *Filson Club Quarterly* 26(1952):112–32. Margaret Campbell, "A History of Tennessee Central Railway," (M.A. thesis, George Peabody College for Teachers, 1927), summarizes the struggle of Jere Baxter's "Liberty Line." John F. Stover, *The Railroads of the South, 1865–1900: A Study in Finance and Control* (Chapel Hill, 1955), provides a broad overview of the subject. The history of the Cumberland River steamboats and their struggle to survive in the railroad era has been told in a fine account: Byrd Douglas, *Steamboatin' on the Cumberland* (Nashville, 1961). The Byrd Douglas Papers in Tennessee State Library and Archives are also helpful.

The history of Nashville's commercial and industrial life has rarely been studied for this period, and the history of labor in Nashville is virtually unexplored territory. Arch Trawick, "An Old Time Drummer Talks About the Grocery Business, 1846–1946," and Trawick, "Things Remembered, 1872–1935," typescripts in Trawick Papers, Tennessee State Library and Archives are good accounts of the grocery trade and the drummers who extended Nashville's wholesale markets in this era. There exists a trove of industrial studies done at Peabody College before World War II, the most useful of which included: Clarence Colton Dawson, "History of the Flour Milling Industry of Nashville, Tennessee" (M.A. thesis, George Peabody College for Teachers, 1931), Laura Kate Miller, "Geographical Influences in the Growth of Nashville," (M.A. thesis, George Peabody College for Teachers, 1923); Louis Garfield Kennamer, "The Woodworking Industries of Nashville" (M.A. thesis, George Peabody College for Teachers, 1922); and Glenn Rogers, "Localization of a Few Selective Industries in Nashville" (M.A. thesis, George Peabody College for Teachers, 1932). In the same vein are M.J. Danner, B.H. Leubke, and B.D. Raskopf, *Development and Present Importance of Nashville Livestock Market*, Rural Research Series 205 (Knoxville: Department of Agricultural Economics and Rural Sociology, Agricultural Experiment Station, Univ. of Tennessee, July 30, 1946), and *Agricultural Trends in Tennessee: A Record of Tennessee Crop and Livestock Statistics, 1866–1947* (Nashville, 1948). Justin Fuller, "History of the Tennessee Coal, Iron and Railroad Company, 1852–1907" (Ph.D. diss., Univ. of North Carolina, 1966), and Ethel Armes, *The Story of Coal and Iron in Alabama* (Birmingham, 1910), deal with Nashville as an early center for capital and enterprise in an industry that soon found a more profitable home in rival Birmingham. Kendrick Walker, *Life and*

Achievements of Alfred Montgomery Shook (Birmingham, 1952), and J.B. Killebrew, *Life and Character of James Cartwright Warner* (Nashville, 1897), deal with two of Nashville's most important contributors to the southern iron and steel industry.

In addition to the numerous publications of the city's commercial associations cited in the footnotes, the minute books and other records of the Board of Trade and Chamber of Commerce provide valuable details on business leadership behind the scenes, beginning c. 1910. The originals are in the Chamber of Commerce offices, and most are now on microfilm in the Tennessee State Library and Archives.

The story of banking, insurance, and finance in the "Wall Street of the South" has been left mostly to uncritical company histories. James R. Kellam, Jr., *Bootstraps: A History of Commerce Union Bank, 1916–1966* ([Nashville, 1966]); Jesse Hill Ford, *Mr. Potter and His Bank: A Life of Edward Potter, Jr.* (Nashville, 1978); Third National Bank, *Nashville, 1927–52: Twenty Five Years of Progress* (Nashville, 1952); Margaret Dick, "Survival of the Fittest: Nashville City Bank at the Crossroads," *Nashville! Magazine,* July 1978, all offer laudatory accounts of individual banks. James E. Caldwell, *Recollections of a Lifetime* (Nashville, 1923), is the author's story of his rise to wealth as the head of First and Fourth National Bank. John B. McFerrin, *Caldwell and Company: A Southern Financial Empire* (1939; rev., Nashville, 1969), is a scholarly and condemnatory account of Rogers Caldwell's rise and fall, which includes some general information on the financial world of Nashville and the South. George Barker, "The Rogers Caldwell Story," *Tennessean Sunday Magazine,* Oct. 20, 27, Nov. 3, 1963, is a fascinating reminiscence. Claude A. Campbell, "The Development of Banking in Tennessee" (Ph.D. diss., Vanderbilt Univ., 1932), provides a helpful overview of the evolution of Nashville as a banking center. On Nashville insurance companies see: Powell Stamper, *The National Life Story: A History of the National Life and Accident Insurance Company of Nashville, Tennessee* (New York, 1968), and Era Irene Emmons, *The Thrift Family: A Story of the Life and Casualty Insurance Company, 1903–1943* (Nashville, 1943). The company magazines, National Life's *Our Shield* and Life and Casualty's *Mirror,* both begun in the 1920s, are very revealing of company strategy and the changing social makeup of their clientele. The links between insurance sales and the early years of WSM and the Grand Ole Opry are explored in Richard A. Peterson, "Single Industry Firm to Conglomerate Synergistics: Alternative Strategies for Selling Insurance and Country Music," in *Growing Metropolis: Aspects of Development in Nashville,* ed. James F. Blumstein and Benjamin Walter (Nashville, 1975). The early days of the Opry and country music are skillfully analyzed in Charles K. Wolfe, *The Grand Ole Opry: The Early Years, 1925–35* (London, 1975), and Wolfe, *Tennessee Strings: The Story of Country Music in Tennessee* (Knoxville, 1977).

The physical transformation of the city and the social changes that accompanied that process are ably summarized in Blanche Henry Clark Weaver, "Shifting Residential Patterns of Nashville," *Tennessee Historical Quarterly* 8(1959). John M. Marshall, "Residential Expansion and Central City Change," in *Growing Metropolis*, is a good analysis of the development of the downtown. See also Marshall's "Railroads and Urban Growth," in the same anthology, on the role of railroads in determining the physical features of Nashville. James Summerville, "The City and the Slum: 'Black Bottom' in the Development of South Nashville," *Tennessee Historical Quarterly* 40 (1981), and Don H. Doyle, "Saving Yesterday's City: Nashville's Waterfront," *Tennessee Historical Quarterly* 35(1976), deal with inner-city neighborhoods. The condition of the city's inner ring of slums is revealed in the health statistics and descriptions in the *Reports of Departments of the City of Nashville* . . . (Nashville, 1883–1912), title varies. The emergence of one of Nashville's suburbs is related skillfully in Mark B. Riley, "Edgefield: A Study of an Early Nashville Suburb," *Tennessee Historical Quarterly* 37 (1978). The rise of West Nashville, an industrial suburb, is told in Henry Francis Beaumont, *West Nashville: Manufacturing Metropolis of the South* (Nashville, 1908), and Nashville Land Improvement Company, *West Nashville* (Nashville, [1900?]).

The ethnic subcommunities that helped define the transformation of Nashville's neighborhoods in this period have been summarized intelligently in Benjamin Walter, "Ethnicity and Residential Succession: Nashville, 1850–1920," in Blumstein and Walter, eds., *Growing Metropolis*. On the Germans and Germantown, Robert C.H. Mathews III, "North Nashville: A History of Urban Development" (M.A. thesis, Univ. of North Carolina, 1976), and John Lawrence Connelly, "Old North Nashville and Germantown," *Tennessee Historical Quarterly* 39(1980), are both helpful, well-researched works. Connelly's *North Nashville and Germantown: Yesterday and Today* (Nashville, 1982) is a more comprehensive study of the neighborhood. Ed Huddleston, *Big Wheels and Little Wagons*, reprinted from the *Nashville Banner*, Oct. 5 to Dec. 7, 1959, is a popular account of personalities in old Germantown. Phyllis Hahn, "German Settlers in Nashville, Tennessee" (M.A. thesis, Vanderbilt Univ., 1935), and Joseph T. Macpherson, Jr., "Nashville's German Element" (M.A. thesis, Vanderbilt Univ., 1957), are also useful. The beginnings of Irish Nashville is treated in James Joseph Flanagan, "The Irish Element in Nashville, 1810–1890: An Introductory Survey" (M.A. thesis, Vanderbilt Univ., 1951). George Flanigan, ed., *Catholicity in Tennessee* (Nashville, 1937), focuses on the history of the church, whereas the *Catholic Herald* reports on some secular aspects of the Irish community. The role of the Irish in city politics, particularly after 1890, remains an important but barely explored topic. The history of the Nashville Jewish community has been recorded in Fedora S. Frank, *Five*

Families and Eight Young Men (Nashville, 1962), and Frank, *Beginnings on Market Street: Nashville and Her Jewry, 1861–1901* (Nashville, 1976).

Nashville's black community and the evolution of race relations have been treated in a number of excellent scholarly studies. The best single overview of segregation in the South is C. Vann Woodward, *The Strange Career of Jim Crow* (New York, 1955; rev. ed., 1957). August Meier, *Negro Thought in America, 1880–1915: Racial Ideologies in the Age of Booker T. Washington* (Ann Arbor, 1963), is the standard book on black thought and action in this period. Howard N. Rabinowitz, *Race Relations in the Urban South, 1865–1890* (New York, 1978), includes Nashville in a thorough study of the evolution of segregation and the black subcommunity segregation helped create. See also Rabinowitz, "Half a Loaf: The Shift From White to Black Teachers in the Negro Schools of the Urban South, 1865–1890," *Journal of Southern History* 40(Nov. 1974), for details on that subject. Joseph H. Cartwright, *The Triumph of Jim Crow: Tennessee Race Relations in the 1880s* (Knoxville, 1976), includes a good analysis of urban reform and black political exclusion in Nashville. Lester C. Lamon, *Black Tennesseans, 1900–1930* (Knoxville, 1977), is a well-researched book that includes much on Nashville blacks. Lamon's *Blacks in Tennessee, 1791–1970* (Knoxville, 1982) puts the subject in broader perspective. Faye Wellborn Robbins, "A World within a World: Black Nashville, 1880–1915" (Ph.D. diss., Univ. of Arkansas, 1980), covers some of the same ground as Rabinowitz, Cartwright, and Lamon but has some new material to offer as well. August Meier and Elliott Rudwick, "The Boycott Movement Against Jim Crow Streetcars in the South, 1900–1906," *Journal of Southern History* 55(Mar. 1969), puts the Nashville boycott in perspective. There are few manuscript sources dealing with black Nashville, but the James C. Napier Papers, Special Collections, Fisk University, are a useful collection. The *Globe*, mentioned above, is also an important newspaper for any study of black Nashville.

Most of Nashville's religious history is found in institutional histories of denominations and individual churches. Woolridge's *History of Nashville* and Crabb's *Personality of a City*, mentioned above, summarize much of this institutional history. Less has been done on the social meaning of religion and its connection to reform and politics. Hunter Dickinson Farish, *The Circuit Rider Dismounts: A Social History of Southern Methodism, 1865–1900* (Richmond, 1938), deals with what I believe to have been the most important denomination in Nashville in that period. Milton L. Baughn, "Social Views Reflected in Official Publications of the Cumberland Presbyterian Church, 1875–1900" (Ph.D. diss., Vanderbilt Univ., 1954), and Rufus Buin Spain, *At Ease in Zion: A Social History of Southern Baptists, 1865–1900* (Nashville, 1967), examine the pronouncements of church officials on social issues. Paul E. Isaac, *Prohibition and Politics: Turbulent Decades in Tennes-*

see, 1885–1920 (Knoxville, 1965), studies the impact of Protestant leaders on one of the most important reform movements of the era and draws skillfully on material culled from Nashville's religious presses. James Douglas Flamming, "The Sam Jones Revivals and Social Reform in Nashville, Tennessee, 1885–1900" (M.A. thesis, Vanderbilt Univ., 1983), is a perceptive study of the evolution of the social gospel in Nashville and places it within the context of the city's rapid growth and class tensions. See also Richard L. Wilson, "Sam Jones: An Apostle of the New South," *Georgia Historical Quarterly* 57(1973). Sarah S. Morrow, *The Legacy of Fannie Battle* (Nashville, 1980), treats the city's most important figure in organized philanthropy in this period. Louise L. Davis's articles on Fannie Battle, "She Didn't Look the Other Way," *Tennessean Magazine*, Dec. 14, 1958, and on Sam Watkins, "A Hungry Orphan's Will," *Tennessean Magazine*, July 16, 1972, also reveal much about philanthropy in Nashville. On Watkins, see also Charles T. Wyatt, *History of the Development of Watkins Institute, Nashville, Tennessee* (Nashville, 1935).

Most of the scholarship on Nashville politics is included in broad studies of the state or region. Roger L. Hart, *Redeemers, Bourbons, and Populists: Tennessee, 1870–1896* (Baton Rouge, 1975), is a provocative state study that places Nashville's New South advocates in the context of their battle with conservative Bourbons and agrarian Populists. On one of Nashville's most important New South political spokesmen, see Thomas Woodrow Davis, "Arthur S. Colyar and the New South, 1860–1905," (Ph.D. diss., Univ. of Missouri, 1965). On race and politics in the South, J. Morgan Kousser, *The Shaping of Southern Politics: Suffrage Restriction and the Establishment of the One-Party South, 1880–1910*, Yale Historical Publications, Miscellany, 102 (New Haven, 1974), is a sophisticated state-by-state analysis. Rabinowitz's *Race Relations*, Cartwright's *Triumph of Jim Crow*, and Lamon's *Black Tennesseans*, all cited above, provide more detail on the local context of urban politics in Nashville. The alliance between black voters and the Republican party, particularly Mayor Thomas Kercheval, beg more extensive historical research. David D. Lee, *Tennessee in Turmoil: Politics in the Volunteer State, 1920–1932* (Memphis, 1979), carries the story of Tennessee politics into the 1920s and gives special attention to the role of Luke Lea, based in part on privately held papers of Lea. One of the problems of research into Nashville politics is the dearth of manuscript material, which prevents the historian from penetrating the public pronouncements and denunciations. Major figures like Kercheval, Head, Howse, and Lea have left no accessible papers. The Napier Collection, mentioned above, fills part of the gap for one important black politician, but it is not sufficient. The records of the City Council and other government departments are available in the City Clerk's Vault in the Metro Courthouse, and the *Reports of Departments*, mentioned above, and the several ordinance and charter books summarizing laws and charter amendments are essential to any study of local government.

All future studies of the progressive era in southern politics will begin with Grantham's *Southern Progressivism,* cited above. Students of urban progressivism also would do well to consult John D. Buenker, *Urban Liberalism and Progressive Reform* (New York, 1973), and J. Joseph Huthmacher, "Urban Liberalism and the Age of Reform," *Mississippi Valley Historical Review* 49(Sept. 1962). For the distinction between social reformers, who wanted to improve conditions of the poor through expansion of government services, and structural reformers, who wanted to remodel city government along the lines of the modern business corporation, see Melvin G. Holli, *Reform in Detroit: Hazen S. Pingree and Urban Politics* (New York, 1969). On structural reformers involved with commission government and city managers, see James Weinstein, *The Corporate Ideal and the Liberal State, 1900–1918* (Boston, 1968), and Bradley R. Rice, *Progressive Cities: The Commission Government Movement in America, 1901–1920* (Austin, 1977). Samuel P. Hays, "The Politics of Reform in Municipal Government in the Progressive Era," *Pacific Northwest Quarterly* 55(Oct. 1964), emphasizes the elite origins of structural reform. Nashville's own progressive movement and its leading reformers and politicians have received remarkably little scholarly attention. If there was any single event that launched the local progressive movement, with its emphasis on rational, scientific planning and its notion of enlightened experts uplifting the whole society through education, it was the Tennessee Centennial Exposition, which is usually treated as an isolated curiosity in the city's written histories. The most accessible reference on the Exposition is Herman Justi, ed., *Official History of the Tennessee Centennial Exposition: Opened May 1, and Closed October 30, 1897* (Nashville, 1898). For more details on this subject see the Centennial Exposition Collection, Tennessee State Library and Archives. Even the most important progressive-era political figures, like Mayors James M. Head and Hilary Howse, await biographical treatment. Head's thoughts on municipal ownership and reform are revealed in his articles "Municipal Construction *Versus* the Contract System," *Arena* 31(April 1904): 337–52; "Nashville, Tennessee, Municipal Government," *Arena* 30(April 1903): 345–51; "One Mayor's Experience," *Proceedings of the Atlantic City Conference for Good Government . . .* (1906), 269–79. George L. Sioussat, "Municipal Affairs in Nashville, 1915," *National Municipal Review* 4 (Oct. 1915), and the anonymous "A City in the Hands of a Receiver," *Outlook* (Sept. 1, 1915), are the best summaries of the complicated crisis of 1915 and the aborted reform movement that preceded it in 1913. The newspaper stories surrounding the crisis are conveniently compiled in the Edwin A. Price Scrapbook, Scrapbook Collection, Tennessee State Library and Archives.

On economic and social change in the World War I era and the 1920s, the national scene is ably surveyed by William E. Leuchtenburg, *The Perils of Prosperity, 1914–32*, Chicago History of American Civilization (Chicago, 1958). On the Nashville woman's experience on the World War I homefront, see Rose L. Gilmore, *Davidson County Women in the World War, 1914–1919* (Nashville, 1923). Lou Cretia Owen's "Diary, 1918–1919," in Tennessee State Library and Archives, is a wonderful account of the DuPont powder plant experience by a social worker with a keen sense of the vast social change in which she and the workers were caught up. David Edward Brand, "Fill the Empty Shell: The Story of the Government Munitions Project at Old Hickory, Tennessee, 1918–1919" (M.A. thesis, Vanderbilt Univ., 1971), is a thorough account of this important wartime industry. Ernest Goodrich, "Report of an Industrial Survey of Nashville, Tennessee for the Commercial Club of Nashville," 1920, typescript in Chamber of Commerce, is a candid analysis of Nashville's economic conservatism that acted as a prod to the aggressive boosters and financial gunslingers of the 1920s. Other useful studies of Nashville's economy in this period include: *Analysis of Nashville's Retail Trade* (Nashville, 1932); John A. DeWitt, Jr., "Early Radio Broadcasting in Tennessee," *Tennessee Historical Quarterly* 31 (1972); and Charles E. Allred, et al., *Human and Physical Resources of Tennessee: Financial Institutions [and] Insurance*, Rural Research Series 66, (Knoxville, 1937). McFerrin, *Caldwell and Company*, and Rogers, "Localization of a Few Selected Industries . . . ," both cited above, are also important to Nashville's economic history in this period.

The most helpful source to understanding the business leaders and their way of thinking in the 1920s is Blaine A. Brownell's *Urban Ethos*, cited above. *Nashville This Week* (1925–30) is a chronicle of business and cultural news in the 1920s that proved very informative. The most important unpublished records for this area are the Chamber of Commerce records, particularly the minutes of meetings of the Board of Governors and special committees beginning in 1912, all stored in the Chamber of Commerce offices. These valuable records were in the process of being microfilmed for the Tennessee State Library and Archives after I used them. Many of Nashville's institutions of higher education have received scholarly attention. The most helpful accounts on Vanderbilt are Edwin Mims, *History of Vanderbilt University* (Nashville, 1946); Mims, *Chancellor Kirkland of Vanderbilt* (Nashville, 1940); and Robert A. McGaw, *A Brief History of Vanderbilt University* (Nashville, 1973). Paul Conkin's forthcoming centennial history of Vanderbilt will provide the first critical analysis of that institution's development. Alfred L. Crabb, "The Historical Background of Peabody College: Covering a Period of One Hundred and Fifty-five Years," *Bulletin*, George Peabody College for Teachers 30 (Oct. 1941), is the best summary of that institution's history. On Fisk University see Joe M. Richardson, *A*

History of Fisk University, 1865–1946 (University, Ala., 1980). Meharry Medical College has recently been treated to a fine historical analysis by James Summerville in *Educating Black Doctors: A History of Meharry Medical College* (University, Ala., 1983). Tennessee State University is well served by Samuel H. Shannon in "Agricultural and Industrial Education at Tennessee State University During the Normal School Phase, 1912–1922" (Ph.D. diss., Peabody, 1974), and Shannon's "Land Grant College Legislation and Black Tennesseans: A Case Study in the Politics of Education," *History of Education Quarterly* 22(Summer 1982): 139–57. Eugene Teselle deals with a lesser known black institution in "The Nashville Institute and Roger Williams University: Benevolence, Paternalism, and Black Consciousness, 1867–1928," *Tennessee Historical Quarterly* 41(1982): 360–79.

There is, in addition, a wealth of other periodicals, city directories, biographical compendia, social directories, clippings, scrapbooks, manuscripts, and photographs on most every aspect of Nashville's past in the Tennessee State Library, the Nashville Room of the Ben West Public Library, the Vanderbilt University Library, and Fisk University Library. Churches, businesses, and government agencies often retain their own historical records, as do families, politicians, and other individuals. So long as these records and individual memories are preserved, the written history of Nashville will always find nourishment for future growth and reinterpretation.

INDEX

Nashville in the New South, 1880–1930 was composed into type on a Compugraphic phototypesetter in ten point Trump Medieval with two points of spacing between the lines. Trump and Trump Bold was selected for display. The book was designed by Jim Billingsley, typeset by Metricomp, Inc., printed offset by Thomson-Shore, Inc., and bound by John H. Dekker & Sons. The book is printed on paper designed for an effective life of at least three hundred years.

THE UNIVERSITY OF TENNESSEE PRESS : KNOXVILLE